genius series

MATHEMATICS Olympiad Excellence GUIDE

Salient Features of the Book

- In-depth analysis of each topic, followed by relevant practical and illustrative examples
- Meant for International/National Olympiads, Quizzes, Inter school competitions
- Comprising questions prepared by teachers from various schools of India and abroad
- Selected questions of various National and International Olympiads
- Model Test Papers with Answers
- All the questions are in MCQ format
- Special emphasis on concept and problem solving skills

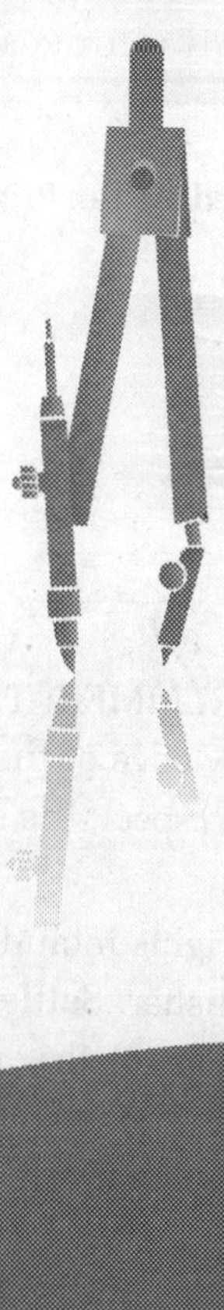

CLASS 1st

Prepared & Published by: **Silverzone Enterprises India Pvt. Ltd.**
B-2 | Ansal Chamber-II, Bhikaji Cama Place
New Delhi-110066(India)
E-mail : info@silverzone.org

Printed by: Tan Prints India Pvt. Ltd., Rohad, Haryana

Olympiad Excellence Guide

genius series

Mathematics

TABLE OF CONTENTS

CHAPTERS

MODEL TEST PAPERS

Chapter 1

Back and Forth Counting

Learning Objectives

- Forth Counting and Back Counting
- What Comes Before
- What Comes After
- Counting in Tens
- Counting in Twenties
- Numbers and Their Names
- Reverse Counting

Forth Counting and Back Counting

Look at the following figures:

(A)

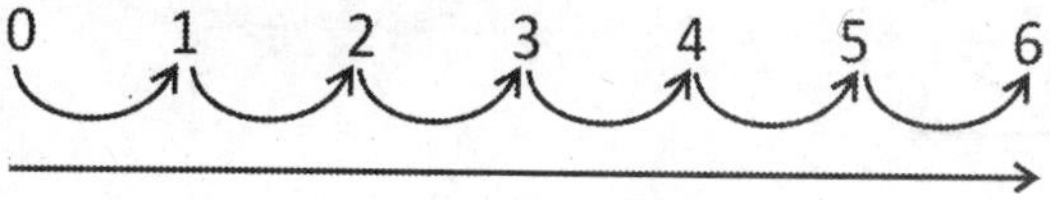

Forth Counting

(B)

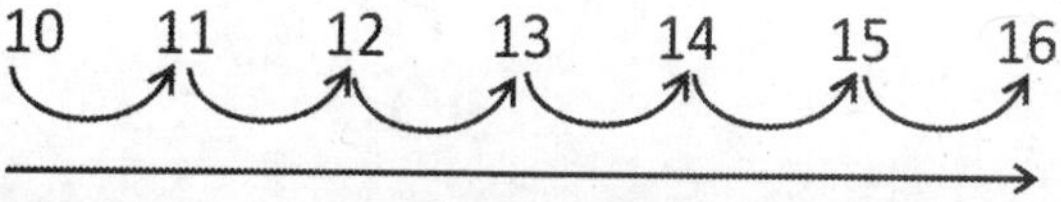

Forth Counting

In forth counting, we count from smaller to greater numbers.

One egg

Two eggs

Three eggs

Four eggs

Five eggs

Look at the following figures:

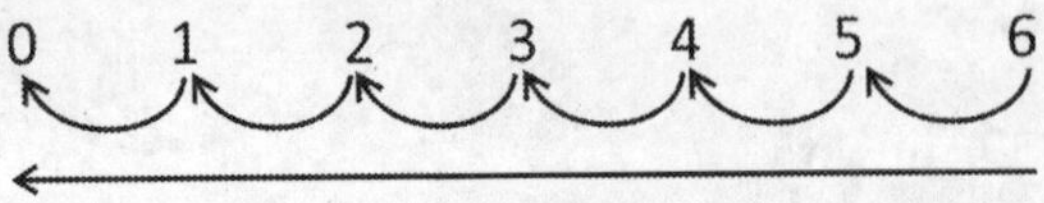

(A)

Back Counting

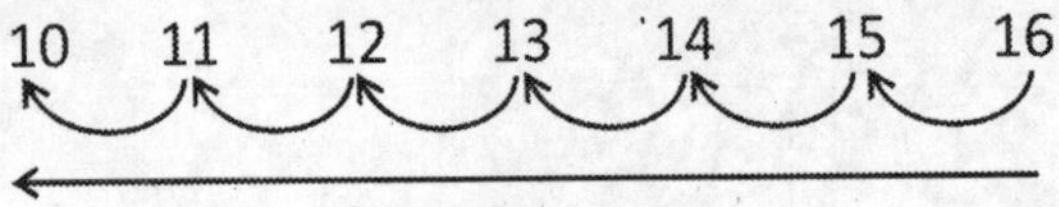

(B)

Back Counting

In back counting we count from greater to smaller numbers.

What Comes Before

In forth counting, smaller number always comes before greater number.

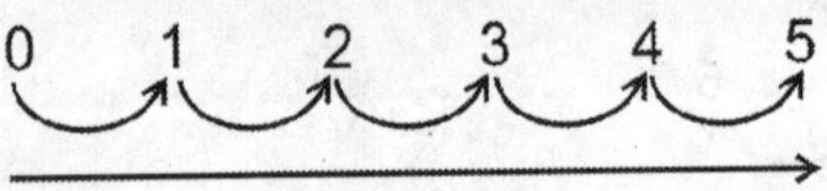

Forth Counting

Here,

1 comes just before 2

2 comes just before 3

3 comes just before 4 &

4 comes just before 5

But,

Numbers coming before 5 are 1 2 3 4

Numbers coming before 4 are 1 2 3

Numbers coming before 3 are 1 2

Example: 1

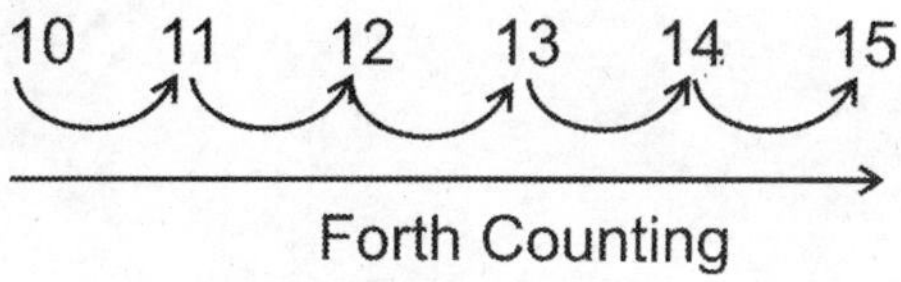

Here,

10 comes just before 11

11 comes just before 12

12 comes just before 13

13 comes just before 14

14 comes just before 15

But,

Numbers coming before 15 are 10 11 12 13 14

Numbers coming before 14 are 10 11 12 13

Numbers coming before 13 are 10 11 12

Numbers coming before 12 are 10 11

In back counting greater number always comes before smaller number.

Example: 2

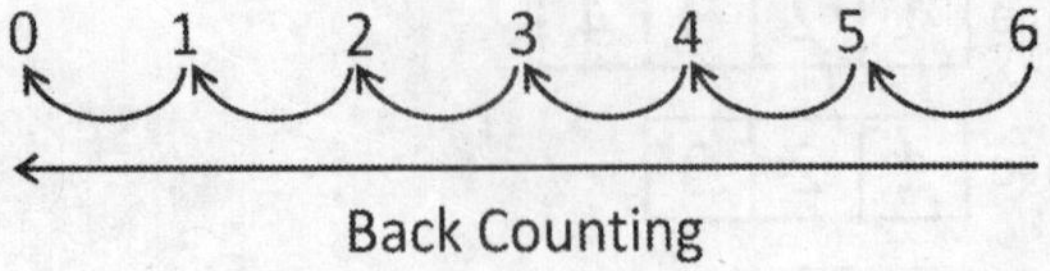

Here,

6 comes just before 5

5 comes just before 4

4 comes just before 3

3 comes just before 2

2 comes just before 1

1 comes just before 0

But in Back Counting,

Numbers coming before 0 are 1 2 3 4 5 6

Numbers coming before 1 are 2 3 4 5 6

Numbers coming before 2 are 3 4 5 6

Numbers coming before 3 are 4 5 6 and

Numbers coming before 4 are 5 6

What Comes After

Just remember that greater number always comes after smaller number in forth counting.

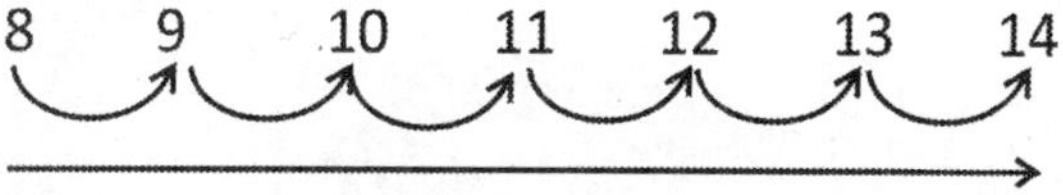

Forth Counting

Here,

9 comes just after 8

10 comes just after 9

11 comes just after 10

12 comes just after 11

13 comes just after 12

14 comes just after 13

But,

Numbers coming after 8 are 9 10 11 12 13 14

Numbers coming after 9 are 10 11 12 13 14

Numbers coming after 10 are 11 12 13 14

Numbers coming after 11 are 12 13 14 and

Numbers coming after 12 are 13 14

Example: 1

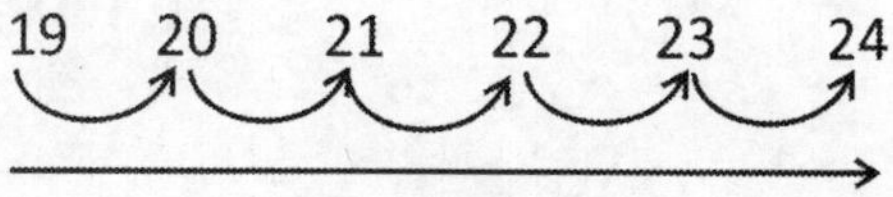

Forth Counting

Here,

20 comes just after 19

21 comes just after 20

22 comes just after 21

23 comes just after 22

24 comes just after 23

But,

Numbers coming after	19	are	20	21	22	23	24
Numbers coming after	20	are	21	22	23	24	
Numbers coming after	21	are	22	23	24		
Numbers coming after	22	are	23	24			

Further, When we do back counting smaller number comes after greater number.

Example: 2

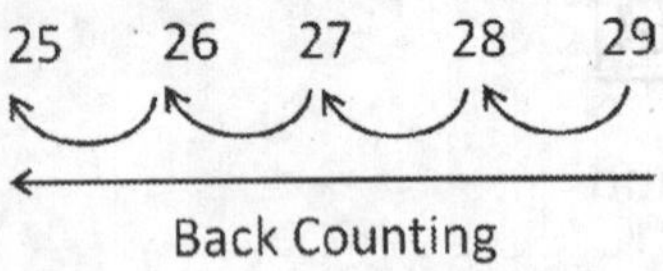

Here,

28 comes just after 29

27 comes just after 28

26 comes just after 27

25 comes just after 26

But,

Numbers coming after 29 are 28 27 26 25

Numbers coming after 28 are 27 26 25 and

Numbers coming after 27 are 26 25

Example: 3

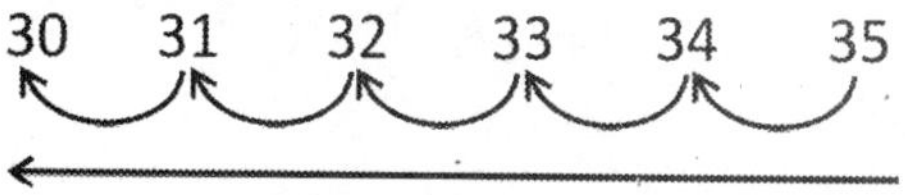

Back Counting

Here,

34 comes just after 35

33 comes just after 34

32 comes just after 33

31 comes just after 32

30 comes just after 31

But,

Numbers coming after 35 are 34 33 32 31 30

Numbers coming after 34 are 33 32 31 30

Numbers coming after 33 are 32 31 30 and

Numbers coming after 32 are 31 30

> **Skip Counting**
>
> Skip counting is counting by a number that is not 1.
>
> eg. 3, 6, 9, 12, ________ is an example of skip counting by 3.

Counting in Tens

Look at the following:

One ten = 1 ten = 10

Two tens = 2 tens = 20

Three tens = 3 tens = 30

Ten tens = 10 tens = 100

Twelve tens = 12 tens = 120

Now, it is clear that,

One ten is one fold of 10 = 10

Two tens is two fold of 10 = 20

Three tens is three fold of 10 = 30

Ten tens is ten fold of 10 = 100

Twelve tens is twelve fold of 10 = 120

Trick:

Just put a single zero (0) in place of ten

One ten = 1 Ten = 10
↓
0

Two tens = 2 Tens = 20
↓
0

Three tens = 3 Tens = 30
↓
0

From the above given explanation, it is clear that while counting in tens, put number left side and a single zero (0) in the right side.

Example:

(A)

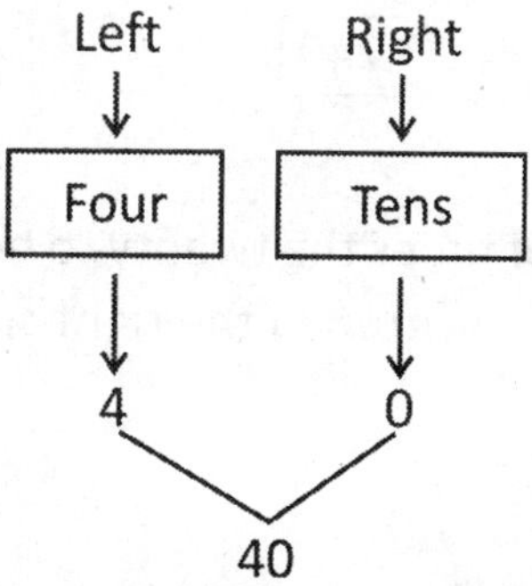

(B)

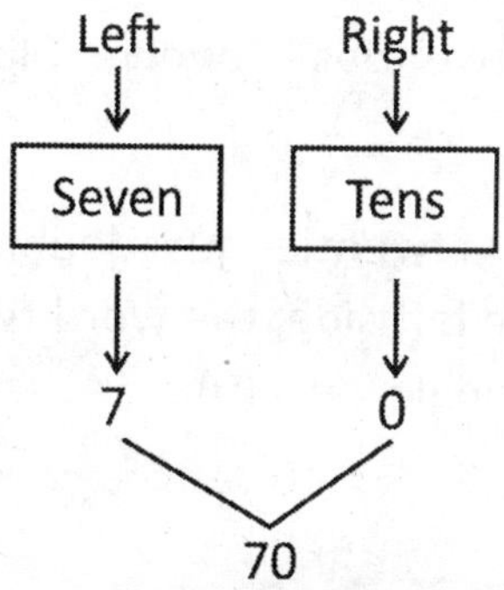

Now, it is clear that counting in 10's goes as:

10, 20, 30, 40, 50, 60, 70, 80, 90, 100 ....and so on.

Counting in Twenties

Look at the following:

One twenty	=	1 twenty	=	20
Two twenties	=	2 twenties	=	40
Three twenties	=	3 twenties	=	60
Five twenties	=	5 twenties	=	100
Twelve twenties	=	12 twenties	=	240

Now, it is clear that

One twenty is one fold of 20 = 20

Two twenties is two fold of 20 = 40

Three twenties is three fold of 20 = 60

Five twenties is five fold of [20] = [100]

Twelve twenties is twelve fold of [20] = [240]

Trick:

While counting in twenties, just double the number of times the twenty to be counted and put it in the left side, the word twenty/twenties written in the right side will be replaced by a single zero (0).

Example:

(A)

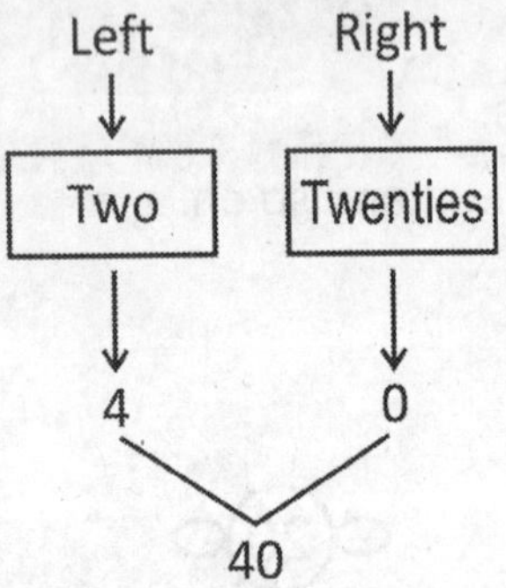

Here, we double the two that becomes [4] and put it in the left while the word twenties written in the right get replaced by zero (0).

(B)

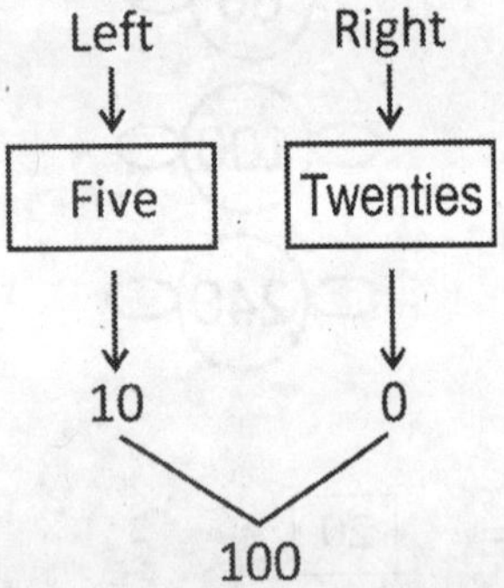

Here, We double the five that becomes [10] and put it in the left while the word twenties written in the right side get replaced by zero (0).

Clearly counting in 20's goes as:

20, 40, 60, 80, 100, 120 ....and so on.

Numbers and Their Names

Let us look at the following patterns:

Number Counting	1	2	3	4	5
Number Name	One	Two	Three	Four	Five

Let us look at the number counting and their appropriate name as given below:

0	1	2	3	4	5	6
Zero	One	Two	Three	Four	Five	Six

7	8	9	10	11	12
Seven	Eight	Nine	Ten	Eleven	Twelve

13	14	15	16	17	18
Thirteen	Fourteen	Fifteen	Sixteen	Seventeen	Eighteen

19	20	21	22	23	24
Ninteen	Twenty	Twenty One	Twenty Two	Twenty Three	Twenty Four

25	26	27	28	29	30
Twenty Five	Twenty Six	Twenty Seven	Twenty Eight	Twenty Nine	Thirty

31	32	33	34	35
Thirty One	Thirty Two	Thirty Three	Thirty Four	Thirty Five

36	37	38	39	40
Thirty Six	Thirty Seven	Thirty Eight	Thirty Nine	Forty
41	42	43	44	45
Forty One	Forty Two	Forty Three	Forty Four	Forty Five
46	47	48	49	50
Forty Six	Forty Seven	Forty Eight	Forty Nine	Fifty
51	52	53	54	55
Fifty One	Fifty Two	Fifty Three	Fifty Four	Fifty Five
56	57	58	59	60
Fifty Six	Fifty Seven	Fifty Eight	Fifty Nine	Sixty
61	62	63	64	65
Sixty One	Sixty Two	Sixty Three	Sixty Four	Sixty Five
66	67	68	69	70
Sixty Six	Sixty Seven	Sixty Eight	Sixty Nine	Seventy
71	72	73	74	75
Seventy One	Seventy Two	Seventy Three	Seventy Four	Seventy Five
76	77	78	79	80
Seventy Six	Seventy Seven	Seventy Eight	Seventy Nine	Eighty

81	82	83	84	85
Eighty One	Eighty Two	Eighty Three	Eighty Four	Eighty Five
86	87	88	89	90
Eighty Six	Eighty Seven	Eighty Eight	Eighty Nine	Ninety
91	92	93	94	95
Ninety One	Ninety Two	Ninety Three	Ninety Four	Ninety Five
96	97	98	99	100
Ninety Six	Ninety Seven	Ninety Eight	Ninety Nine	Hundred

Reverse Counting

Reverse counting is back counting or counting backward and the concept of back counting we have discussed in the beginning of this chapter. The reverse counting goes as following-

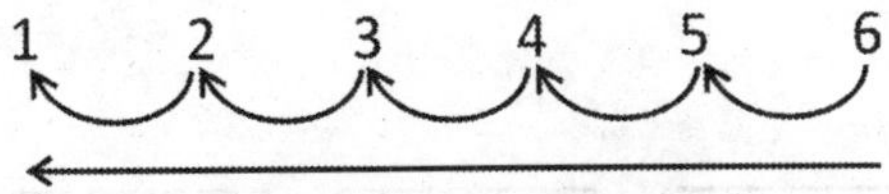

Reverse Counting

or

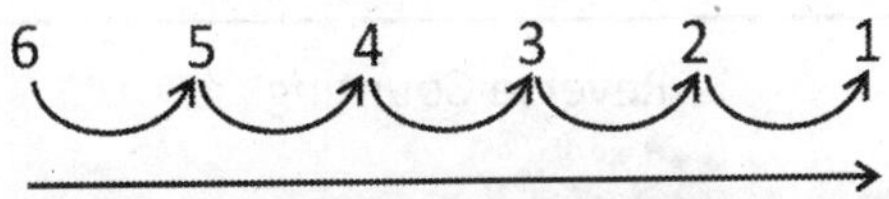

Reverse Counting

Numbers are in reverse counting is one aspect. The another aspect is word in reverse counting.

Look at the following diagram:

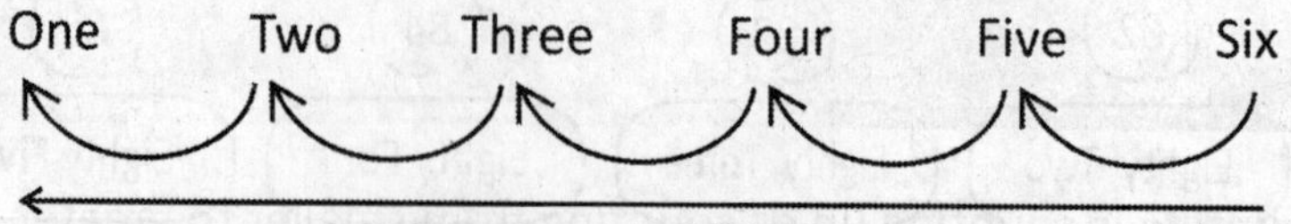

Reverse Counting

or

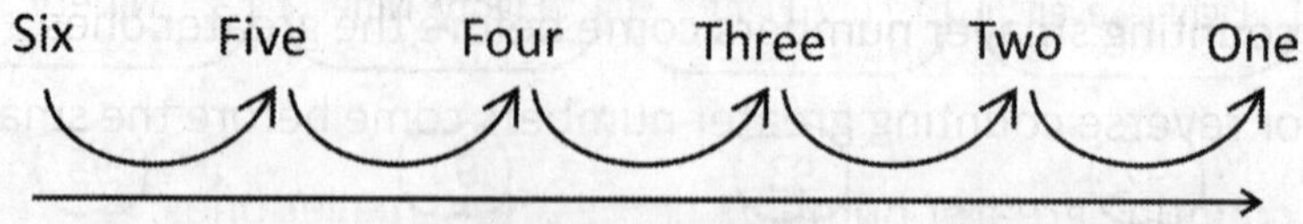

Reverse Counting

Therefore, it is clear that reverse counting goes from greater to smaller.

Take another example if we have to count.

Eleven	Twelve	Ten	Fourteen	Thirteen

In reverse order then the reverse counting diagram goes as:

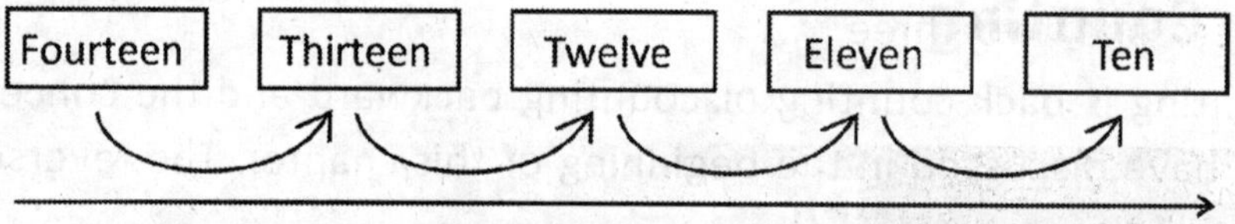

Reverse Counting

or

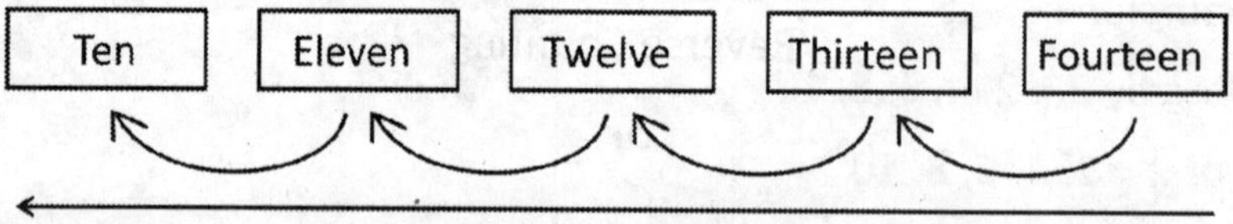

Reverse Counting

Summary

- ❖ Forth counting is counting up or counting from smaller to greater number.
- ❖ Back counting or reverse counting is counting down or counting from greater to smaller number.
- ❖ In forth counting smaller numbers come before the greater ones.
- ❖ In back or reverse counting greater numbers come before the smaller ones.
- ❖ In froth counting greater numbers come after smaller ones.
- ❖ In back or reverse counting smaller numbers come after the greater ones.
- ❖ Counting in tens means counting or collection of 10's like 10, 20, 30, 40, ...and so on.
- ❖ Counting in twenties means counting or collection of 20's like 20, 40, 60, 80, ...and so on.
- ❖ Counting in words means counting of 1, 2, 3..... etc. in the form of one, two, three .... etc. one, two, three, ... are called number names.

Did You Know ?

- ❖ Counting by any number is same as the table of that number.

  For example:
- ❖ Counting by 2 = 2, 4, 6, 8, 10
- ❖ Table of 2 = 2, 4, 6, 8, 10

Solved Problems

1. What comes just before 19 in a forth counting from 14 to 20 ?

(A) 15 (B) 18

(C) 20 (D) 17

(E) None of these

Answer (B)

Explanation: The counting goes as, 14, 15, 16, 17, 18, 19 & 20. In this process we count 18 just before 19.

2. Which one of the following numbers in forth counting will come before 9?

(A) 8 (B) 12

(C) 11 (D) 10

(E) None of these

Answer (A)

3. Steve does forth counting from 0 to 10. What comes just after 5 in this counting ?

(A) 4 (B) 8 (C) 6 (D) 9

(E) None of these

Answer (C)

Explanation: This counting goes as:

0, 1, 2, 3, 4, 5, 6, 7, 8, 9, 10,

4. See the numbers given inside the following box and take out the one that comes just after 7 while doing back counting:

5	2	1
3	6	4
8	0	7

Back counting

(A) 6 (B) 4 (C) 2 (D) 0
(E) None of these

Answer (A)

Explanation:

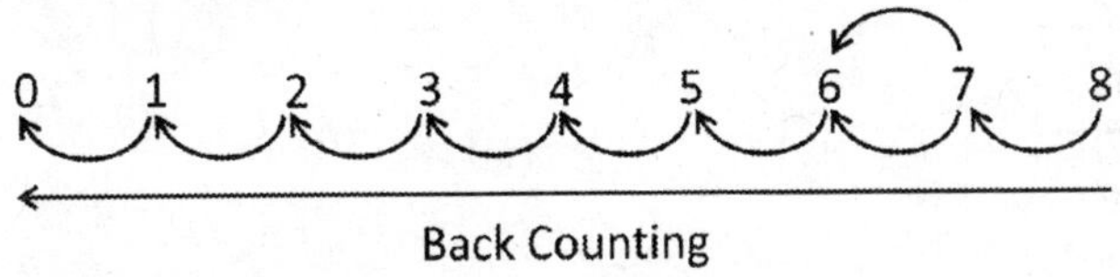

5. Five tens = ?

(A) 40 (B) 50 (C) 60 (D) 80
(E) None of these

Answer (B)

Explanation: Option (B) is correct because it is clear from the following diagram: Therefore, option (B) is correct and rest of the options are incorrect.

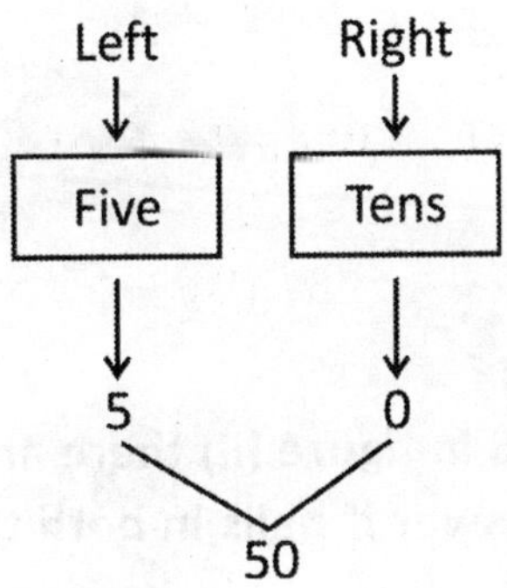

Option: (A) is incorrect as 40 = four tens, it is clear from the following diagram:

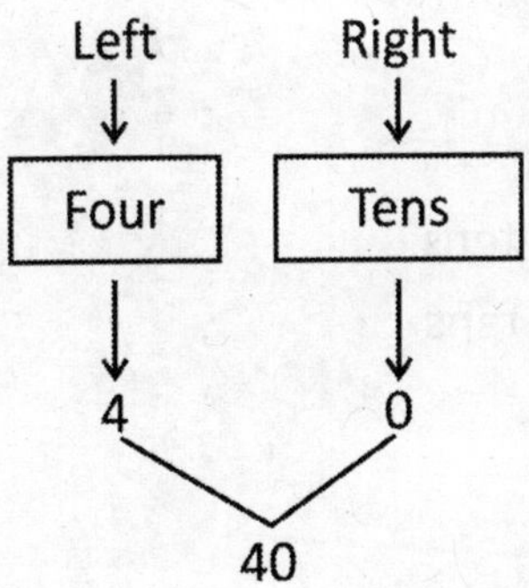

Option: (C) is incorrect because it is equal to [6] tens or Six tens which is clear from the following diagram:

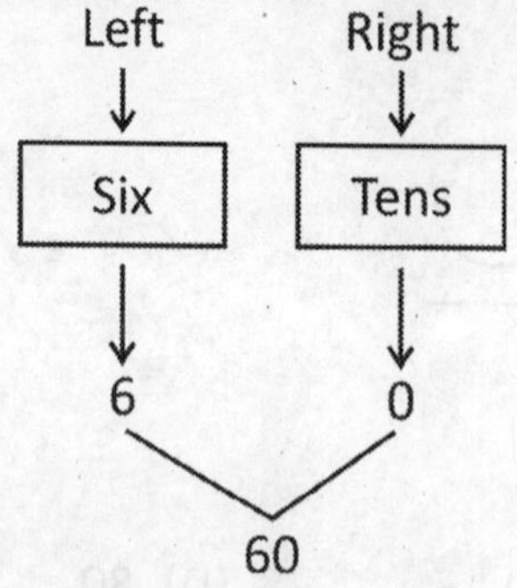

Option (D) is incorrect because it is equal to eight tens which is clear from the following diagram:

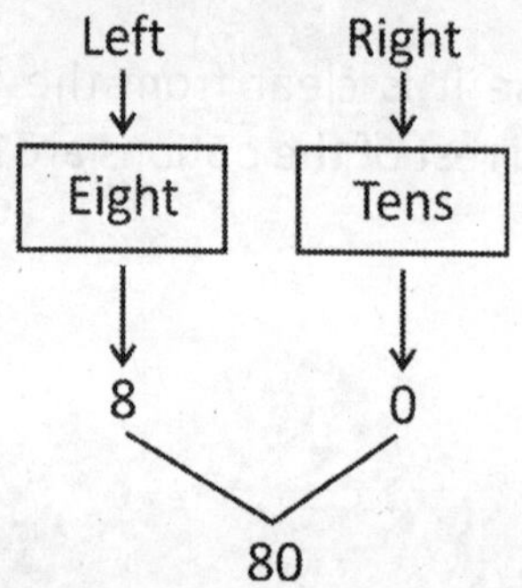

6. In figure (i) there are 10 balls inside a box and in figure (ii) there are also 10 balls inside another box. What will be the answer if balls in both the boxes are counted together?

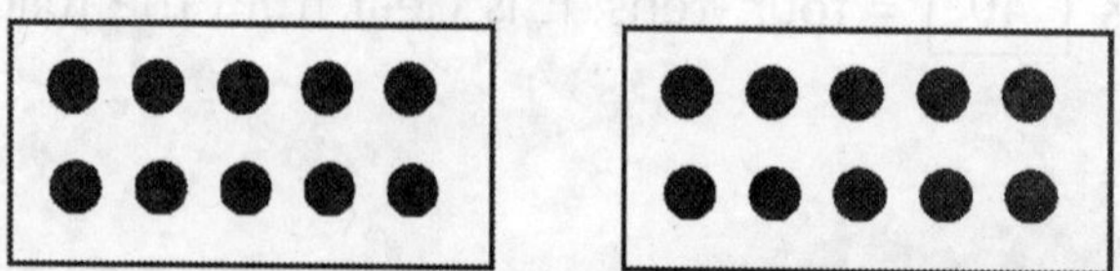

(i) (ii)

(A) Four tens
(B) Five tens
(C) Three tens
(D) Two tens
(E) None of these

Answer (D)

Explanation: While counting together the total number of balls comes to 20 and 20 = 2 fold of 10 = Two tens.

It is clear from the following diagram:

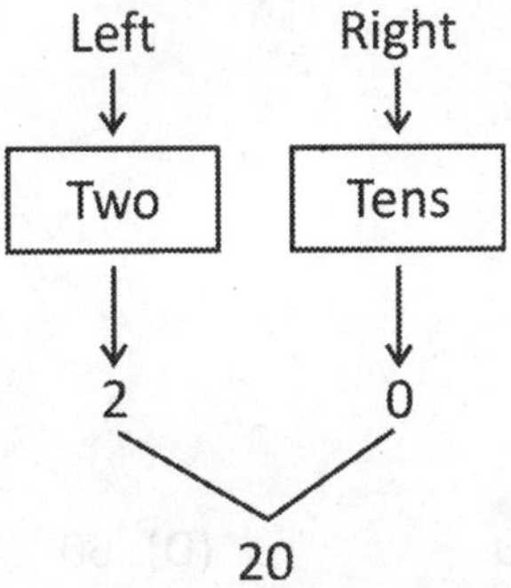

Option (A) is incorrect as four tens = 4 fold of 10 = 40

It is clear from the following diagram :

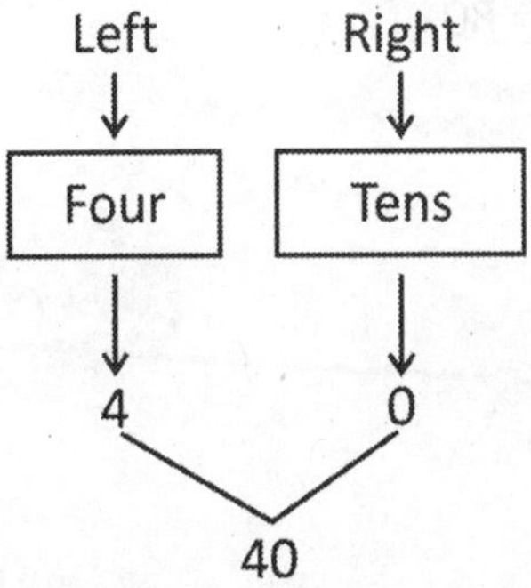

Option (B) is incorrect as five tens = 5 fold of 10 = 50

It is clear from the following diagram :

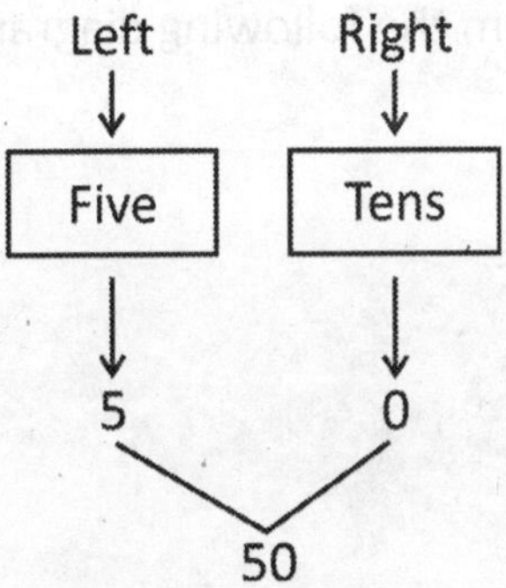

Option (C) is incorrect as three tens = 3 fold of 10 = 30

It is clear from the following diagram:

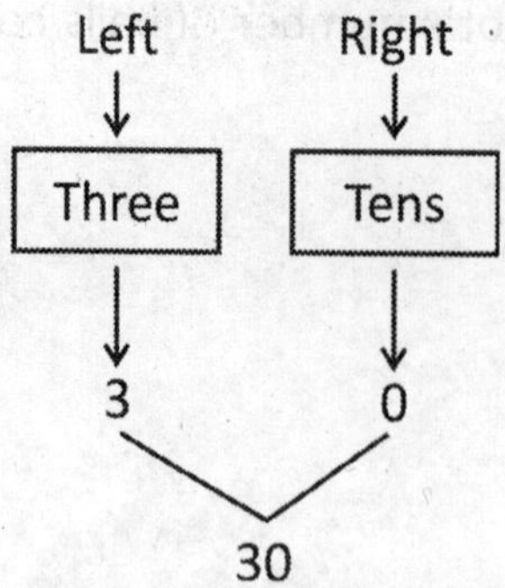

7. **Four twenties = ?**

(A) 140 (B) 80 (C) 40 (D) 60

(E) None of these

Answer (B)

Explanation: 4 twenties is four fold of 20 = 80.

It is clear from the following diagram :

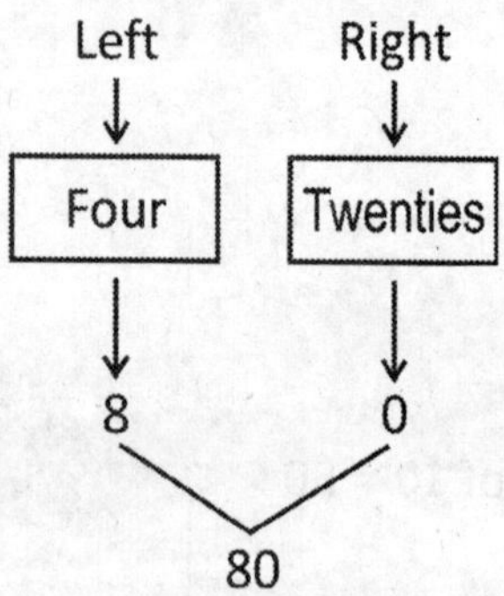

Option (A) is incorrect because it is clear from the following diagram that 140 is equal to seven twenties:

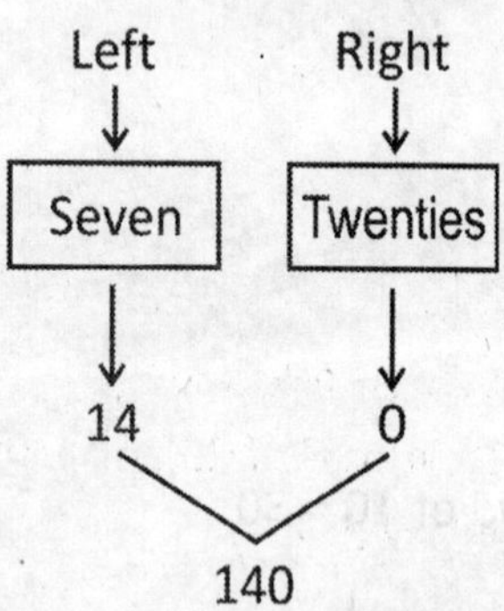

Option (C) is incorrect because it is clear from the following diagram that 40 is equal to two twenties:

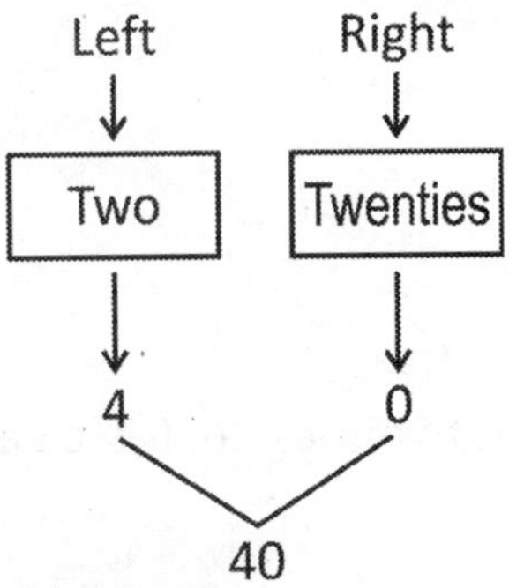

Option (D) is incorrect because it is clear from the following diagram that 60 is equal to three twenties:

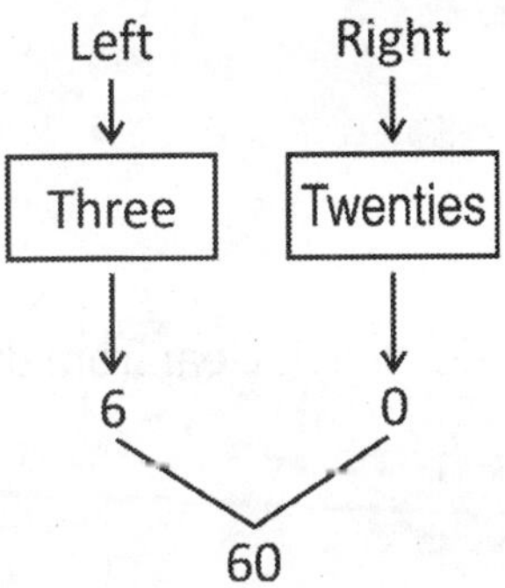

8. Counting in twenties is given below. Fill the blank box with suitable number.

20	40	60	80	100	120	140	

(A) 160
(B) 180
(C) 200
(D) 60
(E) None of these

Answer (A)

Explanation: Here, we have to find the value of 8th box. It means that we need the value of eight twenties which is eight fold of 20 and eight fold of 20 is equal to 160. It is clear from the following diagram:

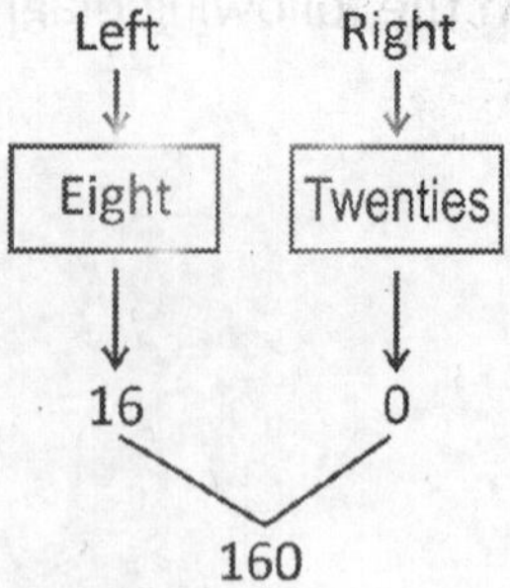

Option (B) is incorrect because 180 = Nine twenties that is clear from the following diagram:

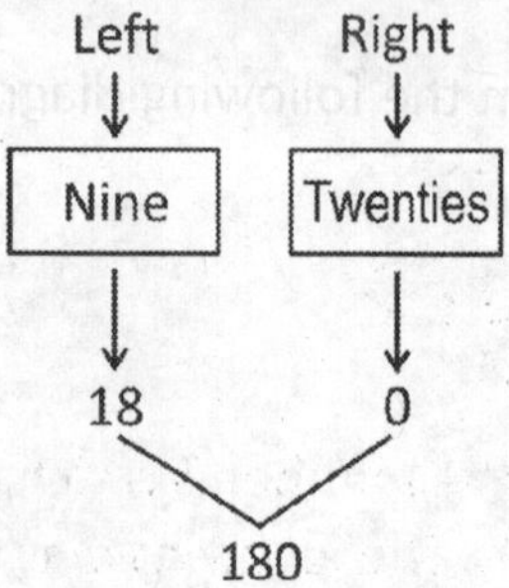

Option (C) is incorrect because 200 = 10 twenties that is clear from the following diagram:

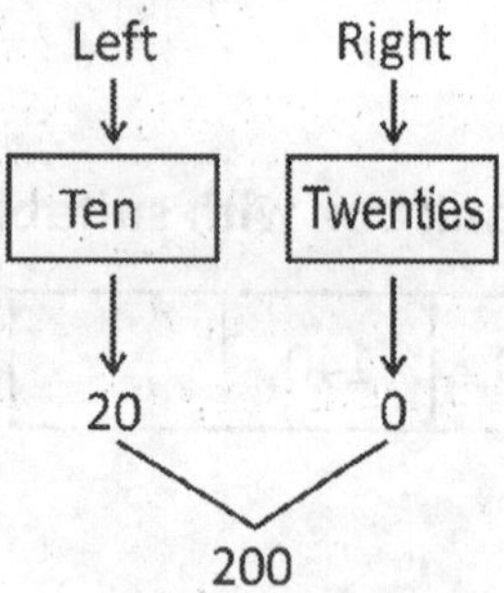

Option (D) is incorrect because 60 = three twenties that is clear from the following diagram:

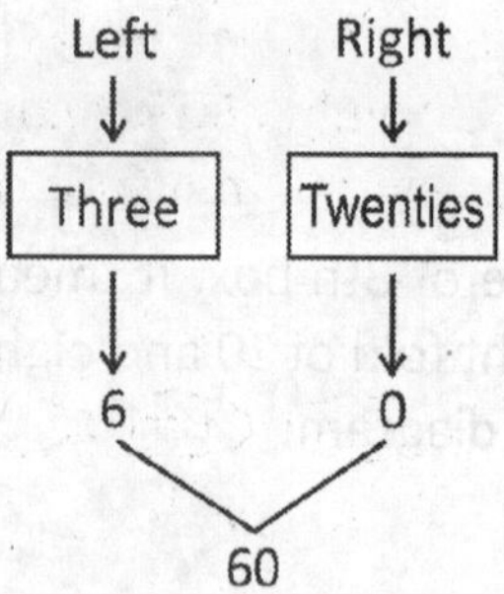

9. Fill the blank box with one of the following options:

One	Two		Four	Five	Six

(A) Seven (B) Three

(C) Eight (D) Nine

(E) None of these

Answer (B)

Explanation: Option (B) is correct because three means the number 3 that comes just after two or 2 and just before 4 (four). It is clear from the following diagram:

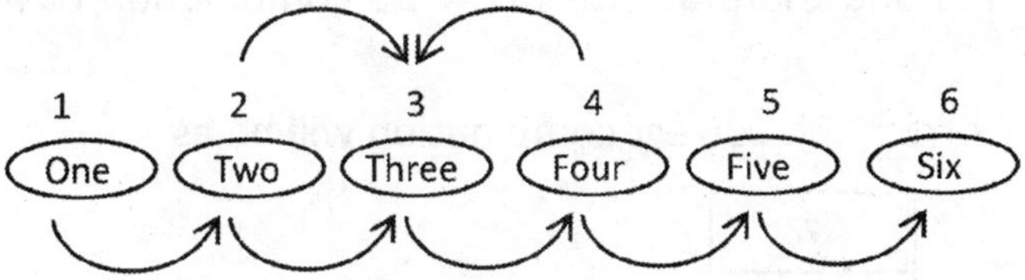

Option (A) is incorrect because seven means the number 7 which comes just after 6 (six) and just before the number 8 (eight). The following diagram makes it more clear :

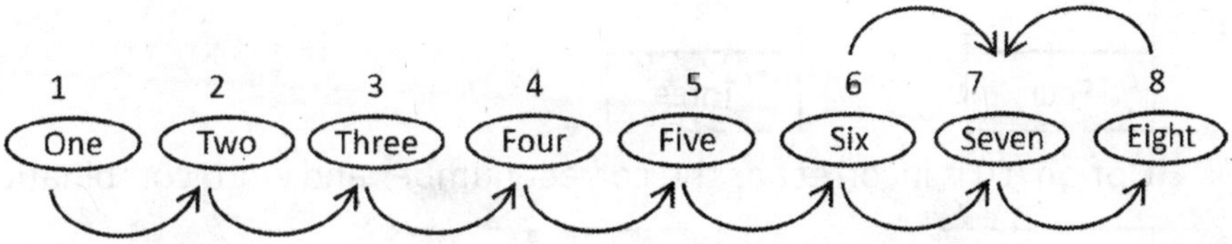

Option (C) is incorrect because eight means the number 8 that comes just after 7 (seven) and just before 9 (nine). The following diagram makes it more clear:

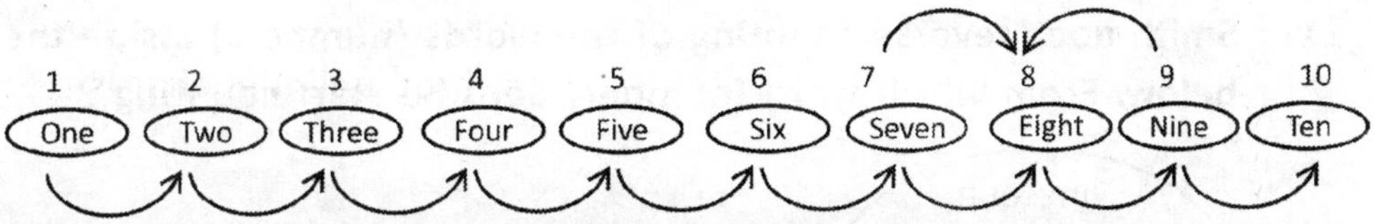

Option (D) is incorrect because nine means the number 9 that comes after 8 (eight) and just before 10 (ten). The following diagram makes it more clear:

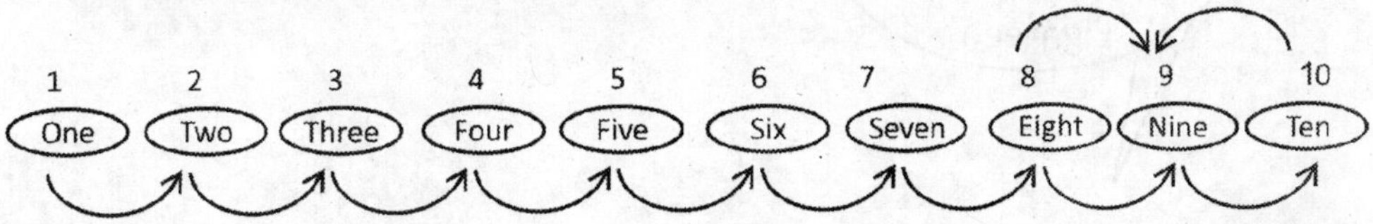

10. Which one of the following options is correctly written?

(A)
7
Nine

(B)
3
Four

(C)
11
Eleven

(D)
20
Thirteen

(E) None of these

Answer (C)

Explanation: Option (C) is correct because the number 11 is written as "Eleven" in words and therefore, this is write combination of number and word.

Option (A) is incorrect the correct combination will be as

9
Nine

or

7
Seven

Option (B) is incorrect as the correct number and word combination will be as

4
Four

or

3
Three

Option (D) is incorrect as the correct number and word combination will be as

13
Thirteen

or

20
Twenty

11. Smith does reverse counting of the words (numbers) inside the egg given below. From which word (number) does he start counting ?

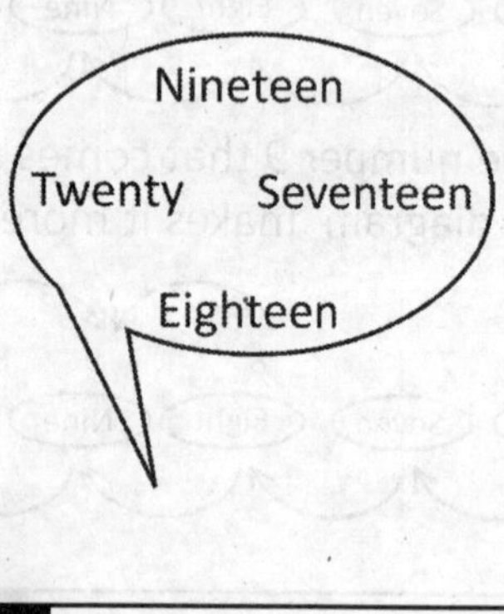

(A) Seventeen (B) Nineteen

(C) Twenty (D) Eighteen

(E) None of these

Answer (C)

Explanation: The counting goes as the following:

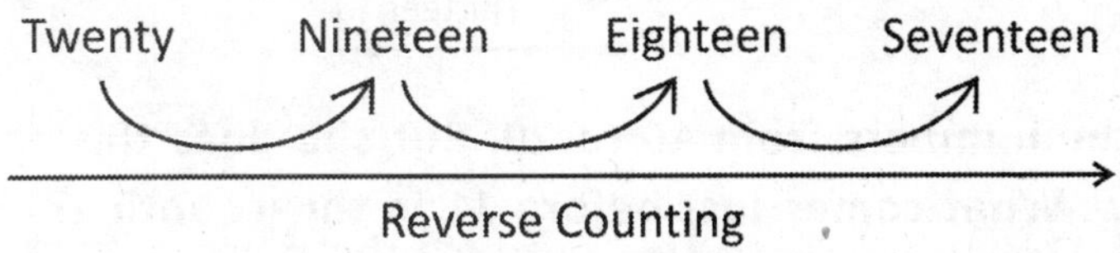

or

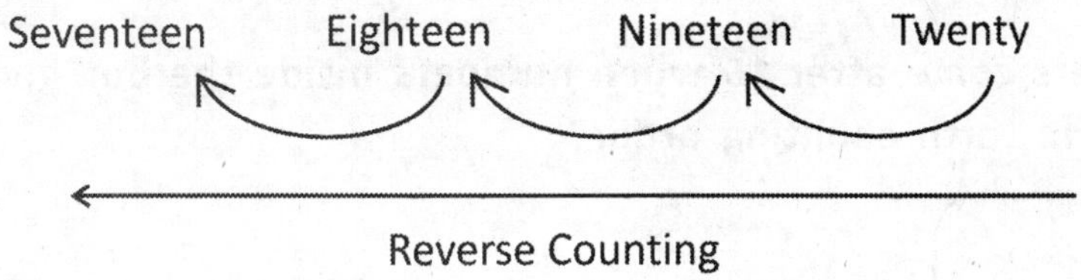

12. Which one of the following box has numbers in the reverse counting order?

(A) 9, 8, 7, 6 (B) 6, 8, 9, 7

(C) 8, 7, 6, 9 (D) 7, 9, 8, 6

(E) None of these

Answer (A)

Practice Exercise 1

1. What comes just before 10 while doing forth counting from number 5 to 10?

(A) 5 (B) 6 (C) 7 (D) 9

(E) None of these

2. Serena counts the numbers from 10 to 20. But she does this counting as reverse counting. What comes just before 11 in this counting?

(A) 13 (B) 18 (C) 12 (D) 17

(E) None of these

3. What numbers come after 15 when numbers inside the box given below are counted in forth counting order?

15 13 11

12 14 17

16

(A) 16 & 17 (B) 12 & 13 (C) 13 & 14 (D) Only 16

(E) None of these

4. Smith arranges 20, 19, 21 and 22 in the order of back counting. What comes just after 21?

(A) 20 (B) 19 (C) 22 (D) 21

(E) None of these

5. Which one of the following options is correct?

(A) One ten = 20

(B) Three tens = 30

(C) Two tens = 30

(D) Five tens = 40

(E) None of these

6. Which one of the following statements is true?

(A) 100 means six tens. (B) Seven tens means 60

(C) Seven tens means 80 (D) Nine tens means 90

(E) None of these

7. Maria does counting from 20 onwards. She starts with 20 and counts three more numbers one after another. What number she counts third time?

(A) 21 (B) 22 (C) 23 (D) 24

(E) None of these

8. In the figure given below, the number that will not be taken while counting in twenties is_______.

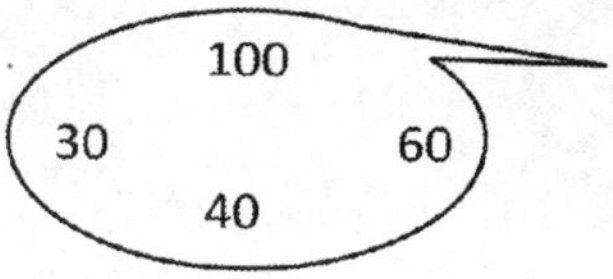

(A) 40 (B) 100 (C) 60 (D) 30

(E) None of these

9. Which one of the following options is a counting in words?

(A)

One	Two	Three

(B)

1	2	3

(C)

0	1	2

(D)

3	2	1

(E) None of these

10. If the numbers 11, 12, 13 & 14 are counted in words then what will come third in forth counting.

(A) Fourteen (B) Eleven

(C) Thirteen (D) Twelve

(E) None of these

Chapter

2 Ones and Tens

Learning Objectives

- Identifying Ones in a Number
- Identifying Tens in a Number

Identifying Ones in a Number

In any number, first digit from right is called ones and second digit from right is called tens. For example,

In [35] first digit from right is [5]. Thus the digit at one's place is [5]. It is also said that [35] has [5] ones.

Similarly in [52] the first digit from right is [2]. Thus the digit at one's place is [2] and it is said [52] has [2] ones.

Now We Can Say:

[12] has [2] ones.

[23] has [3] ones.

[25] has [5] ones.

This method goes the same for every number.

Identifying Tens in a Number

Here [21] is a number. In [21], [2] is at tens place. Second digit from right is the digit at tens place. For example,

In [23] the 2nd digit from right is [2] and hence, it is the digit at tens place. In this case it is also said [23] has [2] tens.

In [32] the 2nd digit from right is [3] and so it is tens place digit in [32].

This is also said that [32] has [3] tens.

Now we can say that

[18] has one tens.

[29] has two tens.

[38] has three tens.

This rule goes the same for every two or more digit numbers.

Summary

- 1st digit from right is at the ones place in a number.
- 2nd digit from right is at the tens place in a number.

Did You Know?

- The digit 0 to 9 was invented in India.
- 0 to 9 is the base of all the numbers.

Solved Problems

1. **18 has [ ] ones.**

(A) 4
(B) 8
(C) 5
(D) 7
(E) None of these

Answer (B)

Explanation: In [18] the first digit from right is [8].

2. **Find out the number at ones place in [27].**

(A) 7
(B) 2
(C) 8
(D) 9
(E) None of these

Answer (A)

Explanation: The [1st] digit from right in [27] is [7] and there fore, it is the digit at ones place.

3. **How many tens are there in [20] ?**

(A) It has 2 tens
(B) It has 5 tens
(C) It has 3 tens
(D) It has 1 ten
(E) None of these

Answer (A)

Explanation: In [20] the 2nd digit from right is [2].

Therefore, [2] is at tens place or it can be said that [20] has [2] tens.

4. How many tens are there in 34 ?

(A) 4 (B) 3

(C) 5 (D) 2

(E) None of these

Answer (B)

Explanation:

In 34 the 2nd digit from right is 3 and hence, it is at tens place.

Practice Exercise 2

1. **Which one of the following is correct statement?**

(A) 24 has 4 ones
(B) 24 has 2 ones
(C) 24 has 3 ones
(D) 24 has 5 ones
(E) None of these

2. **37 has ☐ ones.**

(A) 8
(B) 3
(C) 7
(D) 6
(E) None of these

3. **How many tens are there in 59 ?**

(A) 5
(B) 9
(C) 6
(D) 8
(E) None of these

4. **12 and 17 has ☐ at tens places.**

(A) 2
(B) 7
(C) 1
(D) 5
(E) None of these

5. **Add the following: 10 + 40 + 34.**

(A) 84
(B) 48
(C) 34
(D) 35
(E) None of these

6. **Steve has 5 tens and James has 6 ones. Steve gives 2 tens to James. Find the number James has:**

(A) 56
(B) 26
(C) 36
(D) All of these
(E) None of these

7. **Add the following:**

6 tens + 5 tens + 14 ones

(A) 114
(B) 1114
(C) 124
(D) All of these
(E) None of these

8. **Subtract the following:**

19 tens and 4 ones – 15 tens and 2 ones.

(A) 2 tens and 2 ones
(B) 4 tens and 2 ones
(C) 3 tens and 2 ones
(D) All of these
(E) None of these

9. **Find the digit at tens place in the following:**

46728

(A) 8
(B) 2
(C) 4
(D) 7
(E) None of these

10 **10 tens + 5 ones + 15 tens + 5 ones is equal to how many tens?**

(A) 25
(B) 31
(C) 26
(D) All of these
(E) None of these

Chapter 3

Addition

Learning Objectives

- Concept of Addition
- Addition of Two Numbers
- Addition of Three Numbers
- Addition of Figures
- Addition of Images
- Addition in Column
- Word Problems Based on Addition

Concept of Addition

Addition means collection other than one unit together and counting them as single unit.

Let's understand this through an example:

There are three balls in box A

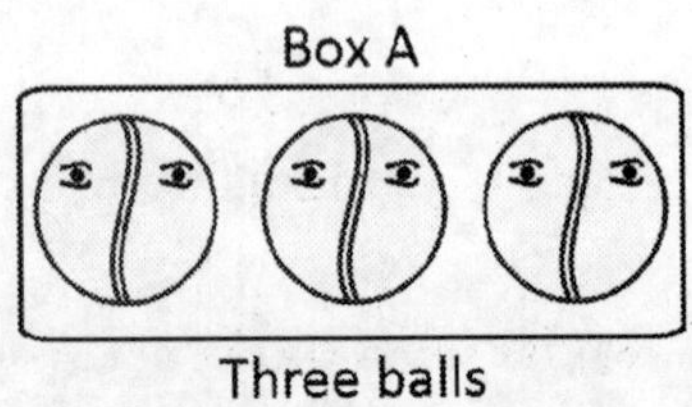

There is one ball in another box B

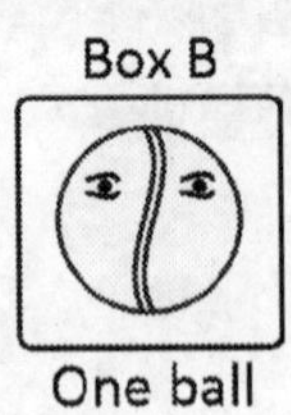

Now,

How many balls are there in both the boxes together?

For this, we put the balls from both the boxes in a single box C as shown below :

Box C

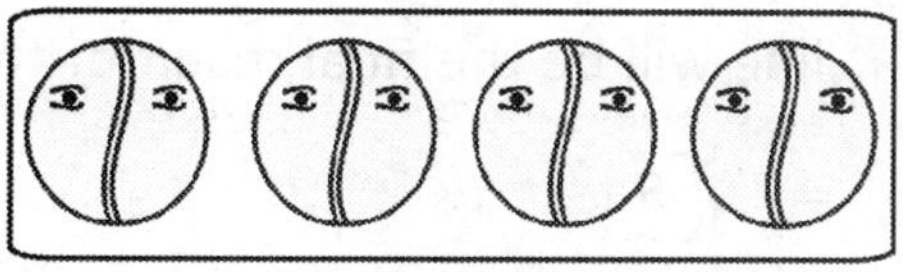

Four balls

Therefore, the third box has three balls of box A and one ball of box B and they are together 4 balls.

Let's understand it in another way:

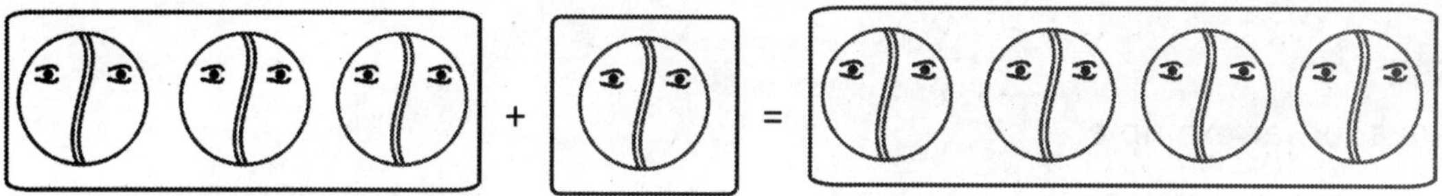

Three balls + One ball = Four balls

or

$$\boxed{3} + \boxed{1} = \boxed{4}$$

Where '+' is sign of addition and it is read as 'plus' and '=' is the sign of 'is equal to' or 'is same as'

Thus,

$\boxed{3} + \boxed{1} = \boxed{4}$ is read as:

'Three + One is equal to Four'

or 'Three + One is same as Four'

Addition of Two Numbers

It is the grouping of two numbers together and counting them as a single number.

$$\boxed{2} + \boxed{3} = \boxed{5}$$

It is also written as:

$$\begin{array}{r} 2 \\ +\,3 \\ \hline 5 \end{array}$$

Trick: Put two vertical lines for 2 and three vertical lines for 3. After this count all the lines together and that line will be the final result of this addition.

$\boxed{2} + \boxed{3} = \boxed{5}$

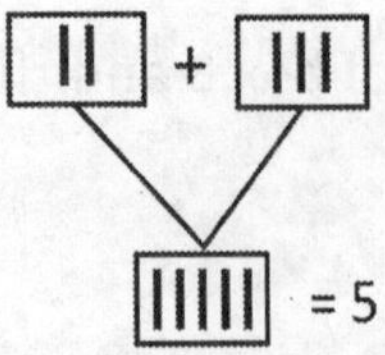

or

$$\begin{array}{r} 2 \\ +3 \\ \hline \boxed{?} \end{array} = \begin{array}{r} \text{II} \\ +\,\text{III} \\ \hline \text{IIIII} \end{array} = 5$$

Now,

Take another example

$\boxed{5} + \boxed{1} = \boxed{?}$

Now, we follow the trick:

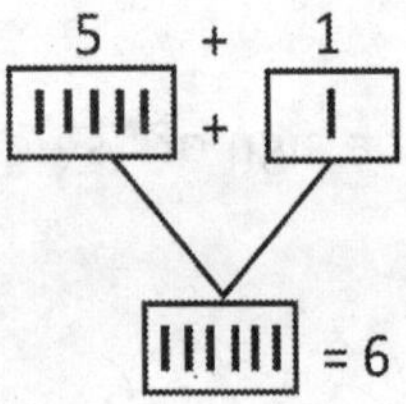

or

$$\begin{array}{r} 5 \\ +1 \\ \hline \boxed{?} \end{array} = \begin{array}{r} \text{IIIII} \\ +\ \ \text{I} \\ \hline \boxed{\text{IIIIII}} \end{array} = 6$$

Addition of Three Numbers

It is grouping of three numbers and counting them as a single unit.

$\boxed{1} + \boxed{2} + \boxed{3} = \boxed{6}$

It is also written as

$$\begin{array}{r} 1 \\ 2 \\ +3 \\ \hline 6 \end{array}$$

Points to remember:

Here,

we apply the same method of putting vertical lines.

1 + 2 + 3 = 6

To check it we follow the vertical line trick:

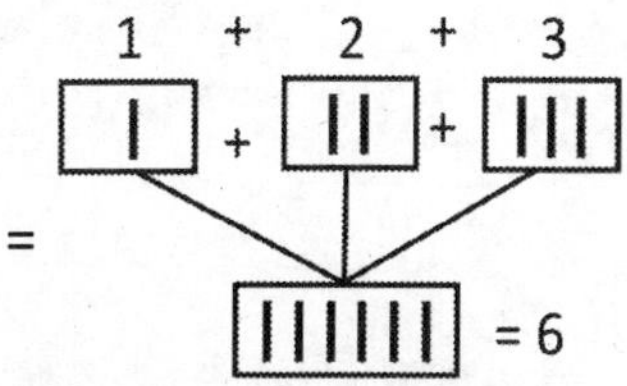

Take another example

4 + 5 + 6 = ?

Now,

We follow the trick

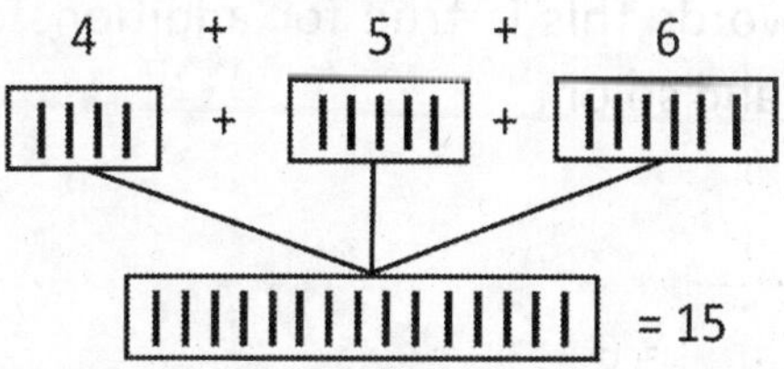

Points to Remember

1st number + 2nd number + 3rd number

= (3rd) number + (2nd) number + (1st) number

= (2nd) number + (3rd) number + (1st) number

= (2nd) number + (1st) number + (3rd) number

= (1st) number + (3rd) number + (2nd) number

= (3rd) number + (1st) number + (2nd) number

In all cases result will be the same.

Example:

[2] + [3] + [6] = [6] + [3] + [2]

= [3] + [2] + [6] = [2] + [6] + [3]

= [3] + [6] + [2] = [2] + [3] + [6]

Therefore, it is clear that in addition, numbers can be added in any order but the result is the same. In another words addition by changing the order of the given numbers dose not affect the result.

Note: This is not only true for addition of three numbers. But it is true for any two or more number's addition also. In another words this is true for additions of four numbers, five numbers, six numbers_______and so on.

Addition of Figures

Figure

Let's consider about 2, 4, 11, 10, etc. In fact these are simply numbers.

But, when we say:

[2] Mangoes

[4] Kilogram

[11] Letters

[10] hours

[10] Rupees

Then the numbers represent a figure. Therefore, it is clear that when numbers come in form of representing something, then they become a figure.

Now, we add figures with simple method of addition we have learned so far.

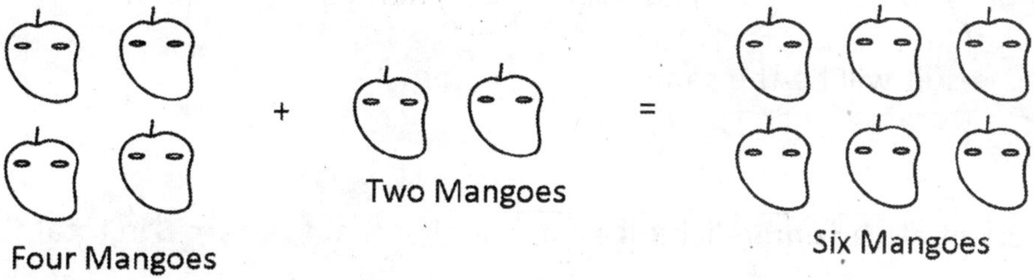

Trick: = 4 Mangoes + 2 Mangoes

[IIII] + [II]

[IIIIII] = 6 Mangoes

Take another example

[3] **kg rice +** [1] **kg pulse +** [2] **kg sugar = ?**

Trick:

3 Kg + 1 Kg + 2 Kg

= [III] + [I] + [II]

[IIIIII] = 6 Kg

Addition of Images

It does mean grouping of two or more pictures together.

[3] pictures + [1] picture = [4] pictures.

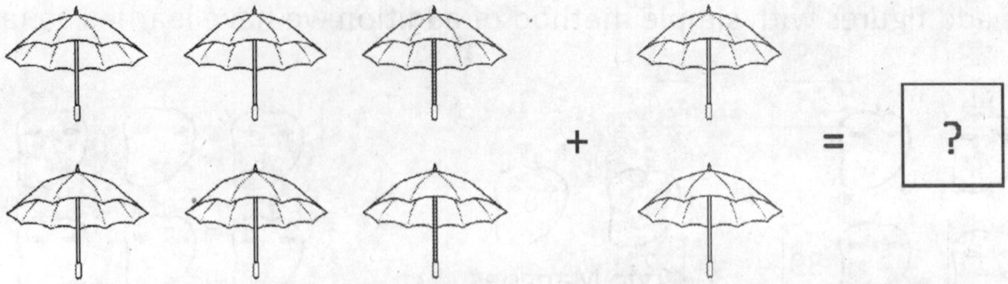

Here, we count all the umbrellas together and find that they are 8 in total.

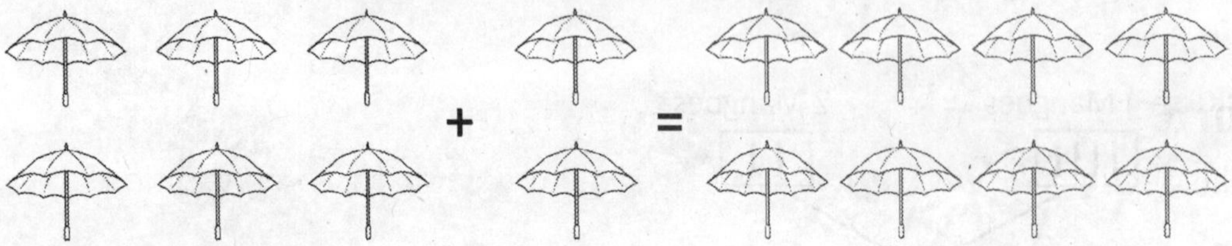

Six umbrellas **Two umbrellas** **Eight umbrellas**

[6] umbrellas + [2] umbrellas = [8] umbrellas.

Addition in Column

Addition in column is done by adding the numbers in column. See the given below examples:

Example: 1

$$\begin{array}{r} 7 \\ +4 \\ \hline 11 \end{array} \qquad \begin{array}{r} 3 \\ +8 \\ \hline 11 \end{array} \qquad \begin{array}{r} 4 \\ +5 \\ \hline 9 \end{array} \qquad \begin{array}{r} 9 \\ +8 \\ \hline 17 \end{array}$$

Example: 2

$$\begin{array}{r} 35 \\ +25 \\ \hline 60 \end{array} \qquad \begin{array}{r} 12 \\ +15 \\ \hline 27 \end{array} \qquad \begin{array}{r} 17 \\ +15 \\ \hline 32 \end{array}$$

Example: 3

```
  27     34     19
 +29    +17    +23
 ---    ---    ---
  56     51     42
```

Example: 4

```
  11     39     22
 +19    +29    +23
 ---    ---    ---
  30     68     45
```

Word Problems Based on Addition

In this section, we will learn about some real problems based on addition.

Example: 1

Steve has 12 toffees. His father gives him 10 more toffees. How many toffees does Steve have now?

(A) 2 toffees
(B) 10 toffees
(C) 12 toffees
(D) 22 toffees
(E) None of these

Answer (D)

Explanation:

12 + 10 = 22 toffees.

Example: 2

There are 4 legs in a chair. In a room there are 3 chairs. How many legs do these three chairs have?

(A) 7 legs
(B) 11 legs
(C) 12 legs
(D) All of these
(E) None of these

Answer (C)

Explanation:

[4] + [4] + [4] = [12] legs

Example: 3

A teacher draws 9 lines on the blackboard. After sometime she again draws 8 lines. How many lines does she draw in all?

(A) 9 lines
(B) 17 lines
(C) 8 lines
(D) All of these
(E) None of these

Answer (B)

Explanation:

[9] + [8] = [17] lines

Example: 4

In a garden there are [4] plants of marigold, [3] plants of jasmine and [7] plants of roses. How many plants are there in all in the garden?

(A) 14 plants
(B) 12 plants
(C) 16 plants
(D) 18 plants
(E) None of these

Answer (A)

Explanation:

[4] + [3] + [7] = [14] plants

Example: 5

Steve has a number which is [4] more than [7]. Find the number.

(A) 11
(B) 12
(C) 16
(D) All of these
(E) None of these

Answer (A)

Explanation:

7 + 4 = 11

Example: 6

Smith is 6 years old now. What will be his age after 15 years from now?

(A) 15 years
(B) 21 years
(C) 18 years
(D) All of these
(E) None of these

Answer (B)

Explanation:

15 + 6 = 21 years

Example: 6

There are 35 students in 1A, 30 students in 1B and 25 students in 1C. How many students are there in 1 class?

(A) 16 students
(B) 80 students
(C) 90 students
(D) All of these
(E) None of these

Answer (C)

Explanation:

35 + 30 + 25 = 90 students.

Example: 7

Serena bought [1] dozen of eggs. Her father told her to buy half dozen more eggs. How many eggs did she buy in all?

(A) 3 eggs
(B) 12 eggs
(C) 18 eggs
(D) 24 eggs
(E) None of these

Answer (C)

Explanation:

[1] dozen = [12] eggs

[$\frac{1}{2}$] dozen = [6] eggs

[12] + [6] = [18] eggs

Example: 8

Zacob has [15] bananas. Lina has [5] + [3] more bananas than Zacob. How many bananas does Lina have?

(A) 23 bananas
(B) 24 bananas
(C) 18 bananas
(D) All of these
(E) None of these

Answer (A)

Explanation:

[15] + [5] + [3] = [23] bananas

Example: 9

Maria has a sticker of number [5]. James has a sticker which has a number that is [17] more than Maria. Find the number of James.

(A) 12
(B) 15
(C) 16
(D) 22
(E) None of these

Answer (D)

Explanation:

| 17 | + | 5 | = | 22 |

Summary

- Addition is the grouping of two or more objects together.
- If any number is added to zero the result is the number itself.

| 0 | + | 5 | = | 5 |

| 0 | + | 2 | = | 2 |

| 2 | + | 0 | = | 2 |

- Result of the addition is called addition fact.

If | 0 | + | 5 | = | 5 |

Then 5 = addition fact

- Sign of addition = '+' and it is read as 'Plus'

| 0 | + | 0 | = | 0 |

Did You Know?

- If you add 0 to a number it remains unchanged.
- Addition represents combining collection of objects together into a larger collection.

Solved Problems

1. Add the numbers inside the egg given below.

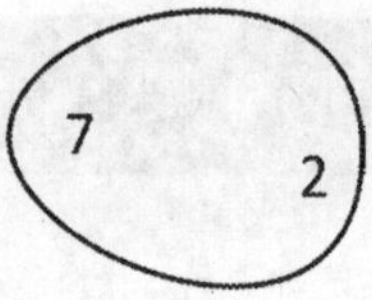

(A) 8 (B) 6
(C) 12 (D) 9
(E) None of these

Answer (D)

Explanation:

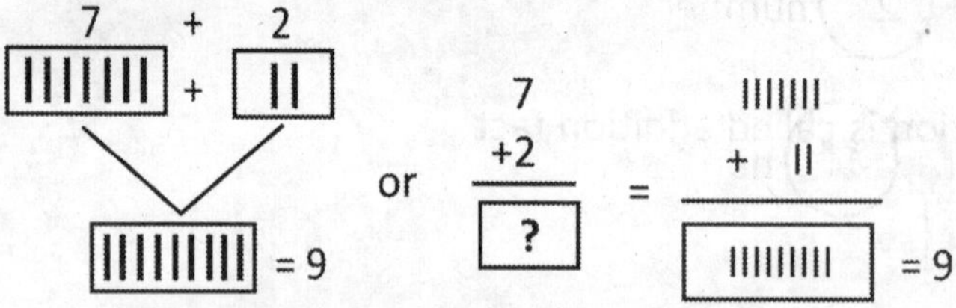

2. [7] + [2] = [?]

(A) [2] + [7] (B) [1] + [5]

(C) [6] + [1] (D) [8] + [2]

(E) None of these

Answer (A)

Explanation: In addition, if two or more numbers are added in any order the result is the same. In another words 1st number + 2nd number = 2nd number + 1st number

Therefore, 7 + 2 = 2 + 7

Further, we can check from the method:

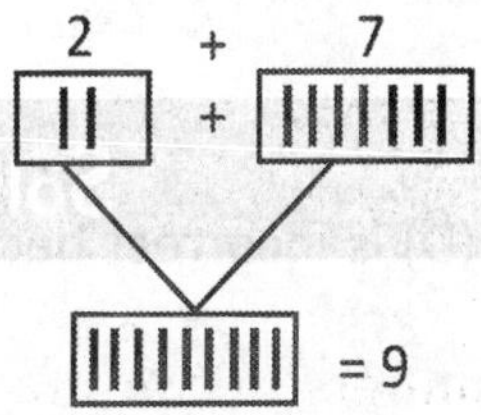

Again, =

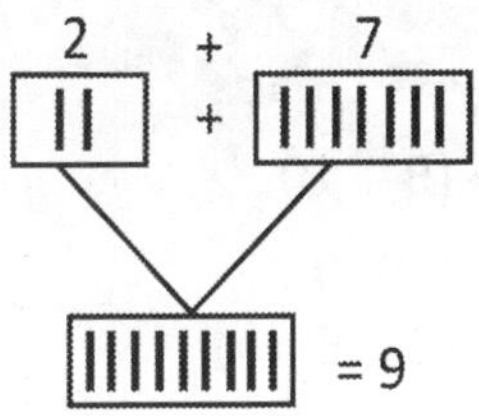

Therefore, 7 + 2 = 2 + 7

Points to remember:

(1st) number + (2nd) number

= (2nd) number + (1st) number

Option (B) is incorrect because =

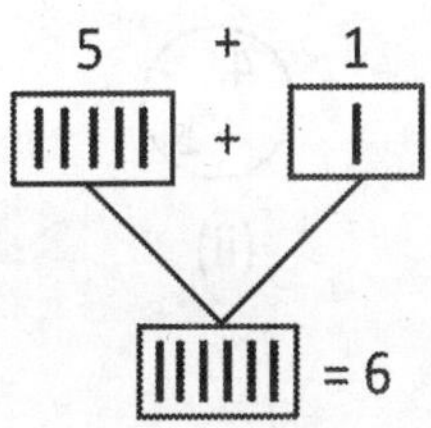

Option (C) is incorrect because =

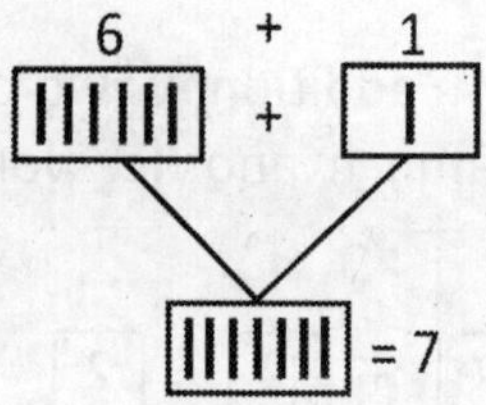

Option (D) is incorrect because =

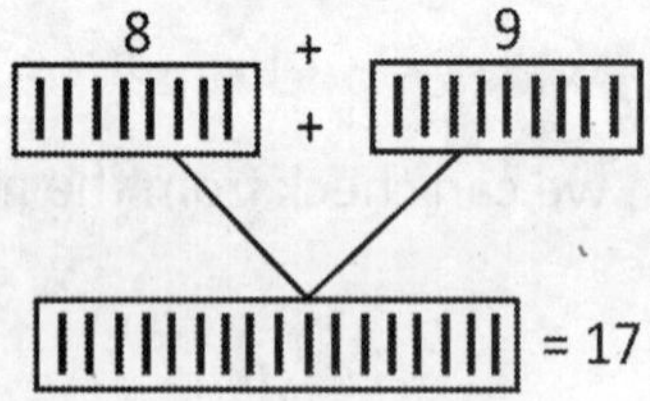

3. 6 + 4 + 1 = ?

(A) 12 (B) 10

(C) 11 (D) 9

(E) None of these

Answer (C)

Explanation:

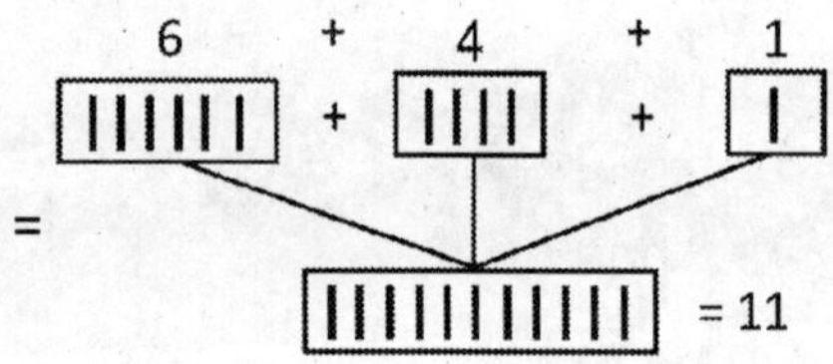

4. Add the number given in figure (i) and figure (ii).

(i)

(ii)

(A) 7 (B) 8

(C) 9 (D) 6

(E) None of these

Answer (B)

Explanation:

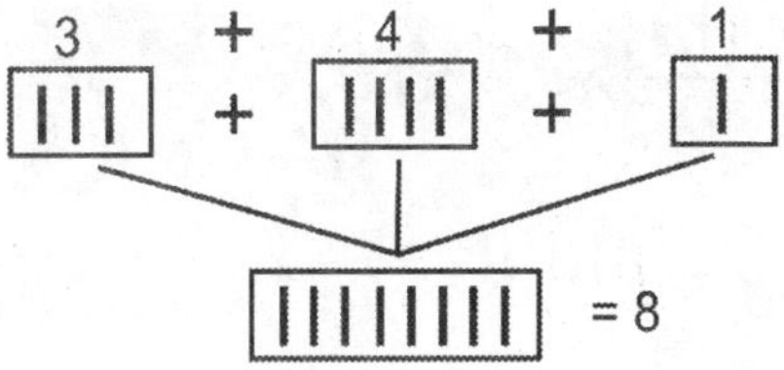

5. **Smith adds rupees 5 and rupees 6. What is the result of this addition?**

(A) 11 rupees
(B) 10 rupees
(C) 12 rupees
(D) 14 rupees
(E) None of these

Answer (A)

Explanation:

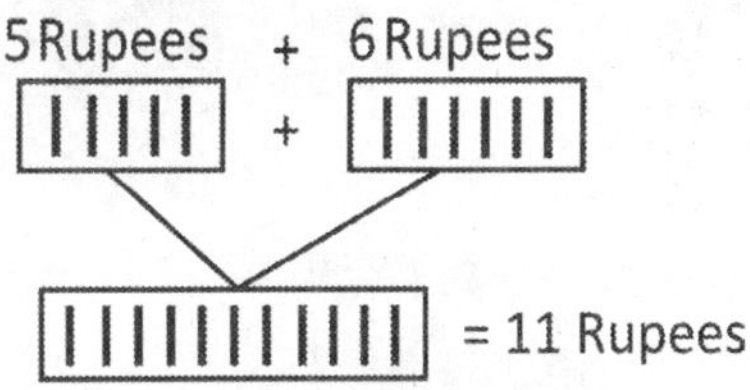

6. **4 books + 3 books + 1 book = ?**

(A) 7 books
(B) 6 books
(C) 5 books
(D) 8 books
(E) None of these

Answer (D)

Explanation:

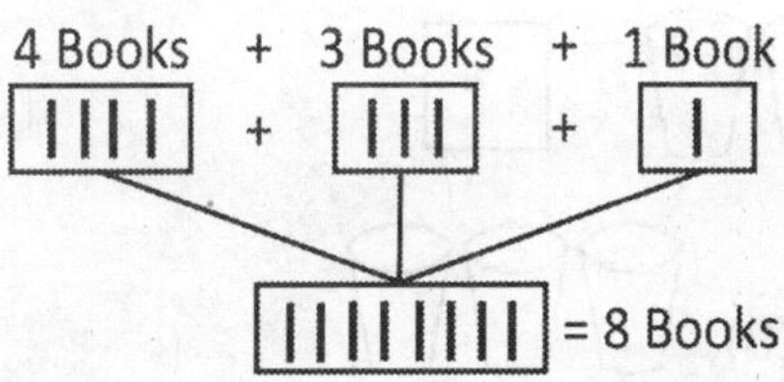

7. **Add the balloons given below and choose the correct option.**

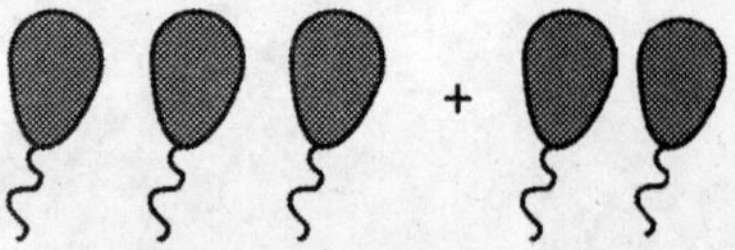

= ?

(A) 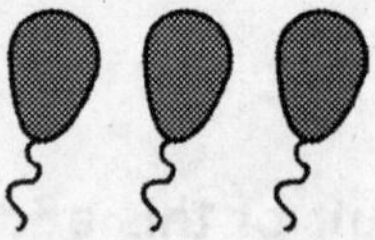

(B) 

(C) 

(D) 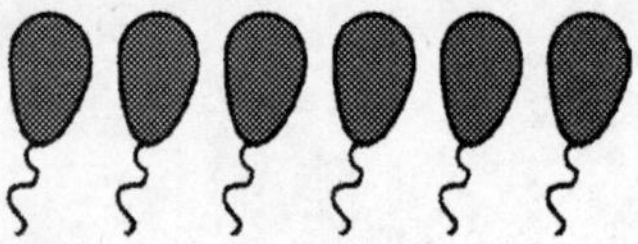

(E) None of these

Answer (C)

Explanation:

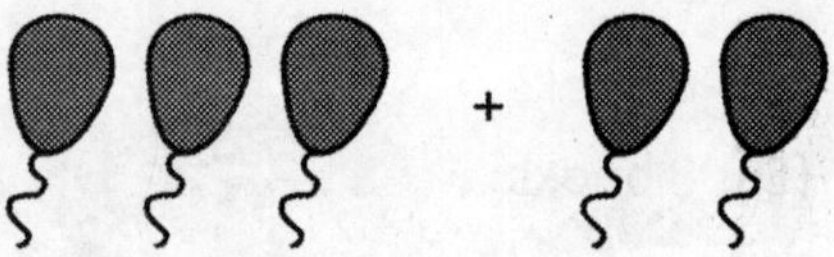

3 Balloons + 2 Balloons

It becomes a group of 3 + 2 = 5 Balloons.

8. 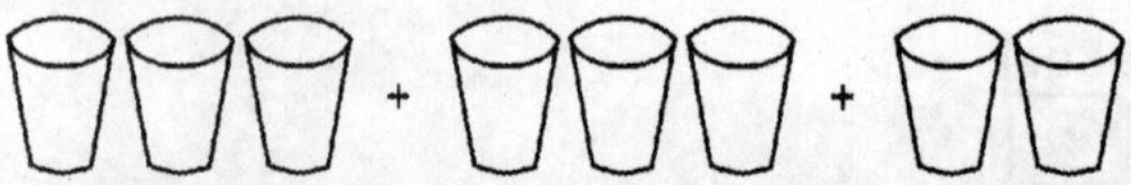 = ?

(A) 

(B) 

(C) 

(D) 

(E) None of these

Answer (C)

Explanation:

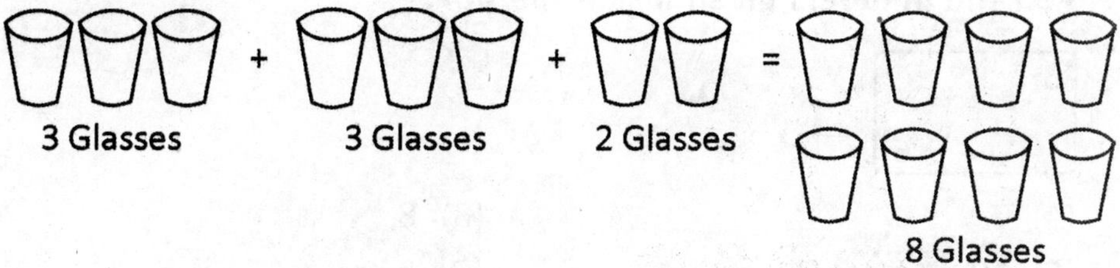

Practice Exercise 3

1. 6 + 8 = ?

(A) 14 (B) 13
(C) 18 (D) 12
(E) None of these

2. **Add the numbers given inside the box:**

3	
	6

(A) 7 (B) 8
(C) 10 (D) 9
(E) None of these

3. **Steve adds the numbers 2, 1 and 4. What is the final result of this addition?**

(A) 7 (B) 8
(C) 9 (D) 5
(E) None of these

4. **1 + 4 + 8 = ?**

(A) 12 (B) 13
(C) 15 (D) 16
(E) None of these

5. **Add ₹3 and ₹6**

(A) 9 rupees (B) 8 rupees
(C) 4 rupees (D) 3 rupees
(E) None of these

6. **1 Banana + 2 Bananas + 4 Bananas = ?**

(A) 7 Bananas (B) 6 Bananas

(C) 35 bananas (D) 39 bananas

(E) None of these

7. Add the following  = ?

(A) 

(B) 

(C) 

(D) 

(E) None of these

8. Ricky adds the eggs kept in the two boxes and put this addition in a single box. What is the result of this addition?

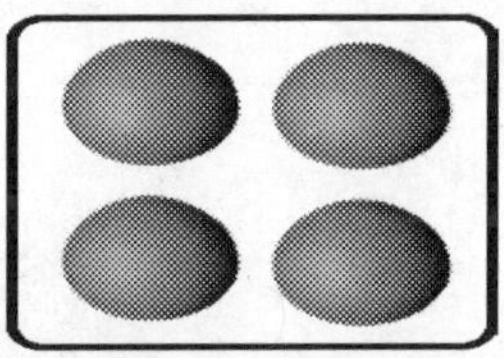

Box (i)

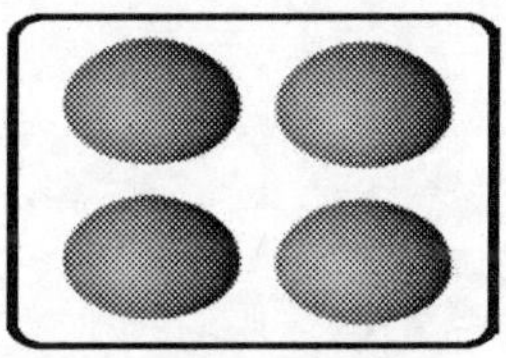

Box (ii)

(A) 

(B) 

(C) 

(D) 

(E) None of these

9. Steve buys 1 dozen eggs, James buys 9 eggs and Ricky buys 2 dozen eggs. How many eggs are bought by all the three people together.

(A) 40 eggs
(B) 42 eggs
(C) 44 eggs
(D) 45 eggs
(E) None of these

10. Lina has 17 dolls and Serena has 15 dolls. Lina buys 18 more dolls. How many dolls they have in all?

(A) 45 dolls
(B) 48 dolls
(C) 50 dolls
(D) All of these
(E) None of these

Chapter

4 Subtraction

Learning Objectives

- Introduction
- Subtraction of Two Numbers
- Subtraction of Three Numbers
- Subtraction of Figures
- Subtraction of Images
- Subtraction in Column
- Word Problems Based on Subtraction
- Mixed Problems

Introduction

Subtraction means taking out something from some longer unit and in this process finding the outcome as left over.

Let's understand this through an example:

There are three eggs in the box given below:

Three eggs

From this box Steve eats one egg then how many eggs are left?

Steve eats one egg then one egg will disappear from the box as shown below:

Two eggs

Now two eggs are seen in the box. Therefore, this means two eggs are left over and the outcome of this subtraction process is 2.

Let's understand it another way:

Total eggs in the box = 3

1 = egg eaten by Steve = 3 – 1 = 2

And 2 = outcome or left over

Here, '__' is the sign of subtraction and it is read as 'minus', and = is the sign of 'is equal to' or 'is same as'.

Thus,

3 – 1 = 2

It is read as

'three minus one is equal to two' or 'three minus one is same as two'.

Subtraction of Two Numbers

It is the process of taking away smaller number from the greater one.

4 – 3 = 1

TRICK:

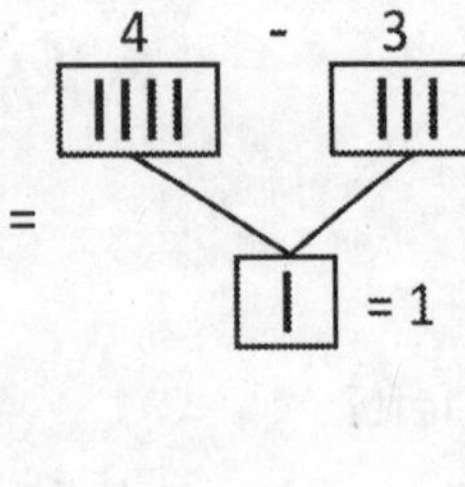

Here, it is clear that if we have to subtract 3 then we cut three vertical lines from 4. It means number of vertical lines to be cut is equal for both greater and smaller numbers and number of vertical lines to be cut for each greater and smaller number is equal to the number to be subtracted.

Similarly, if 2 has to be subtracted then number of vertical lines to be cut from greater number is 2 and from smaller number is also 2

And if 4 has to be subtracted then 4 vertical lines are cut.

Take another example:

5 – 3 = ?

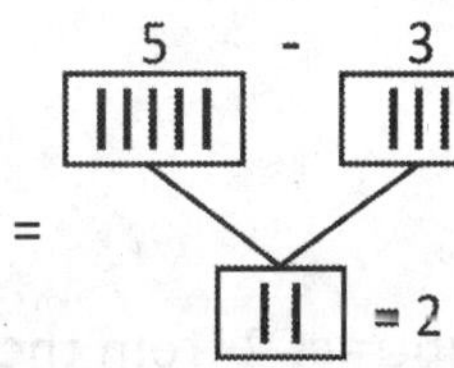

Subtraction of Three Numbers

Let's see the given below example:

Example: 1

4 – 2 – 1 = ?

Here we shall subtract the numbers 2 and 1 from 4, since the numbers 2 and 1 have '–' sign.

Now,

Step 1: Add the numbers with '–' sign.

Step 2: Do subtraction as subtraction of two numbers.

$4 - (2 + 1)$

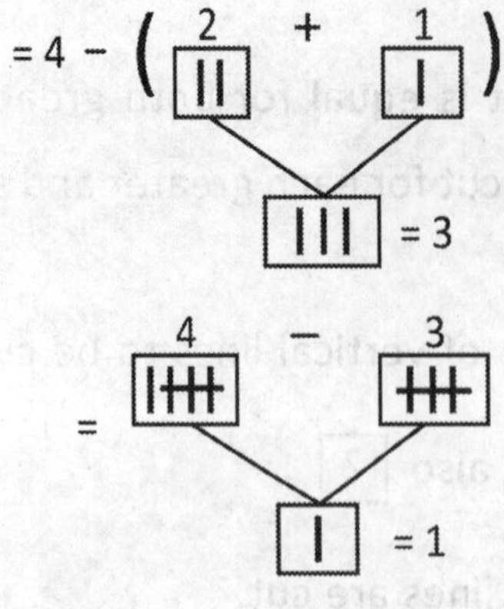

Thus,

4 – (2 +1) = 4 - 3 = 1

Take another example:

Example: 2

4 – 2 + 1 = ?

Here, we will add two numbers 4 and 1 and then we will subtract 2 from the sum.

Step 1: Add numbers with ' + ' sign

Step 2: Do the subtraction as subtraction of two numbers.

Thus,

(4 + 1) – 2

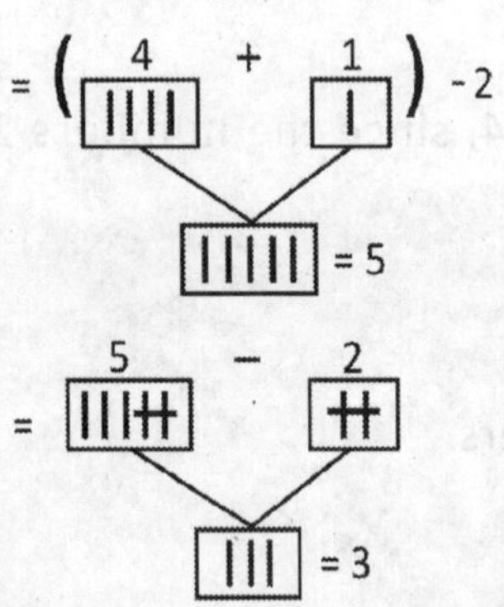

Therefore, above given two examples make the concept of subtraction of three numbers clear.

Subtraction of Figures

Numbers = 2, 1, 5 & 6, etc.

Figures = 2 rupees, 3 books, 1 kg, 6 hours, etc.

Now, how to subtract figures?

In fact, we subtract figures with simple method of subtraction we have learned so far.

Example:

5 hours – 2 hours = 3 hours

Trick:

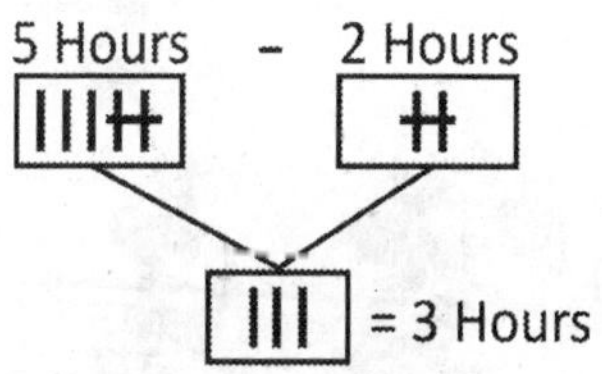

Take another example:

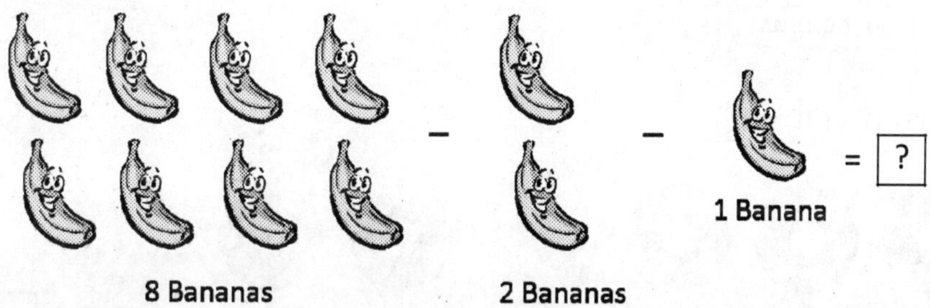

Trick:

8 bananas – 2 bananas – 1 banana

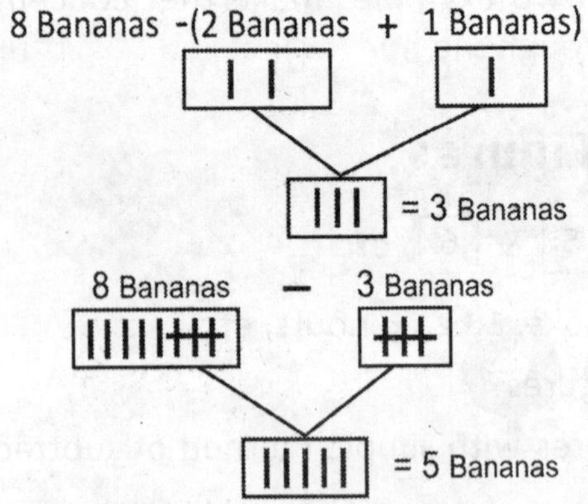

Subtraction of Images

It means taking out picture or pictures from group of pictures and finding the remaining as the result of the subtraction.

Take another example:

Here, we count the flowers given before the sign of minus and after the sign of minus. We subtract it through the normal method of subtraction.

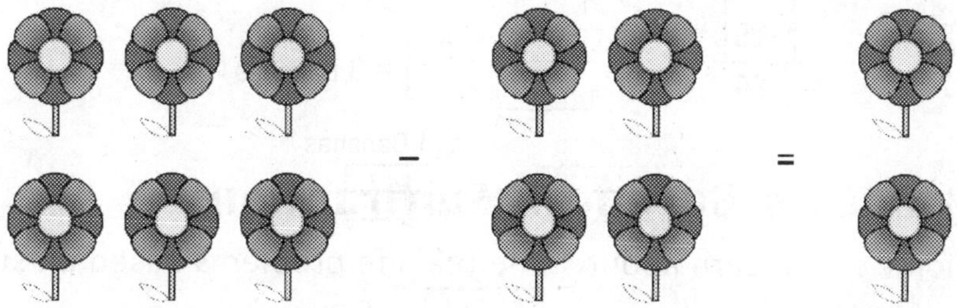

6 Flowers 4 Flowers 2 Flowers

Subtraction in Column

Subtraction in column is done by subtracting the numbers in column. See the given below examples:

Example: 1

$$\begin{array}{r} 27 \\ 19 \\ \hline 08 \end{array} \qquad \begin{array}{r} 39 \\ -17 \\ \hline 22 \end{array} \qquad \begin{array}{r} 24 \\ -12 \\ \hline 12 \end{array} \qquad \begin{array}{r} 19 \\ -8 \\ \hline 11 \end{array}$$

Example: 2

$$\begin{array}{r} 49 \\ -36 \\ \hline 13 \end{array} \qquad \begin{array}{r} 42 \\ -27 \\ \hline 15 \end{array} \qquad \begin{array}{r} 37 \\ -17 \\ \hline 20 \end{array}$$

Example: 3

$$\begin{array}{r} 31 \\ -15 \\ \hline 16 \end{array} \qquad \begin{array}{r} 65 \\ -56 \\ \hline 09 \end{array} \qquad \begin{array}{r} 19 \\ -7 \\ \hline 12 \end{array}$$

Example: 4

38	39	28
−17	−15	−17
21	24	11

Word Problems Based on Subtraction

In this section we will learn about some real life problems based on subtraction.

Example: 1

James purchased 18 balloons on his birthday and gave 1 balloon to each of his friends. He has 7 friends. How many balloons were left with him?

(A) 11 balloons
(B) 10 balloons
(C) 12 balloons
(D) All of these
(E) None of these

Answer (A)

Explanation:

18 − 7 = 11 balloons

Example: 2

Smith is 4 years younger than Lina. If the age of Lina is 9 years then find the age of Smith?

(A) 4 years
(B) 5 years
(C) 6 years
(D) All of these
(E) None of these

Answer (B)

Explanation:

9 − 4 = 5 years

Example: 3

A number is [9] less than [35]. Find the number.

(A) 15 (B) 18

(C) 26 (D) 12

(E) None of these

Answer (C)

Explanation:

[35] – [9] = [26]

Example: 4

Which one of the following numbers she will get?

1. **Serena puts [25] in a magic box.**
2. **If 3 is subtracted three times from it.**

(A) 14 (B) 15

(C) 16 (D) 18

(E) None of these

Answer (C)

Explanation:

[25] – [3] – [3] – [3] = [25] – ([3] + [3] + [3])

[25] – [9] = [16]

Example: 5

A student brought 1 dozen toffees on his birthday in the school. He distributed half dozen toffees among his friends. How many toffees were left with him?

(A) 4 toffees (B) 6 toffees

(C) 8 toffees (D) All of these

(E) None of these

Answer (B)

Explanation:

1 dozen toffees = 12 toffees

$\frac{1}{2}$ dozen toffees = 6 toffees

12 – 6 = 6 toffees

Example: 6

Smith says that he has a number. If you subtract 5 from it, the result will be 7. Find the number.

(A) 11
(B) 13
(C) 15
(D) 12
(E) None of these

Answer (D)

Explanation:

12 – 5 = 7

Example: 7

In a school there are 35 students in 1A and 25 students in 1C . Which section has more students and by how much?

(A) Section A by 9
(B) Section C by 9
(C) Section A by 10
(D) Section C by 10
(E) None of these

Answer (C)

Explanation:

Section A has 10 more students than section C .

Example: 8

There are [18] mangoes in the basket. William eats [2] mangoes daily. How many mangoes are left after [5] days?

(A) 10 mangoes (B) 8 mangoes
(C) 12 mangoes (D) 15 mangoes
(E) None of these

Answer (B)

Explanation: Mangoes eaten by William in [5] days

= [2] + [2] + [2] + [2] + [2] = [10]

Mangoes left = [18] – [10] = [8] mangoes.

Example: 9

A number when subtracted from [18] gives the result [7]. Find the number.

(A) 11 (B) 12 (C) 9 (D) All of these
(E) None of these

Answer (A)

Explanation:

[18] – [11] = [7]

Example: 10

The sum of two numbers is [16]. If bigger number is [9] then find the smaller number.

(A) 8 (B) 7 (C) 6 (D) All of these
(E) None of these

Answer (B)

Explanation: [16] – [9] = [7]

Summary

- Subtraction is the process of taking away smaller unit from bigger one.
- If zero is subtracted from any number the result is the number itself.
- (1 – 0 = 1), (5 – 0 = 5), (8 – 0 = 8).
- Result of subtraction is called subtraction fact.

  That is 5 – 4 = 1
- Sign of subtraction is '—' and it is read as 'minus'.
- If any number is subtracted from itself, the result is 0.

  (8 – 8 = 0), (5 – 5 = 0),(10 – 10 = 0).

Did You Know?

- Subtraction means taking away number of objects from a given collection.
- If you subtract 0 from a number the number remains unchanged.

Solved Problems

1. **Solve** 5 + 7 + 8 − 9

Solution:

To solve this sum, first add the numbers with + sign.

That is 5 + 7 + 8 = 20

Now subtract 9 from 20. That is 20 − 9 = 11.

So the answer is 11.

2. **Solve** 19 − 8 − 4 − 2

Solution:

To solve this sum first write 19 then add all the numbers with negative sign.

That is − 8 − 4 − 2 = − 14

Now subtract 14 from 19. That is 19 − 14 = 5.

So the answer is 5.

3. **Solve** 5 + 4 − 3 + 7 − 2

Solution:

To solve this sum first add the numbers with + sign.

That is 5 + 4 + 7 = 16.

Then add the numbers with − sign. That is −3 + −2 = −5.

Now subtract 5 from 16. That is 16 − 5 = 11.

4. **Steve takes a number 12 and add 9 to it and then subtract 7 from it. Find the number.**

Solution:

To solve this sum first add 12 and 9. That is 12 + 9 = 21.

Now subtract 7 from 21. That is 21 – 7 = 14.

5. **Steve has ₹ 5 + ₹ 10 + ₹ 2 and Smith has ₹ 2 + ₹ 5, find how much more money Steve has than Smith?**

Solution:

To solve this sum first add the money Steve has.

That is 5 + 10 + 2 = ₹ 17.

Now add the money Smith has. That is 2 + 5 = ₹ 7.

Now subtract ₹ 7 from ₹ 17. That is ₹ 17 – ₹ 7 = ₹ 10.

So Steve has ₹ 10 more than Smith.

6. **Serena has 5 apples and she eats 3 apples. How many apples she has now?**

(A) 1 (B) 4

(C) 3 (D) 2

(E) None of these

Answer (D)

Explanation:

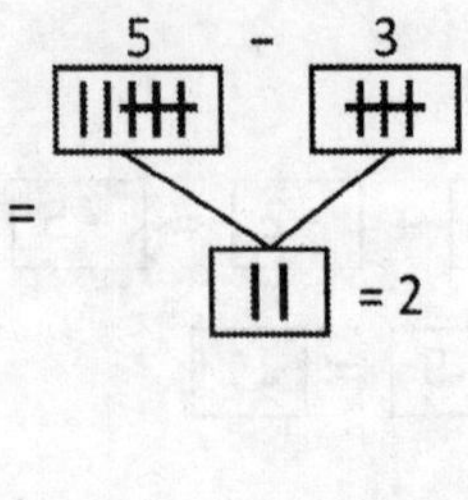

7. **9 – 5 = ?**

(A) 3 (B) 4

(C) 6 (D) 5

(E) None of these

Answer (B)

Explanation:

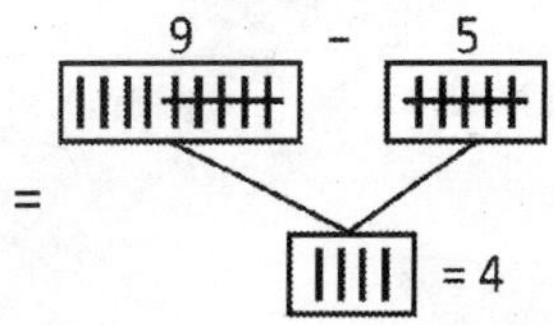

8. **Jack has 6 Chocolates, he eats 2 chocolates in the morning and again 2 in the evening, how many chocolates he has now?**

(A) 3 (B) 1

(C) 5 (D) 2

(E) None of these

Answer (D)

Explanation:

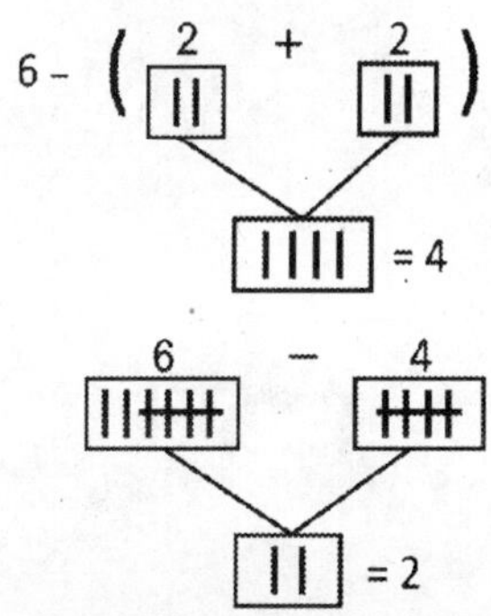

9. **7 – 3 + 5 = ?**

(A) 9 (B) 6

(C) 5 (D) 8

(E) None of these

Answer (A)

Explanation:

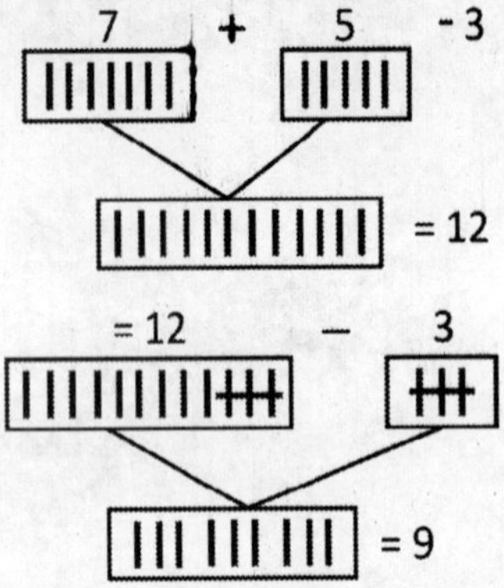

10. Zacob subtracts 4 rupees out of 8 rupees. Find the result.

(A) 5 rupees

(B) 3 rupees

(C) 2 rupees

(D) 4 rupees

(E) None of these

Answer (D)

Explanation:

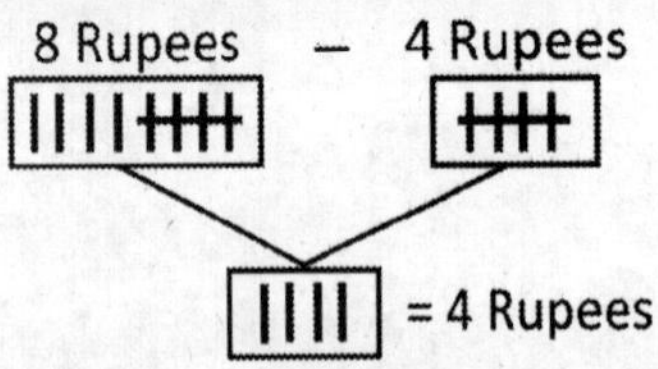

11. 7 kg + 1 kg – 3 kg = ?

(A) 2 kg

(B) 3 kg

(C) 5 kg

(D) 6 kg

(E) None of these

Answer (C)

Explanation:

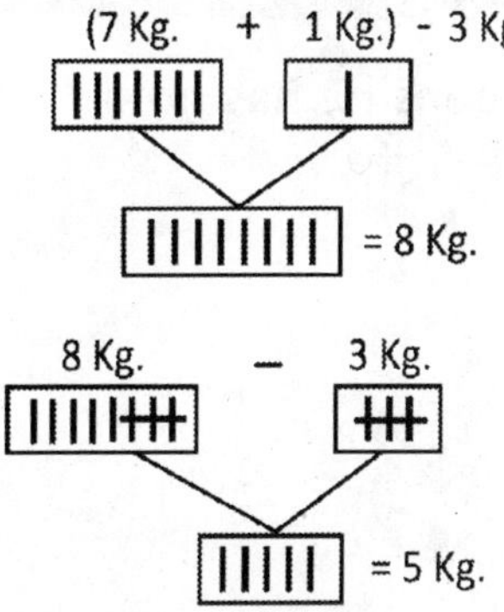

12. 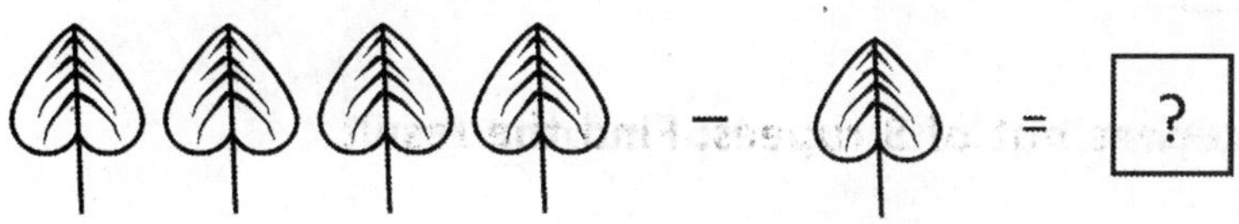

(A) 

(B) 

(C) 

(D) 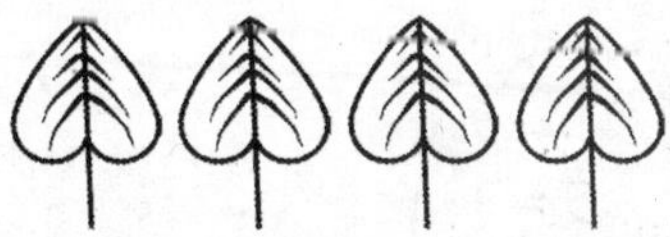

(E) None of these

Answer (C)

Explanation:

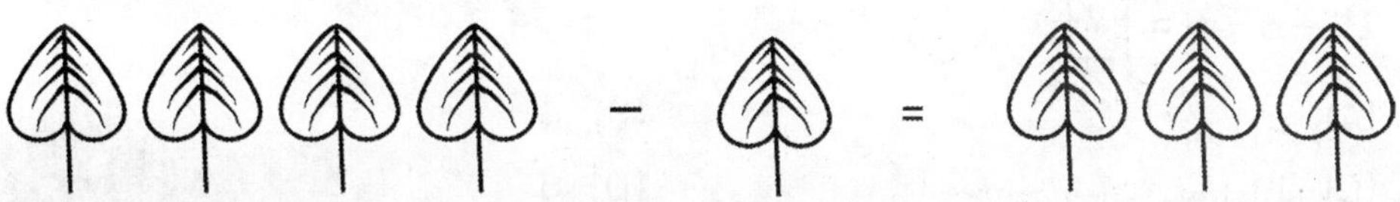

4 Leaves 4 Leaf 3 Leaves

Practice Exercise 4

1. Steve had 6 Pens. He lost 2 pens. How many pens he has now ?

(A) 5 (B) 4
(C) 3 (D) 2
(E) None of these

2. 8 + 1 – 9 = [?]

(A) 5 (B) 0
(C) 4 (D) 3
(E) None of these

3. Which one of the following options is not correct ?

(A) 4 – 3 = 1 (B) 4 – 4 = 0
(C) 7 – 5 = 2 (D) 3 – 3 = 3
(E) None of these

4. 15 – 8 – 6 = [?]

(A) 2 (B) 4
(C) 1 (D) 6
(E) None of these

5. Jack subtracts 5 hours from 8 hours. What is the result of this subtraction?

(A) 4 hours (B) 3 hours
(C) 2 hours (D) 5 hours
(E) None of these

6. **5 pencils + 2 pencils – 1 pencil = ?**

(A) 5 pencils (B) 4 pencils
(C) 3 pencils (D) 6 pencils
(E) None of these

7. ↑↑↑↑↑
↑↑↑↑↑ – ↑↑↑↑↑ = ?

(A) ↑↑↑↑↑ (B) ↑↑↑↑
(C) ↑↑↑↑↑↑ (D) ↑↑↑↑↑↑↑
(E) None of these

8. **Mr. Collin gives ₹250 to his son as a pocket money. His son spends ₹75 in a week. How much money is left with him?**

(A) ₹150 (B) ₹175
(C) ₹200 (D) All of these
(E) None of these

9. **On a tree there are 48 birds. After some time 10 more birds come and sit on the tree and 7 birds flyaway. How many birds are there on the tree now?**

(A) 51 (B) 49
(C) 41 (D) All of these
(E) None of these

10. **Solve the following:**

4 + 8 – 9 + 7 – 2

(A) 6 (B) 7
(C) 8 (D) All of these
(E) None of these

Chapter

5 Comparison

Learning Objectives

- Introduction
- Comparison of Numbers
- Comparison of Images (Size)
- Ascending and Descending Order

Introduction

Comparison enables us to identify what is greater or smaller between two objects and what is greatest and smallest among more than two objects.

For example, if we compare 1 & 2, it is clear that 2 is bigger number but if we compare

1, 2 & 3 then

1 is the smallest and 3 is the biggest number.

While 2 comes between 1 & 3 therefore, it is greater or bigger than 1 but smaller or less than 3.

Comparison of Numbers

Let us see the examples given below:

Example: 1

3 > 2

It means that 3 is greater than 2 and '>' is the sign of 'greater than' or bigger than' or more than'

3 > 2 is read as:

(A) 3 is greater than 2

(B) 3 is bigger than 2

(C) 3 is more than 2

3 > 2 is also written as 2 < 3 and read as 2 is less than 3

Therefore, it is clear that the mouth of the sign '>' is open to the side of the greater or bigger number.

Example: 2

How 3 is a greater number between 2 and 3 ?

For that we apply vertical line trick:

3	2
= III	II

When counted III (3) is more than II (2)

Hence 3 > 2

Take another example:

Example: 3

Which one is bigger between 4 and 6 ?

4	6
||||	||||||

Clearly \|\|\|\|\|\| (6) is more than \|\|\|\| (4)

6 > 4 or 4 < 6

Example: 4

10 and 7

10 > 7 or 7 < 10

It means the number 10 has two digits and the number 7 has 1 digit.

Therefore, 10 is greater than 7

Take another example:

Example: 5

If we compare 85 and 100

Then

100 > 85 or 85 < 100

100 has three digits and 85 has two digits.

Therefore, 100 is greater than 85 .

If the two numbers have equal number of digits then the digits at extreme left are compared and the number with greater digit is greater.

Example: 6

If we compare 20 and 10 then:

20 > 10 or 10 < 20

To find this result we compare the two numbers.

While comparing two digit numbers, if extreme left digits are equal or same then we compare the next digits to the right and so on. In this case also the number with greater digit is greater.

Example: 7

When we compare

42 and 49

49 > 42 or 42 < 49

Therefore, 49 > 42

Smaller Numbers

See the following examples:

Example: 1

2 < 3

It means 2 is less than 3 and '<' is the sign of 'less than' or 'smaller than'.

Hence, 2 < 3 is read as:

(A) 2 is smaller than 3

(B) 2 is less than 3

2 < 3 is also written as 3 > 2. So it is clear that the mouth of the sign '<'

is closed to the side of the smaller number.

How [2] is smaller in [2] < [3] ?

For this, Let's see the vertical line trick:

2		3
II	|	III

When counted [II] (2) is less than [III] (3)

Hence, [2] < [3]

Take another example:

Example: 2

Which one is smaller when

[3] and [6] are compared?

Here we have

3		6
III	|	IIIIII

Clearly [III] (3) is less than [IIIIII] (6)

Hence, [3] < [6] or [6] > [3]

Other Rules

Rule1: If a number has less digits than another, it is smaller of the two.

If we have [8] and [14]

Then

[8] < [14] or [14] > [8]

Let us take another example:

If we compare 25 **and** 100

Then

25 < 100 or 100 > 25

Rule2: If the two numbers have equal number of digits then the digits on extreme left are compared and the number with smaller digit is smaller.

When 15 **and** 26 **are compared then** 15 < 26 is true.

To know how is it possible just see the trick given below:

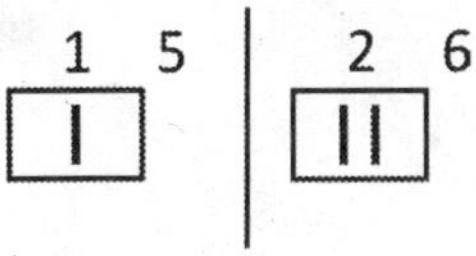

Thus 1 < 2

And hence, 15 < 26

Rule3: While comparing two digit numbers, if extreme left digits are same then we compare the second digit from left. In this case also, the number with smaller digit is smaller.

When we compare 32 and 35

Then

32 < 35 or 35 > 32

Trick:

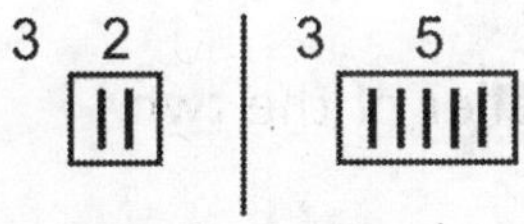

Here 2 < 5

Hence, 32 < 35

Equal Numbers

Equal means neither greater nor less than.

Let's consider

1 and 01

These numbers are equal because if one or more zeroes is put before any number, the number remains unchanged. Thus 1 and 01 can be written as:

1 = 01 or 01 = 1

Where '=' is the sign of equal

And 1 = 01 is read as,

1 is equal to 01

Similarly take another example:

04 and 004 are equal and they can be written as

04 = 004 or 004 = 04

Comparison of Images (Size)

The comparison is done through pictures.

Size Comparison

Let's understand it through an example:

(A) Small

(B) Big

In the above mentioned pictures (A) is smaller and (B) is bigger. Therefore, (A) is smaller in comparison of (B) while (B) is bigger in comparison of (A).

Thus we can present it as:

(A) Big (B) Small (A) Small (B) Big

Take another example:

(A) Small (A) Big

Here again picture (A) is smaller in comparison of (B) and picture (B) is bigger in comparison of (A)

Thus we can present it as

(A) Big (B) Small (A) Small (B) Big

Comparison of (Number) Images

Just see the two groups of pictures given below:

Group A Group B

Here group A has four keys and group B has two keys. Therefore, group A is greater than group B and this can be presented as:

or

Take another example:

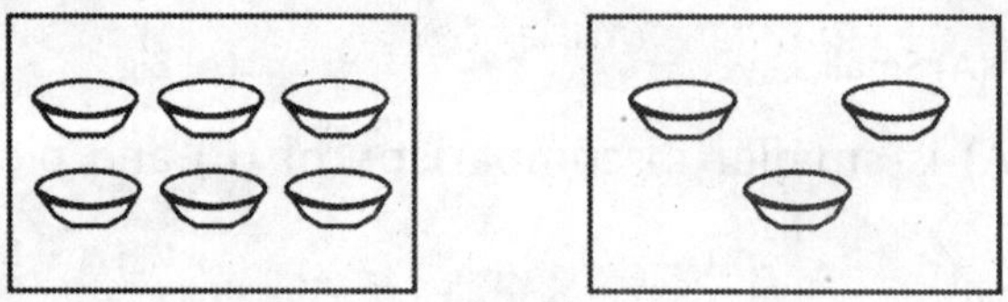

(A) (B)

Here box (A) has 6 bowls while (B) has 3 bowls. Thus box (A) has more number of bowls in comparison of box (B). It can be presented as:

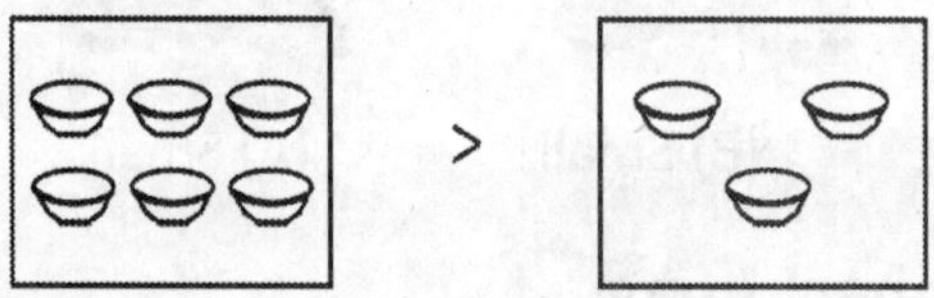

or

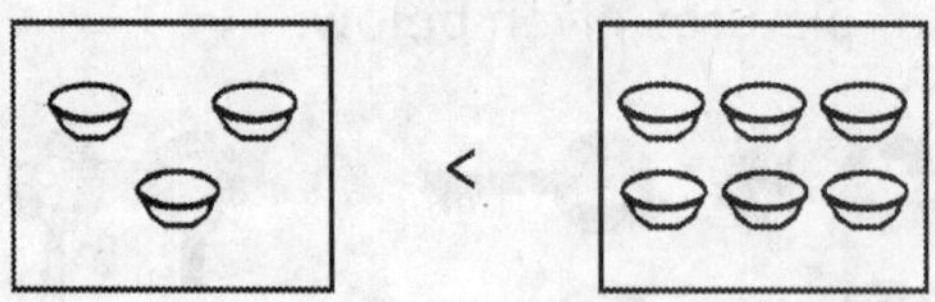

Ascending and Descending Order

Numbers can be arranged in ascending or descending order. In other words you can say that numbers can be arranged from smallest to greatest or greatest to smallest.

Ascending Order

In ascending order numbers are arranged in the order from smallest to greatest.

For example: [2], [4], [6], [8], [10], [12] are in ascending order.

Example: 1

Arrange the following numbers in ascending order:

[3], [9], [7], [16], [15]

The correct answer is [3], [7], [9], [15], [16].

To solve this first we write smallest number that is [3]. Then again write the smallest number from the remaining numbers that is [7] and thus continue in the same way. The numbers are arranged in the ascending order.

Example: 2

Arrange the following numbers in ascending order:

[19], [8], [15], [12], [21]

The correct answer is [8], [12], [15], [19], [21]

To solve this first we write smallest number that is [8]. Then again write the smallest number from the remaining numbers that is [12] and thus continue in the same way. The numbers are arranged in the ascending order.

Descending Order

In descending order numbers are written from greatest to smallest.

For example: [18], [17], [14], [9], [8] are in descending order.

Example: 1

Arrange the following numbers in descending order:

3, 9, 7, 16, 15

The correct answer is 16, 15, 9, 7, 3

To solve this first we write greatest number that is 16. Then again write the greatest number from the remaining numbers that is 15 and thus continue in the same way. The numbers are arranged in the descending order.

Example: 2

Arrange the following numbers in descending order:

19, 8, 15, 12, 21

The correct answer is 21, 19, 15, 12, 8

To solve this first we write greatest number that is 21. Then again write the greatest number from the remaining numbers that is 19 and thus continue in the same way. The numbers are arranged in the descending order.

Summary

- Comparison means which one is greater or more and smaller than other.
- Sign of greater or bigger or more is '>'.
- Sign of smaller or less is '<'.
- Equal numbers are neither greater than nor smaller or less than each other.
- If one or more zeroes are put before any number, then number remains un-changed. For example 06 and 6 are equal.
- Comparison of images is the pictorial comparison.
- Ascending order means smallest to greatest.
- Descending order means greatest to smallest.

Did You Know?

- We can compare the things on the basis of colour, size, shape, appearance, etc.

Solved Problems

1. Which one of the given options below is false?

(A) 1 > 9 (B) 4 > 3

(C) 5 > 3 (D) 9 > 8

(E) None of these

Answer (A)

Explanation: Option (A) is correct because:

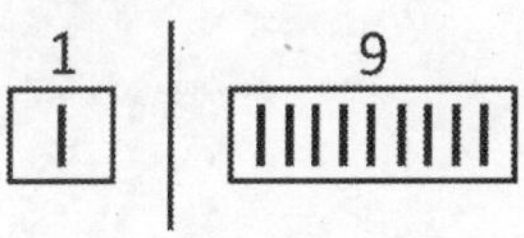

Hence, 9 > 1

Option (B) is incorrect as it is true. Let's check :

4	3
||||	|||

Hence, 4 > 3

Option (C) is incorrect as it is true. Let's check :

5	3
|||||	|||

Hence, 5 > 3

Option (D) is incorrect as it is true. Let us check :

9	8
|||||||||	||||||||

Hence, 9 > 8

2. 14 > 10 will be read as________.

(A) 10 is greater than 14
(B) 14 is less than 10
(C) 10 is bigger than 14
(D) 14 is greater than 10
(E) None of these

Answer (D)

Explanation:

14 > 10 is read as "14 is greater than 10"

3. Just see the numbers inside the egg given below and find out which one is the smallest ?

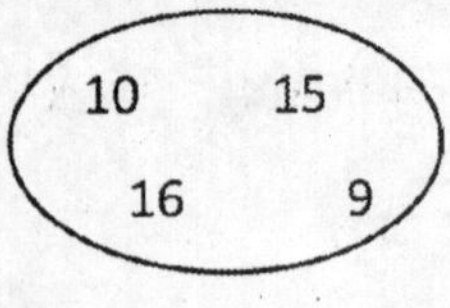

(A) 15 (B) 16

(C) 10 (D) 9

(E) None of these

Answer (D)

Explanation: The only single digit number given. Rest of the options is incorrect because they are double digit numbers and therefore, bigger than 9

4. Which one is wrong ?

(A) $3 < 9$ (B) $5 < 10$

(C) $4 < 7$ (D) $5 < 3$

(E) None of these

Answer (D)

Explanation: Option (D) is correct because it is wrong.

Let's check

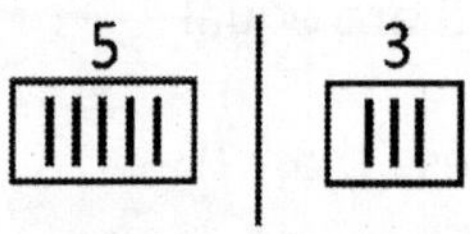

Hence, $3 < 5$ or $5 > 3$

Option (A) is incorrect because it is true.

Let's check:

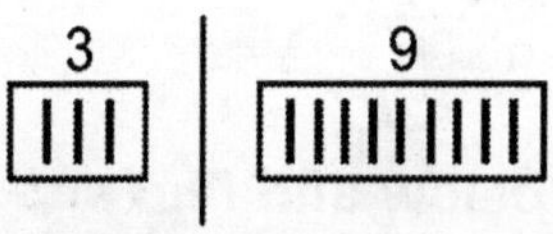

Hence, $3 < 9$

Option (B) is incorrect because it is true. In fact 2 digits number 10 is greater than 5.

Option (C) is incorrect because it is true

Let's check:

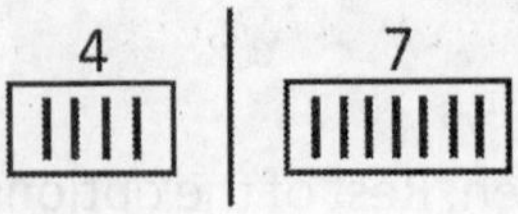

Hence, 4 < 7 or 7 > 4

5. Which one of the following pair of numbers is not equal ?

(A) 2 and 02 (B) 02 and 2

(C) 002 and 2 (D) 20 and 2

(E) None of these

Answer (D)

Explanation:

20 is a double digit number and 2 is a single digit number. So 20 > 2.

6. Choose the incorrect statement.

(A) 05 and 5 are equal (B) 60 and 06 are equal

(C) 07 and 007 are equal (D) 08 and 8 are equal

(E) None of these

Answer (B)

Explanation:

06 is equal to 6 and 60 > 06 or 6

7. Which one of the following is not true?

(A) 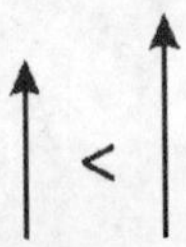

(B) 

(C) 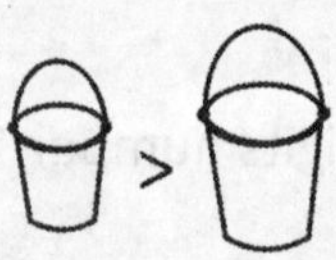

(D) 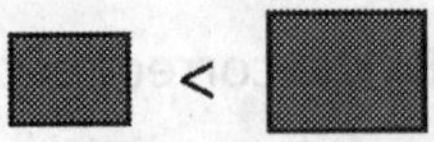

(E) None of these

Answer (C)

Explanation: Picture in left is smaller than the picture in right.

8. The following picture is greater than which one of the following options? Calculate in term of numbers.

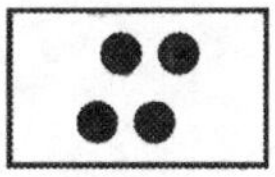

(A) 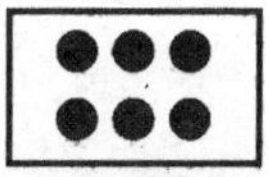

(B) 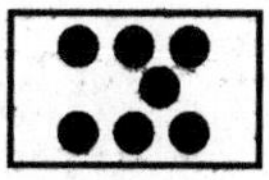

(C) 

(D) 

(E) None of these

Answer (D)

9. Arrange the following numbers in ascending order:
65, 98, 58, 49, 36, 62.

(A) 36, 49, 58, 62, 65, 98

(B) 36, 49, 58, 98, 65, 62

(C) 49, 36, 58, 62, 65, 98

(D) 36, 49, 62, 58, 65, 98

(E) None of these

Answer (A)

10. Arrange the following numbers in ascending order:
89, 91, 87, 86, 95, 79

(A) 79, 86, 87, 89, 95, 91

(B) 79, 86, 87, 91, 89, 95

(C) 89, 86, 87, 79, 91, 95

(D) 79, 86, 87, 89, 91, 95

(E) None of these

Answer (D)

11. Arrange the following numbers in descending order:

65, 98, 58, 49, 36, 62

(A) 36, 49, 58, 62, 65, 98

(B) 98, 65, 62, 58, 49, 36

(C) 98, 65, 62, 58, 36, 49

(D) 98, 62, 65, 58, 49, 36

(E) None of these

Answer (B)

12. Arrange the following numbers in descending order:

89, 91, 87, 86, 95, 79

(A) 95, 91, 89, 87, 86, 79

(B) 95, 89, 91, 87, 86, 79

(C) 89, 95, 91, 89, 87 86, 79

(D) 79, 86, 87, 89, 91, 95

(E) None of these

Answer (A)

Practice Exercise 5

1. **Choose the false option.**
   (A) 12 > 9
   (B) 15 > 5
   (C) 16 > 4
   (D) 6 > 17
   (E) None of these

2. **Pick up the true statement.**
   (A) 3 is greater than 8
   (B) 9 is greater than 10
   (C) 18 is greater than 7
   (D) 4 is greater than 13
   (E) None of these

3. $\boxed{9}$ **is less than which one of the following options?**
   (A) 5
   (B) 14
   (C) 3
   (D) 8
   (E) None of these

4. **16 is less than______.**
   (A) 14
   (B) 10
   (C) 8
   (D) 18
   (E) None of these

5. **05 is equal to which one of the following numbers?**
   (A) 5
   (B) 50
   (C) 06
   (D) 07
   (E) None of these

6. **Which one of the following is not equal to 8?**
   (A) 08
   (B) 008
   (C) 0008
   (D) 80
   (E) None of these

7. Choose the false option.

(A) 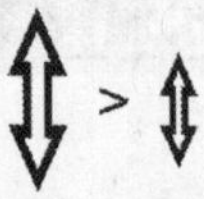

(B) 8 < 8

(C) 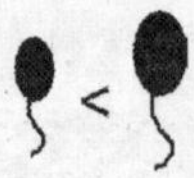

(D) 

(E) None of these

8. Identify the option that is greater than the picture given below. Do numberwise comparison.

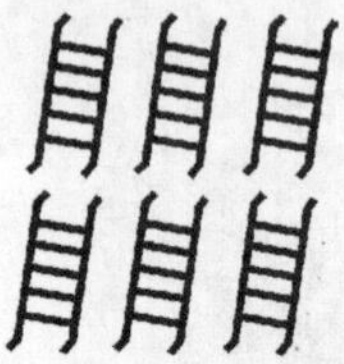

(A) 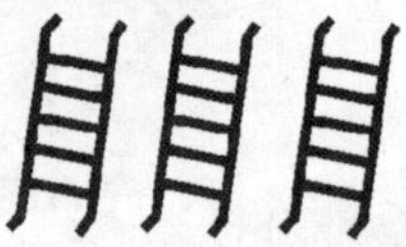

(B) 

(C) 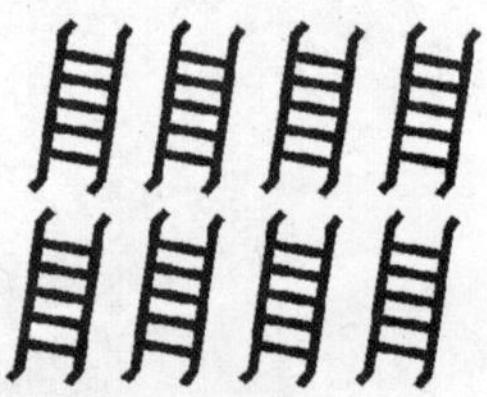

(D) 

(E) None of these

9. Steve has 27 pens and Smith has 19 pens. Who has more pens and by how much?

(A) Steve, by 9

(B) Smith, by 8

(C) Steve, by 8

(D) All of these

(E) None of these

10. There are three buildings called P, Q and R . P is of 20 storeys, Q is of 18 storeys and R is of 25 storeys. Which building has maximum height?

(A) P

(B) Q

(C) R

(D) All of these

(E) None of these

Chapter

6 Time and Calendar

Learning Objectives

- Introduction
- Hours, Minutes and Seconds
- Knowing Time
- Time Indicating Watches
- Reading Time From a Clock
- Calendar

Introduction

A day is divided into hours and an hour is divided into minutes and a minute is divided into seconds. See the following examples:

A train reaches Patna in one day hence 'one day period' is a time.

The examination time is for 3 hours hence 3 hour is a period of time.

Hours, Minutes and Seconds

Hours, minutes and seconds are units for the measurement of time.

For example we can say:

2 hours; 2 minutes; 2 seconds

Now just remember

24 hours = 1 day

1 hour = 60 minutes

1 minute = 60 seconds

Hence 1 day = 24 hours or 1 time of 24 hours

Therefore,

2 days = 2 times of 24 hours

3 days = 3 times of 24 hours

4 days = 4 times of 24 hours and so on.

Similarly,

1 hour = 60 minutes or 1 time of 60 minutes

2 hours = 2 times of 60 minutes

3 hours = 3 times of 60 minutes and so on.

Again 1 minute = 60 seconds or 1 time of 60 seconds

Hence, 2 minutes = 2 times of 60 seconds

3 minutes = 3 time of 60 seconds and so on.

Knowing Time

Knowing time means knowing period or duration of a certain event. For example,

A man goes to a certain distance in 60 minutes, then we can say that he takes

[1] hour and one hour is equal to [60] minutes.

Let's take another example:

If one minute is taken to cook Maggi then time taken in seconds is equal to [60] seconds.

Time Indicating Watches

Let's see the face of the clock given below:

CLOCK

In the above mentioned clock, the number [1] to [12] are marked.

The space between two consecutive numbers is divided into [5] equal parts.

Thus the face or dial of the clock is divided into [60] small divisions.

This is also clear from the picture of the clock that it has two hands.

One is the shorter hand that is called hour hand and the other is the longer hand that is called minute hand.

The minute hand moves from one small division to another small division in one minute or [60] seconds. It means it goes around the dial of the clock in [1] hour.

CLOCK

As minute hand covers two small divisions in [1] hour

therefore, [1] hour = [60] minutes

It must be noted also that the minute hand moves from one number to another in [5] minutes.

Important Points

- The hour hand moves from one number to the next in [1] hour.
- The hour hand takes two complete rounds in a day.
- The hour hand takes [12] hours to complete one round.

Reading Time From a Clock

When the minute hand is at [12] then the actual time is the number that is indicated by the shorter or hour hand. For example, just see the following:

Here the longer or the minute hand is at 12 and hour or shorter hand indicates 9. Therefore, the time is 9 or 9 O ' clock.

Similarly, in the clock shown below. The time is 4 or 4 O'clock.

When the minute hand is at any number we do counting in 5 like.

5 , 10 , 15 , 20 , 25 , 30 , 35 , 40 , 45 and 50

If minute hand is at 1 it shows 5 minutes.

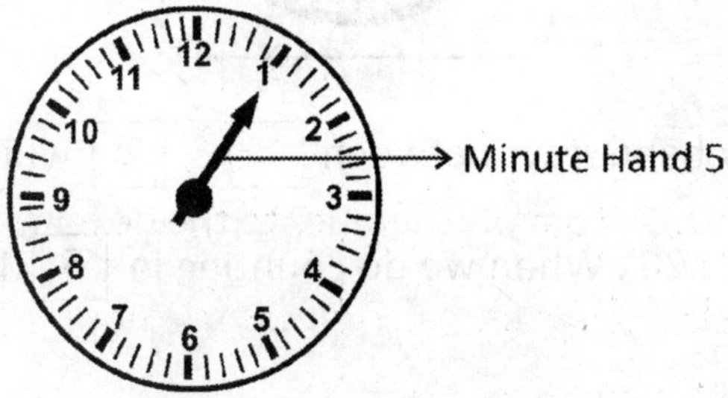

CLOCK

If minute hand is at 2 it shows 10 minutes.

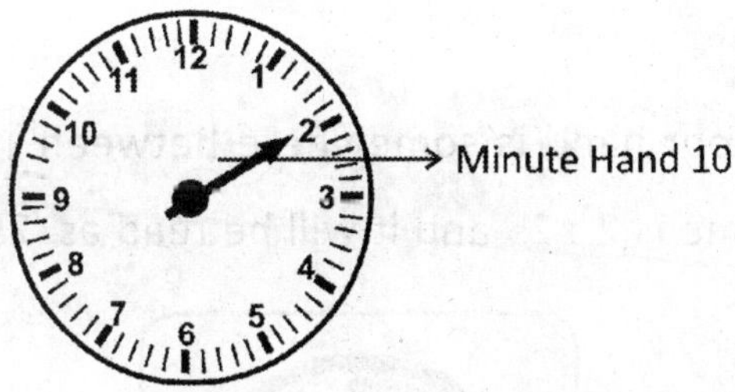

CLOCK

If minute hand is at 3 it shows 15 minutes.

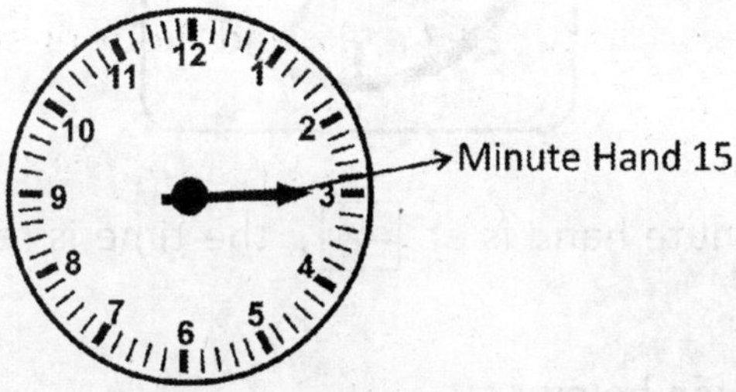

CLOCK

And this process goes on

Let's look at the picture given below:

Here the shorter or hour hand stays between [1] & [2] while minute hand indicates [4] . So the time is 01 : 20 . When we do counting in [5] for [4] it goes as [5] , [10] , [15] and [20] .

Thus the longer hand indicates [20] minutes.

It does mean the actual time is 1 : 20 and we read it as
20 minutes past 1.

Similarly if shorter or hour hand is somewhere between [2] & [3] and minute hand is at 5 then the time is 2 : 25 and it will be read as '25' minutes past 2.

When the longer or minute hand is at [6] , the time is read as the half past the hour.

Let's see the picture given below:

Here the hour or shorter hand is somewhere between 1 & 2 and minute hand is at 6. Therefore, the time is 1 : 30 and it is read as 'half past 1'

Similarly if the hour hand is somewhere between 4 & 5 and minute hand is at 6 then the actual time is 4 : 30 and it is read as 'half past 4'

Calendar

In a week there are seven days. They are the following:

Days	Description
Monday	Monday is called the first day of the week
Tuesday	Tuesday is called the second day of the week
Wednesday	Wednesday is called the third day of the week
Thursday	Thursday is called the fourth day of the week
Friday	Friday is called the fifth day of the week
Saturday	Saturday is called the sixth day of the week
Sunday	Sunday is called the seventh day of the week

Months in a Year

There are 12 months in a year. The name of the months is given in the following table:

	Months	Short Form (days)	Description
1	January	Jan (31)	It is the first month of the year
2	February	Feb (28/29)	It is the second month of the year
3	March	Mar (31)	It is the third month of the year
4	April	Apr (30)	It is the fourth month of the year
5	May	May (31)	It is the fifth month of the year
6	June	Jun (30)	It is the sixth month of the year
7	July	Jul (31)	It is the seventh month of the year
8	August	Aug (31)	It is the eighth month of the year
9	September	Sep (30)	It is the nineth month of the year
10	October	Oct (31)	It is the tenth month of the year
11	November	Nov (30)	It is the eleventh month of the year
12	December	Dec (31)	It is the last month of the year

February is the only month in which number of days varies. Otherwise all the months have fixed number of days. In a year there are 365 days. Every leap year has 366 days. So 1 extra day is added in the month of February. Leap year comes after every four years.

Summary

- Time is a period or duration of certain event.
- Hours, minutes and seconds are the units of time.

  [24] Hours = [1] day

  [1] Hour = [60] minutes

  [1] minute = [60] seconds

- A clock has numbers [1] to [12]
- A clock has shorter or hour hand and minute or longer hand.
- A clock has [5] minutes spaces between two consecutive numbers.
- The dial of a clock has [60] small divisions.
- In a week there are 7 days.
- In a year there are 12 months.

Did You Know?

- 10 years is called decade and 100 years is called century.

Solved Problems

1. 24 hours + 24 hours = [?]

(A) 4 days (B) 2 days

(C) 3 days (D) 5 days

(E) None of these

Answer (B)

Explanation:

[24] hours + [24] hours = [1] day + [1] day = [2] days

2. 5 minutes means_____times of 60 seconds.

(A) 5　　(B) 4

(C) 6　　(D) 8

(E) None of these

Answer (A)

Explanation:

[1] minute = [1] time of [60] seconds

Hence,

[5] minutes = [5] times of [60] seconds

Let's check it:

[5] minutes can be written as

1 Minute	1 Minute	1 Minute	1 Minute	1 Minute
60 Seconds	60 Seconds	60 Seconds	60 Seconds	60 Seconds

There are [5] sixties in it .

3. Which one of the following represents 3 hours ?

(A) 60 minutes, 60 minutes

(B) 60 minutes, 60 minutes, 60 minutes

(C) 60 minutes, 60 minutes, 60 minutes, 60 minutes

(D) 60 minutes

(E) None of these

Answer (B)

4. Jennifer takes one minute to eat a bread while Steve takes 4 minutes to eat a bread. Who takes more time ?

(A) Jennifer takes more time

(B) Steve takes less time

(C) Jennifer and Steve take equal time

(D) Jennifer takes less time and Steve takes more time.

(E) None of these

Answer (D)

5. What is the time shown by the watch given below:

(A) 7 O'clock (B) 5 O'clock

(C) 9 O'clock (D) 8 O'clock

(E) None of these

Answer (D)

Explanation: Hour hand is at 8 and minute hand is at 12 (see trick 1).

Rest of the options is incorrect because of the correctness of option (D).

Therefore, option (D) is correct and rest of the options are incorrect.

6. Which one of the following watches shows the time 05 : 05?

(A)  (B) 

(C) 

(D) 

(E) None of these

Answer (C)

7. What comes two days after Sunday?

(A) Monday (B) Tuesday (C) Wednesday (D) Thursday

(E) None of these

Answer (C)

Explanation: Two days after Sunday is Wednesday

8. How many months in a year have 31 days?

(A) 5 months (B) 6 months

(C) 7 months (D) 8 months

(E) None of these

Answer (C)

Explanation: In a year there are 7 months which have 31 days.

9. Which one of the following months is the second last month of the year?

(A) October (B) November

(C) December (D) All of these

(E) None of these

Answer (B)

Explanation: November is the second last month of the year.

10. Which day comes before Friday?

(A) Monday (B) Tuesday (C) Wednesday (D) Thursday

(E) None of these

Answer (D)

Explanation: Thursday comes before Friday.

Practice Exercise 6

1. Which one of the following represents 3 days ?

(A) 24 hours + 24 hours + 24 hours
(B) 24 hours + 24 hours
(C) 24 hours
(D) 24 hours + 24 hours + 24 hours + 24 hours
(E) None of these

2. Read the statements given below and choose the true one.

(A) 6 minutes is equal to 6 times of 60 seconds.
(B) 5 minutes is equal to 5 times of 50 seconds.
(C) 4 minutes is equal to 4 times of 40 seconds.
(D) 3 minutes is equal to 3 times of 30 seconds.
(E) None of these

3. Steve drives a car to reach a certain distance in two hours. Find the time taken in mInutes.

(A) 3 times of 60 minutes
(B) 4 times of 60 minutes
(C) 2 times of 60 minutes
(D) 5 times of 60 minutes
(E) None of these

4. James goes out for morning walk at 5 O'clock and comes back in one hour. At what time he cómes back ?

(A) 8 O'clock
(B) 4 O'clock
(C) 6 O'clock
(D) 7 O'clock.
(E) None of these

5. When I get up in the morning it was 6 O'clock and at that time the minute hand was at_______.

(A) 6
(B) 7
(C) 8
(D) 12
(E) None of these

6. **What is the time shown by the clock given below ?**

(A) 3 : 30 (B) 2 : 30
(C) 4 : 30 (D) 5 : 30
(E) None of these

7. **5 minutes means_______times of 60 seconds.**

(A) 5 (B) 4
(C) 6 (D) 8
(E) None of these

8. **A clock shows the time as 7:30. At this time the hour hand is between which of the two numbers ?**

(A) 6 and 7 (B) 5 and 6
(C) 7 and 8 (D) 3 and 4
(E) None of these

9. **Which one of the following options represents 4 hours?**

(A) 60 minutes + 60 minutes + 60 minutes
(B) 60 minutes + 60 minutes
(C) 60 minutes + 60 minutes + 60 minutes + 60 minutes
(D) 60 minutes + 60 minutes + 60 minutes + 60 minutes + 60 minutes
(E) None of these

10. **Tina runs for 60 seconds, then again for 60 seconds and then again for 60 seconds. What is her duration of running ?**

(A) One minute (B) 3 minutes
(C) 2 minutes (D) 4 minutes
(E) None of these

Chapter 7

Money

Learning Objectives

- Concept of Money
- Identifying Coins
- Identifying Notes
- Adding Cost of Things

Concept of Money

We all are familiar with Money. In India or anywhere in the world money is available in the form of coins and notes. We pay money while purchasing any things and receive money by selling goods.

Buying things

Further it must be noted that money in India is counted in terms of paise and rupees.

Let's remember the following:

100 paise = 

1 rupee

50 paise = 

Half rupee

25 paise = 

Half of the half rupee

20 paise = 

One of 5 parts of a rupee

10 paise = 

One of the 10 parts of a rupee

5 paise = 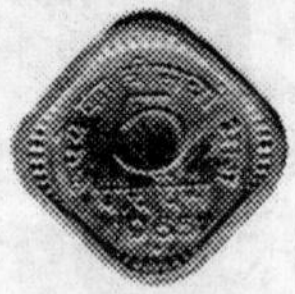

One of the 20 parts of a rupee

One 1 rupee =

1 rupee

Two 1 rupee =

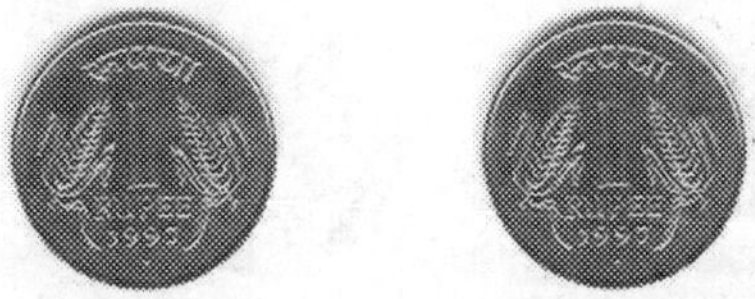

1 rupee 1 rupee

Three 1 rupee =

1 rupee 1 rupee 1 rupee

and so on

One 2 rupees =

2 rupees

Two 2 rupees =

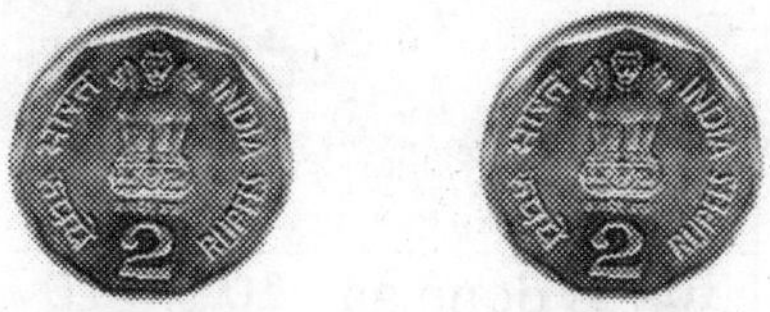

2 rupees 2 rupees

Three 2 rupees =
and so on.

2 rupees 2 rupees 2 rupees

One 5 rupees =

5 rupees

Two 5 rupees =

5 rupees

5 rupees

Three 5 rupees =
and so on.

5 rupees

5 rupees

5 rupees

See another example:

One 4 Rupees	Two 4 Rupees	Three 4 Rupees	Four 4 Rupees
4 Rupees	8 Rupees	12 Rupees	16 Rupees

For [5] rupees counting in [5] is done as:

[5], [10], [15], [20] ..... and so on.

For [10] rupees counting in [10] is done as [10], [20], [30], [40], [50] ...... and so on.

The same rule is applicable in case of paisa.

For [5] paise, the counting is as:

[5], [10], [15], [20] ..... and so on.

For [10] paise the counting is as [10], [20], [30], [40] ...... and so on.

For 20 paise,

the counting is done as 20, 40, 60, 80, 100 .... and so on.

Identifying Coins

All coins are made up of metal. In India 50 paise, 1 rupee, 2 rupees, 5 rupees and 10 rupees coins are there in circulation.

Just see the 50 paise coin given below:

50 paise

50 paise

2 rupees

2 rupees

It is clear from the pictures of the coins given above that denomination of coins is written on it. Therefore, when we see a coin, we find the denomination given on it so that the coin can be identified easily.

Identifying Notes

The information that is required to identify the rupees are written on a paper and is called Notes. In India, 1 rupee, 2 rupees, 5 rupees, 10 rupees, 20 rupees, 50 rupees, 100 rupees, 500 rupees and 1000 rupees Notes are in circulation.

Look at the 1 rupee and 2 rupees notes given below:

1 rupee (One rupee note)

2 rupees (Two rupee note)

It is clear from the picture given above that denomination or value of notes written on it. Therefore, whenever we identify the note we see the denomination or value written on it.

5 rupees (Five rupees note)

10 rupees (Ten rupees note)

20 rupees (Twenty rupees note)

50 rupees (Fifty rupees note)

100 rupees (One hundred rupees note)

200 rupees (Two hundred rupees note)

500 rupees (Five hundred rupees note)

2000 rupees (Two thousand rupees note)

Adding Cost of Things

This is grouping of the costs of two or more things converting them into single money value.

If cost of one apple = 2 rupees

and cost of one banana = 4 rupees

then total cost of both the fruits = cost of one apple + cost of one banana

= [2] rupees + [4] rupees.

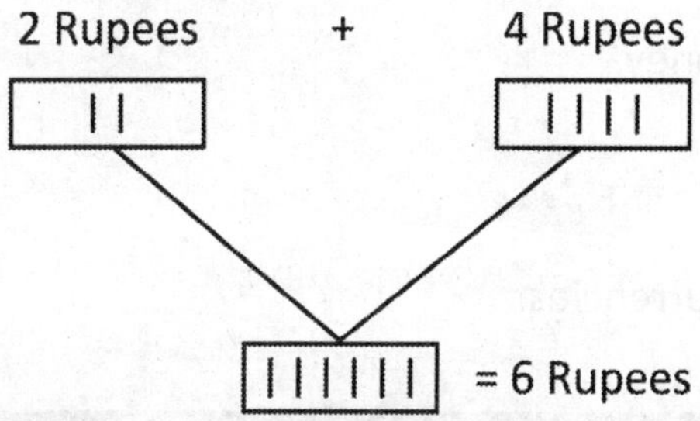

or

2 Rupees [||]
+ 4 Rupees [||||]

6 Rupees = [||||||]

Example:

If cost of one pen = [5] rupees

cost of two pencils = [6] rupees

Cost of one rubber = [2] rupees

then cost of one pen + cost of two pencils + cost of one rubber.

= [5] rupees + [6] rupees + [2] rupees = [13] rupees.

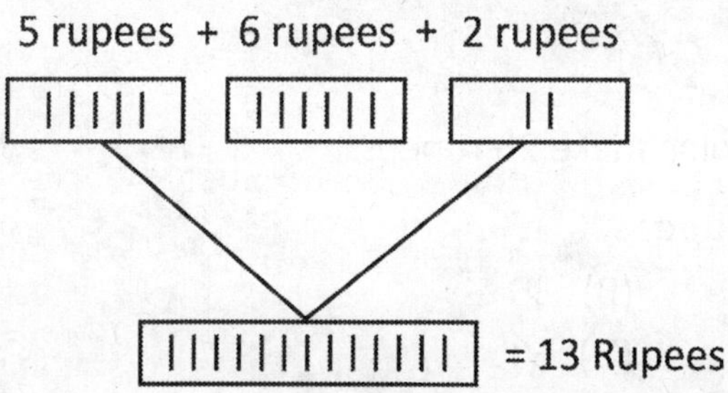

or

5 rupees [|||||]
6 rupees [||||||]
+ 2 rupees [||]

13 rupees = [|||||||||||||]

Summary

- Money is paid while buying things and it is received on selling things.
- Rupees and paise are the units of money.
- Coins are metal form of money.
- Notes are paper form of money.
- Coins and notes are also known as currencies.

Did You Know ?

- In India 1 paisa coin was used.
- ₹ 1000 note has been introduced few years back.

Solved Problems

1. **How many 5 rupees coins make 25 rupees?**

   (A) 4 (B) 5
   (C) 6 (D) 3
   (E) None of these

   Answer (B)

   Explanation: Five 5 rupees coins make 25 rupees.

2. **Five 10 rupees makes_______rupees.**

   (A) 20 (B) 30
   (C) 60 (D) 50
   (E) None of these

   Answer (D)

   Explanation:

   One | 10 | rupee = | 10 | rupees

Two 10 rupee = 20 rupees

Three 10 rupee = 30 rupees

Four 10 rupee = 40 rupees.

Five 10 rupee = 50 rupees

3. Which one of the following options has 5 rupees coin?

(A) 

(B) 

(C) 

(D) 

(E) None of these

Answer (A)

4. Which one of the following is correct?

(A) 5 rupees 

(B) 1 rupee 

(C) 2 rupees 

(D) 2 rupees 

(E) None of these

Answer (C)

5. **Identify the note given in the picture and pick the correct option.**

(A) It is a 20 rupees note
(B) It is a 5 rupees note
(C) It is a 50 rupees note
(D) It is a 10 rupees note
(E) None of these

Answer (D)

6. **Which one of the following options has similar value of the given Note?**

(A) 20 notes of 100 rupees
(B) 5 notes of 500 rupees
(C) 5 notes of 100 rupees
(D) 5 notes of 50 rupees
(E) None of these

Answer (A)

Explanation: The given note is of Rs. 2000 which has similar value of 20 notes of Rs. 100.

7. **4 rupees is the cost of a toy and 3 rupees is the cost of a pen. What is the cost of one toy and one pen?**

(A) 7 rupees
(B) 8 rupees
(C) 6 rupees
(D) 9 rupees
(E) None of these

Answer (A)

Explanation: Cost of one toy + cost of one pen

= 4 rupees + 3 rupees = 7 rupees.

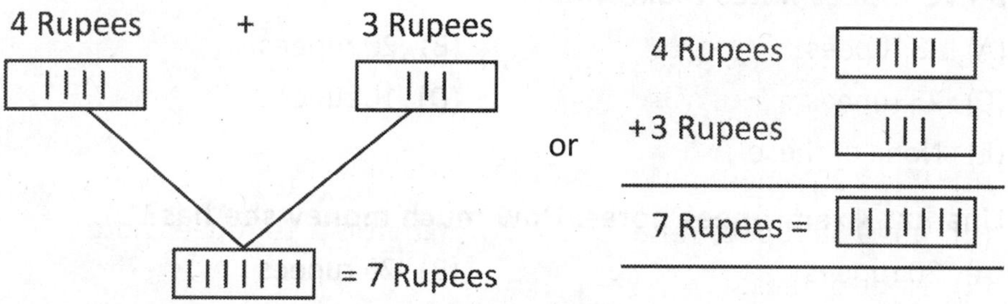

8. The cost of one copy is 5 rupees and the cost of two books is 6 rupees. What is the total cost of one copy and two books?

(A) 15 rupees (B) 9 rupees

(C) 11 rupees (D) 2 rupees

(E) None of these

Answer (C)

Explanation: Option (C) is correct because cost of one copy + cost of 2 books = 5 rupees + 6 rupees = 11 rupees.

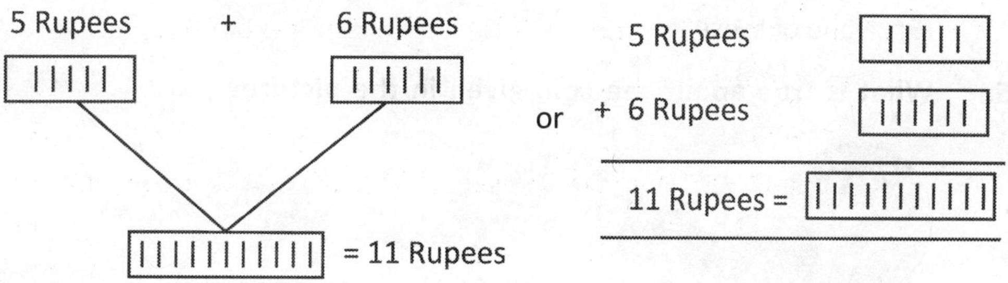

Practice Exercise 7

1. **3 five rupees notes make what?**

(A) 15 rupees
(B) 20 rupees
(C) 25 rupees
(D) 10 rupees
(E) None of these

2. **Lina has 4 ten rupees notes. How much money she has?**

(A) 20 rupees
(B) 25 rupees
(C) 30 rupees
(D) 40 rupees
(E) None of these

3. **30 rupees has________ten rupees.**

(A) 5
(B) 3
(C) 2
(D) 8
(E) None of these

4. **How many 200 rupees notes make 600 rupees?**

(A) 3
(B) 4
(C) 5
(D) 6
(E) None of these

5. **What is true about the coin given in the picture?**

(A) It is 5 rupees coin
(B) It is 6 rupees coin
(C) It is 1 rupees coin
(D) It is 10 rupees coin
(E) None of these

6. **Which one of the following options has 2 rupees coin ?**

(A) 

(B) 

(C) 

(D) 

(E) None of these

7. **Identify the 20 rupees notes out of the options given below:**

(A) 

(B) 

(C) 

(D) 

(E) None of these

8. **Which one out of the following is not a paper money?**

(A) 

(B) 

(C) 

(D) 

(E) None of these

9. If cost of 3 oranges = 50 rupees and cost of 2 apples = 30 rupees then what is the total cost of 3 oranges and 2 apples?

(A) 80 rupees (B) 70 rupees

(C) 100 rupees (D) 90 rupees

(E) None of these

10. Cost of two things is given as 7 rupees and 3 rupees. Add these two costs.

(A) 8 rupees

(B) 10 rupees

(C) 9 rupees

(D) All of these

(E) None of these

Chapter

8 Measurement

Learning Objectives

- Introduction
- Length and Breadth

Introduction

The kilometre, metre, centimetre, inches and foot are the units of distance and length. While kilometre and metre are used for long and average distances, and centimetre, inches and foot are used to measure short distances.

Length and Breadth

Length is longer dimension of an object while breadth is the dimension from side to side.

Let's see the picture given below:

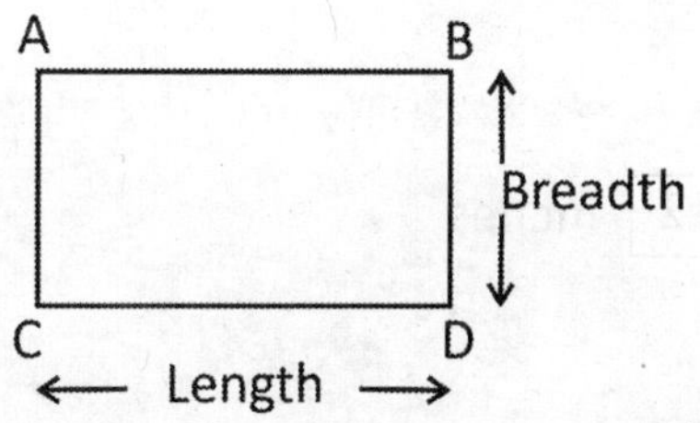

Measurement

In the above mentioned picture, the longer dimension is AB and CD. Hence AB and

CD are lengths. While dimension from side to side are AC and BD and it is called breadth.

Now Remember,

1 kilometre = 1000 metres

1 metre = 100 centimetres

and 1 foot = 12 inches.

Now if 1 kilometre = 1000 metres

then 2 kilometres = Two 1000 metres.

3 Kilometres = Three 1000 metres and the process goes on.

Similarly,

1 metre = 100 centimetres.

2 metres = two 100 centimetres

3 metres = three 100 centimetres and the process goes on.

Again 1 foot = 12 inches.

2 feet = two 12 inches

= 24 inches.

3 feet = three 12 inches

= 36 inches.

Remember again

Short forms:

Kilometre = km

Metre = m

Centimetre = cm

Summary

- Kilometres, metres, centimetres, inches and foot are the units of distances and lengths.
- Length is the longer dimension.
- Breadth is the shorter and side to side dimension.
- Long distances are measured in kilometres, for example distance travelled by trains and buses are calculated in kilometres.
- For measurement of lengths and heights, metre, centimetre, foot and inches are used. For example length of a cloth is measured in metres and centimetres. To measure the height of a person, foot and inches are used as measurement unit.
- Km > m > cm
- Foot > Inch > cm.

Did You Know?

- There are 12 inches in 1 foot.
- Generally the length of a football field is 110 metres but it varies from country to country.

Solved Problems

1. How many kilometres are there in two 1000 metres?

(A) 4 (B) 2

(C) 3 (D) 5

(E) None of these

Answer (B)

Explanation:

[1] kilometre = one [1000] metres then [2] kilometres = two [1000] metres.

2. Which one of the following is the length in the given picture?

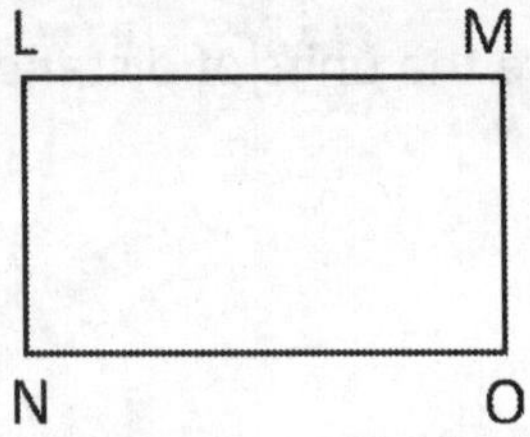

(A) LM (B) LN

(C) MO (D) NL

(E) None of these

Answer (A)

Practice Exercise 8

1. **Steve goes from Delhi to patna. The distance from Delhi to patna will be measured in:**

   (A) Kilometres (B) Inches
   (C) Centimetres (D) Foot
   (E) None of these

2. **Which one of the following is the bigger unit?**

   (A) Metres (B) Centimetres
   (C) Kilometres (D) Inches
   (E) None of these

3. **Find the breadth of the following figure.**

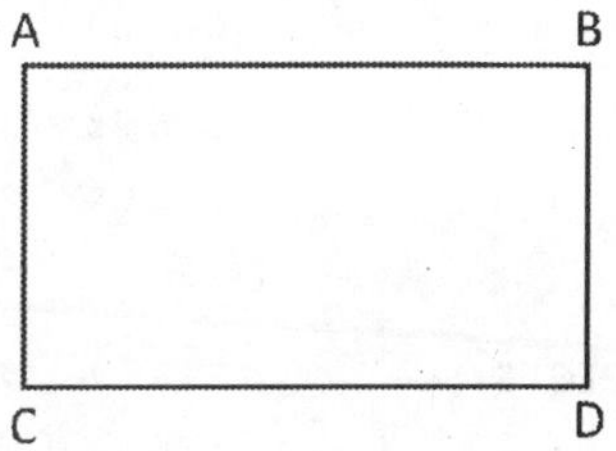

   (A) AC (B) AB
   (C) CD (D) DC
   (E) None of these

4. **Which one of the following is the smaller unit?**

   (A) Centimetre (B) Metre
   (C) Kilometre (D) Inches
   (E) None of these

5. **4 feet makes how many 12 inches?**

   (A) 5 (B) 4
   (C) 3 (D) 6
   (E) None of these

6. Which one of the following is correct?

(A) Cloth is measured in kilometres.

(B) Height is measured in kilometres.

(C) Long distance is measured in centimetres.

(D) Height of a person is measured in foot.

(E) None of these

7. What is the length of the given figure?

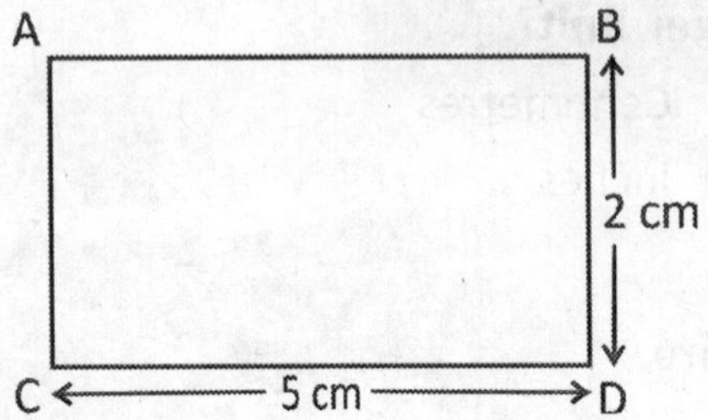

(A) 2 cm
(B) 5 cm
(C) 4 cm
(D) 3 cm
(E) None of these

8. Four hundred centimetres make how many meters?

(A) 5
(B) 3
(C) 4
(D) 7
(E) None of these

9. The length of a house is 7 m more than its breadth. The breadth of the house is 15 m. Find the length of the house.

(A) 15 m
(B) 7 m
(C) 22 m
(D) All of these
(E) None of these

10. How many centimetres are there in 4 metres and 50 centimetres?

(A) 400 cm
(B) 450 cm
(C) 425 cm
(D) All of these
(E) None of these

Chapter 9

Identification of Geometrical Figures

Learning Objectives

- Line
- Angles
- Triangle
- Quadrilateral
- Rectangle
- Square
- Rhombus

Line

A line is a collection of points. See the picture of lines given below

1. Straight and standing line (Vertical)

2. Straight and sleeping lines (Horizontal)

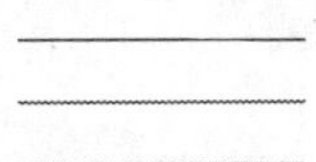

3. Straight and slanting lines

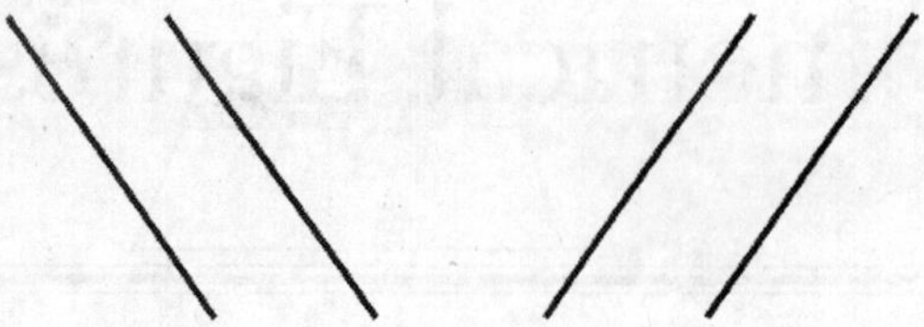

4. Curved lines

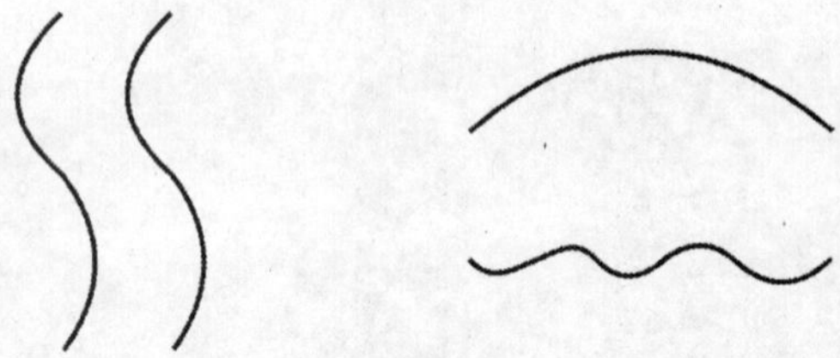

Angles

See the following figure:

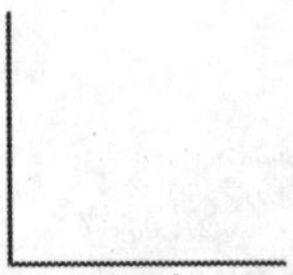

Angle

It is an angle.

Triangle

A triangle has three sides and three angles. Let's see the following figures:

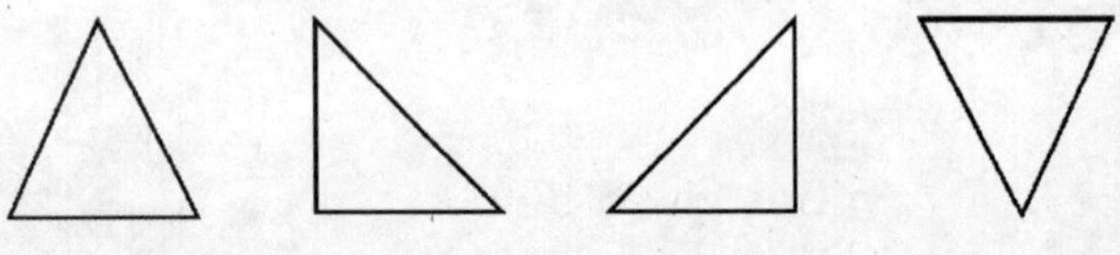

The above given figures have three sides and three angles. Therefore, they are triangles.

Quadrilateral

See the quadrilaterals given below:

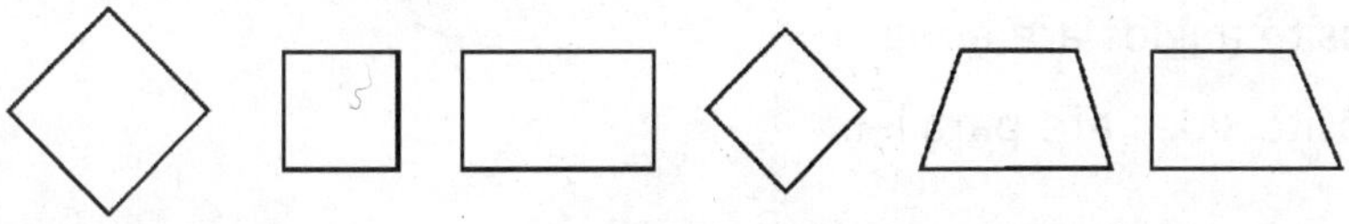

Thus it is clear that a quadrilateral has four sides whether they are equal or not.

Rectangle

Let's see the following rectangles:

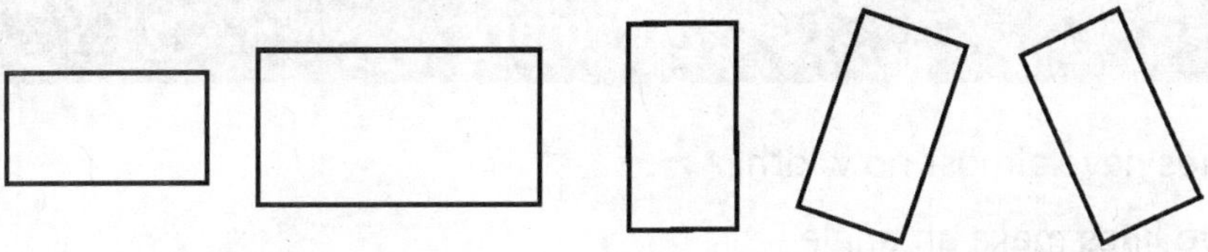

Thus it is clear that a rectangle has equal angles and equal opposite sides.

Square

Let's see the squares given below:

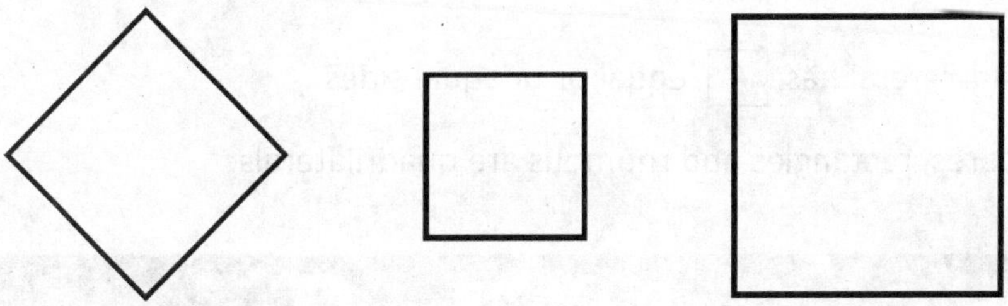

Square has 4 equal sides and 4 angles.

Rhombus

Let's see the pictures of rhombus given below.

In Rhombus

- Four sides are equal.
- Opposite angles are equal.
- Opposite sides are parallel.

Summary

- Lines have almost no width.
- Two lines make an angle.
- Square has four equal sides.
- Rectangle has equal opposite sides.
- Rhombus has four equal sides and opposite equal angles.
- Square is a rhombus.
- Quadrilateral has 4 equal or unequal sides.
- Squares, rectangles and rhombus are quadrilaterals.

Did You Know?

- You can make geometrical shapes using straight line or curve lines.
- Map or design of the building is created using geometrical shapes.

Solved Problems

1. Which one of the following options has curve lines?

(A) 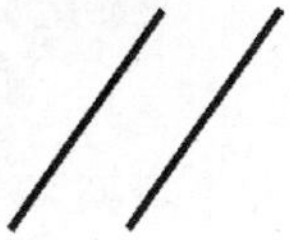

(B) 

(C) 

(D) 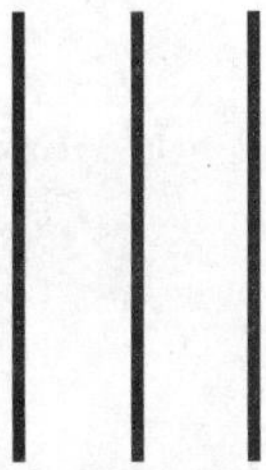

(E) None of these

Answer (B)

2. Choose the straight lines that are slanting.

(A) 

(B) 

(C) 

(D) 

(E) None of these

Answer (D)

3. Which one of the following is not an angle ?

(A) 

(B) 

(C) 

(D) 

(E) None of these

Answer (D)

4. Which one of the following options has two angles?

(A) 

(B) 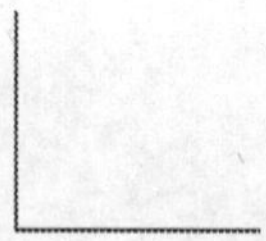

(C) 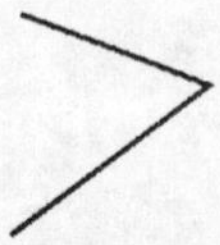

(D) 

(E) None of these

Answer (A)

5. Which one of the following is a triangle?

(A) 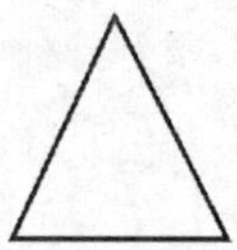

(B) 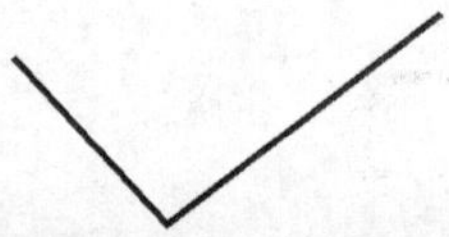

(C) 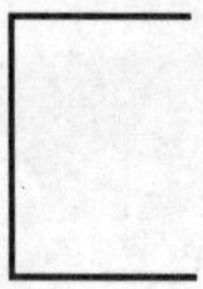

(D) 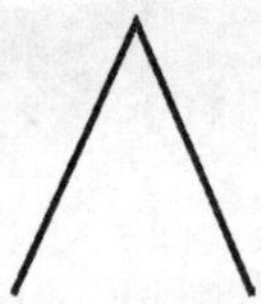

(E) None of these

Answer (A)

6. How many lines are required to make a triangle?

(A) 4

(B) 7

(C) 3

(D) 5

(E) None of these

Answer (C)

7. Which one of the following is a quadrilateral?

(A) 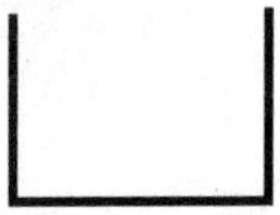

(B) 

(C) 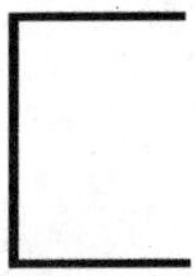

(D) 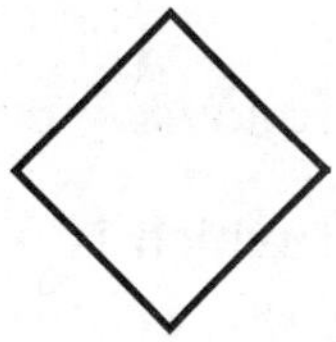

(E) None of these

Answer (D)

8. Choose the option which is not a quadrilateral?

(A) 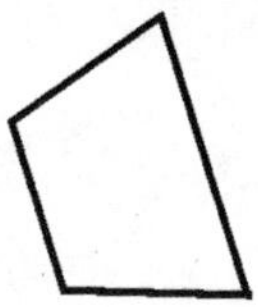

(B) 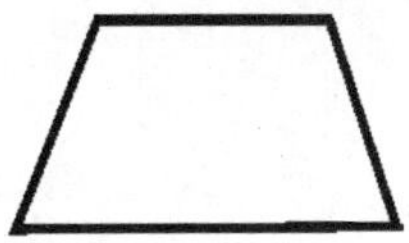

(C) 

(D) 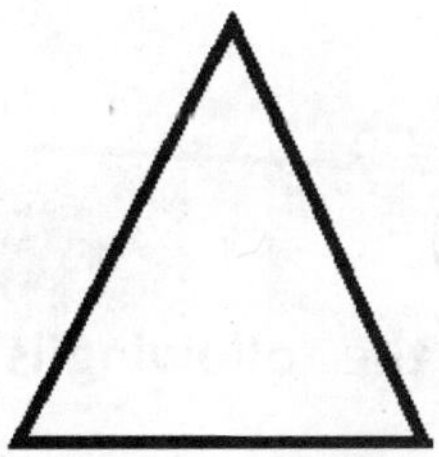

(E) None of these

Answer (D)

9. Which one of the following is a rectangle?

(A) 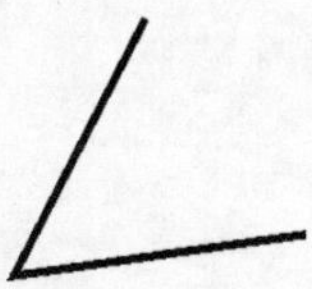

(B) 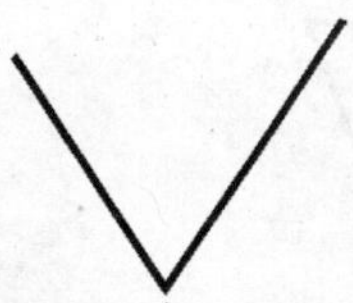

(C) 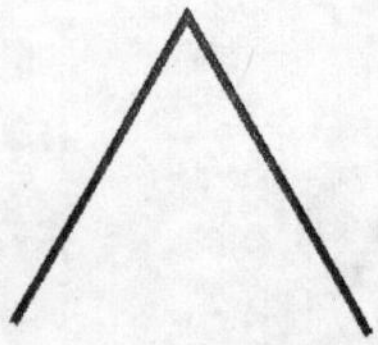

(D) 

(E) None of these

Answer (D)

10. Choose the option which is not a rectangle.

(A) 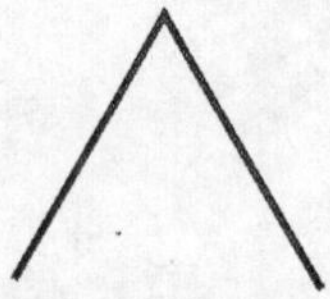

(B) 

(C) 

(D) 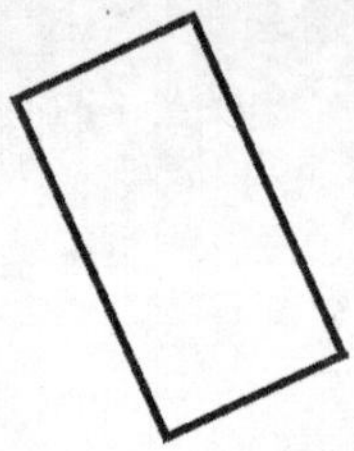

(E) None of these

Answer (A)

11. Which one of the following is a square?

(A) 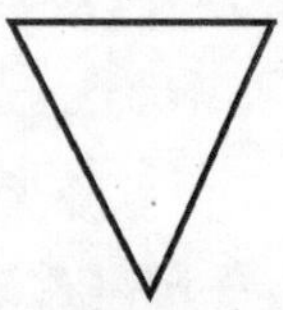

(B) 

(C) 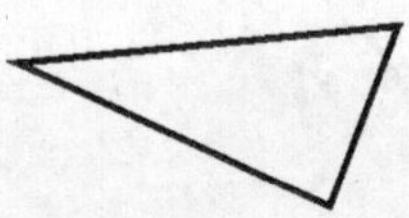

(D) 

(E) None of these

Answer (B)

12. How many lines are required to make 2 square?

(A) 4 (B) 8

(C) 12 (D) 3

(E) None of these

Answer (B)

13. Identify rhombus out of the given options.

(A) 

(B) 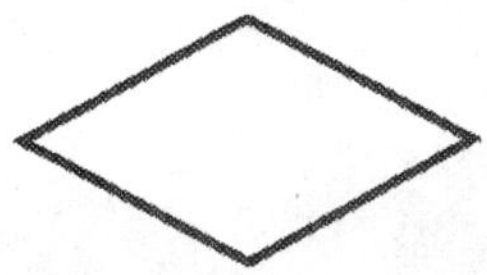

(C) 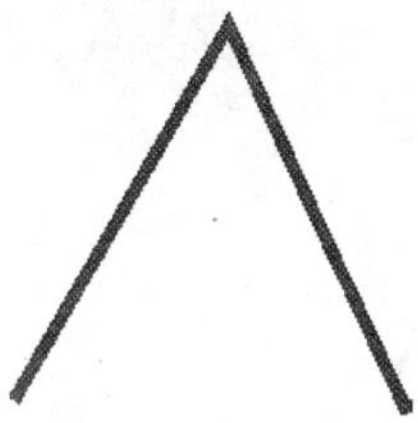

(D) 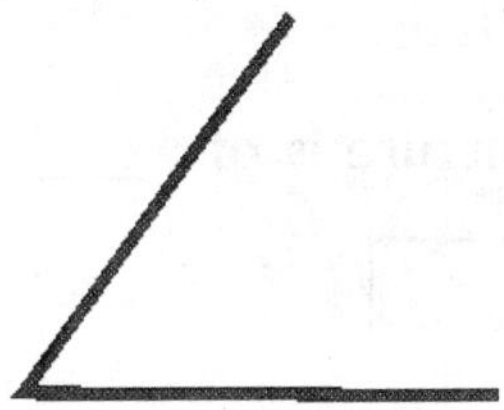

(E) None of these

Answer (B)

14. From 4 equal straight lines, how many rhombus can be made?

(A) 1 (B) 2

(C) 4 (D) 5

(E) None of these

Answer (A)

Practice Exercise 9

1. **Choose the straight lines.**

(A) 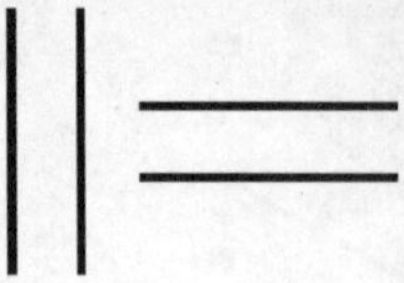

(B) 

(C) 

(D) 

(E) None of these

2. **The given picture is of a________.**

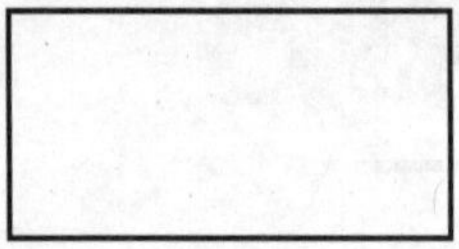

(A) Rectangle
(B) Triangle
(C) Line
(D) Angle
(E) None of these

3. **Which one of the following is an angle?**

(A)

(B) 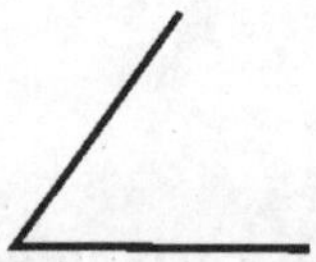

(C) 

(D) 

(E) None of these

4. What is true about a square?

(A) It has 5 sides
(B) It has 6 sides
(C) It has 3 sides
(D) It has 4 sides
(E) None of these

5. Identify the quadrilateral.

(A) 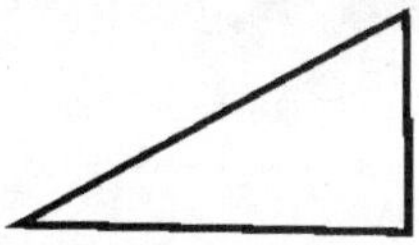

(B) 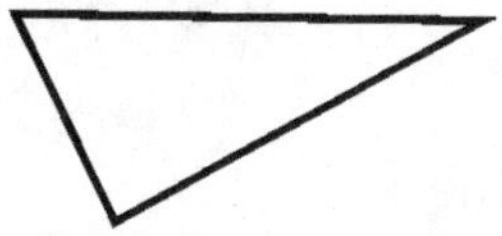

(C) 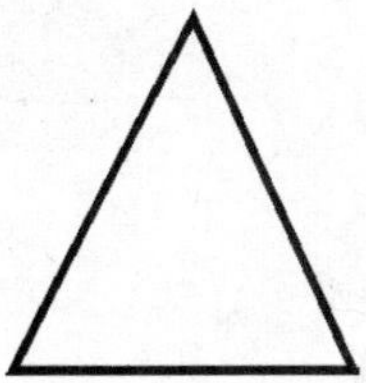

(D) 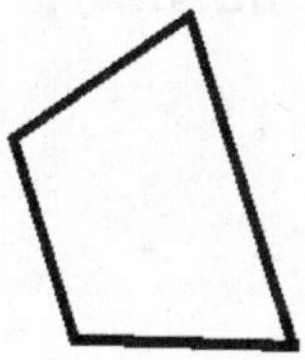

(E) None of these

6. Name the picture given below.

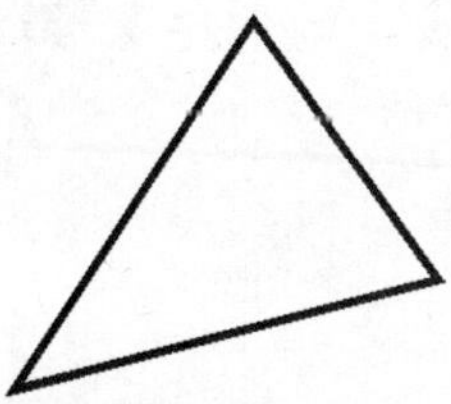

(A) Line
(B) Triangle
(C) Quadrilateral
(D) Rectangle
(E) None of these

7. What is true about a triangle?

(A) It has three sides
(B) It has four sides
(C) It has only two sides
(D) All the above
(E) None of these

8. Standing lines are_______lines.

(A) Horizontal (B) Selecting

(C) Slanting (D) Vertical

(E) None of these

9. Rectangle has_______sides.

(A) 2 (B) 4

(C) 6 (D) 5

(E) None of these

10. Which one of the following is a quadrilateral?

(A) 

(B) 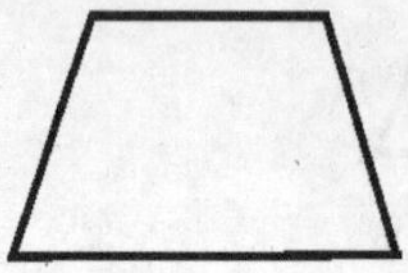

(C) 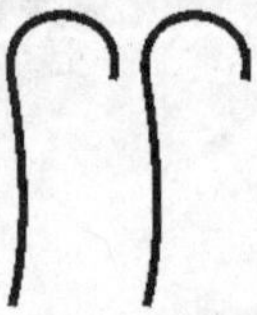

(D) 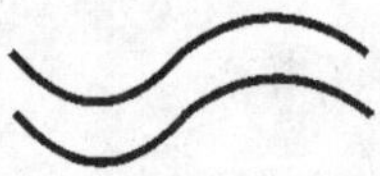

(E) None of these

Chapter

10 Applied Mathematics

Learning Objectives

- Introduction

Introduction

In this chapter, we will apply our mathematical knowledge to solve various problems. Some of these problems, along with their solutions are given below.

Example: 1

How many circles are there in the figure?

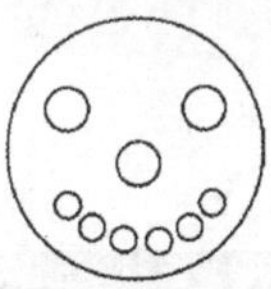

(A) 10 (B) 12

(C) 13 (D) 14

(E) None of these

Answer (A)

Explanation: Clearly in the figure, number of circles are |||||||||| = 10

So, correct option is (A).

Example: 2

Fill in the blanks with correct symbol.

______

(A) <

(B) >

(C) =

(D) All the above

(E) None of these

Answer (A)

Explanation: Clearly left figure is smaller than the right figure.

So, correct option is (A).

Summary

❖ In the number series numbers are arranged in different patterns

Did You Know ?

❖ Numbers are arranged in a pattern based on the addition, subtraction, multiplication, etc.

Solved Problems

1. Solve the following and choose the correct option.

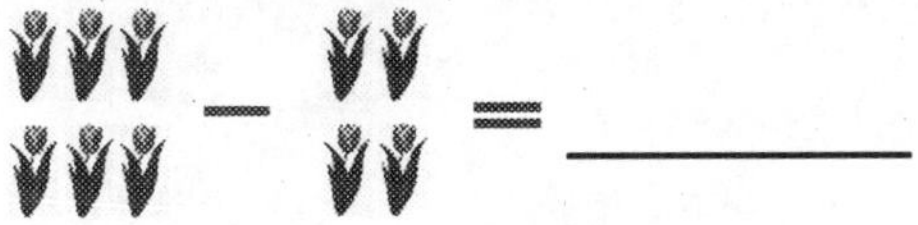

(A) 

(B) 

(C) 

(D) 

(E) None of these

Answer (B)

Explanation: Here, 4 number of roses are removed from 6 number of roses. So, remaining roses are 6 – 4 = 2. Hence option (B) is the answer.

2. Arrange the numbers given in the following circle in ascending order.

22 32
36
35 29

(A) 22, 32, 29, 35, 36
(B) 29, 32, 22, 35, 36
(C) 36, 35, 32, 29, 22
(D) 22, 29, 32, 35, 36
(E) None of these

Answer (D)

Explanation:

In ascending order, we arrange the numbers in their increasing order.

So, the order is 22, 29, 32, 35, 36. Hence option (D) is the answer.

3. Fill in the boxes.

	Tens	+		Ones	=	89

(A) 6, 9 (B) 9, 8

(C) 8, 9 (D) 8, 0

(E) None of these

Answer (C)

Explanation: Since, 8 tens = 80 and 9 ones = 9

∴ 8 tens + 9 ones = 89. Hence option (C) is the answer.

4. Look at the following calendar carefully.

September 2017						
SUN	MON	TUE	WED	THU	FRI	SAT
					1	2
3	4	5	6	7	8	9
10	11	12	13	14	15	16
17	18	19	20	21	22	23
24	25	26	27	28	29	30

Which day will be on 24th September 2017?

(A) Tuesday (B) Saturday

(C) Friday (D) Sunday

(E) None of these

Answer (D)

Explanation: Clearly 24 lies in the column of Sunday so on 24th September, the day will be Sunday.

Hence option (D) is the answer.

Practice Exercise 10

1. Choose the greatest number from each box and then add them.

Box-1	Box-2
1 6 10 3 2 8 12 11	5 7 10 6 11 8 12 9

What is your answer?

(A) 12
(B) 16
(C) 20
(D) 24
(E) None of these

2. Which one of the following options has the greatest number?

(A) 200
(B) 220
(C) 450
(D) 555
(E) None of these

3. Find the missing numbers.

12	14	16	18	20	?	?

(A) 21, 22
(B) 22, 23
(C) 22, 24
(D) All the above
(E) None of these

4. Add the numbers written in the picture.

(A) 18 (B) 17

(C) 20 (D) All the above

(E) None of these

5. Subtract the following.

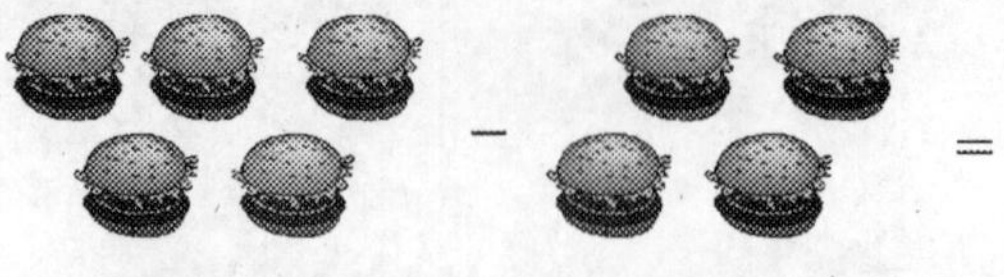

(A) 

(B) 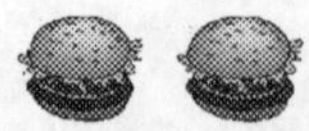

(C) 

(D) 

(E) None of these

6. Find the value of sum of all the coins given below.

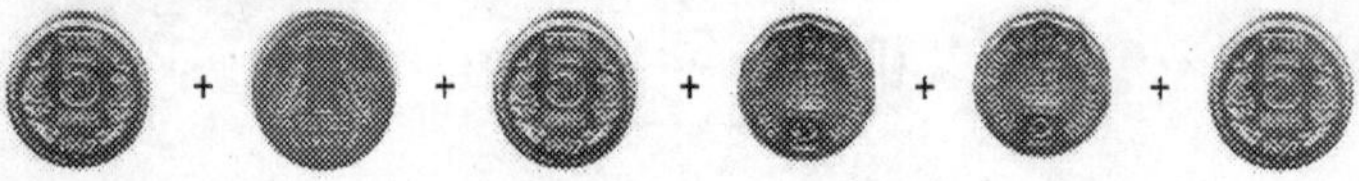

(A) ₹ 10 (B) ₹ 15

(C) ₹ 18 (D) ₹ 20

(E) None of these

7. Find the value of ☐

If ☐ + ☐ = 16

(A) 4 (B) 6

(C) 7 (D) 8

(E) None of these

8. Subtract the following.

(A) 7 (B) 6

(C) 5 (D) 4

(E) None of these

9. Identify the shape of the given figure.

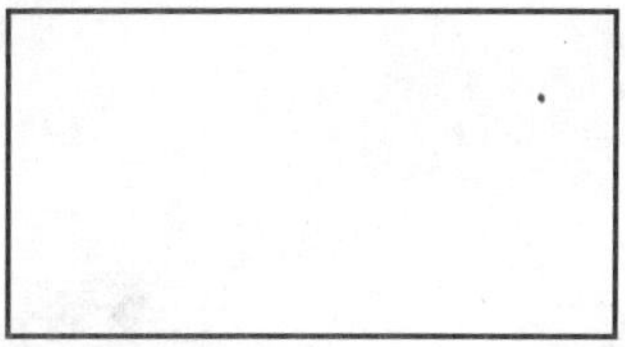

(A) Square (B) Circle

(C) Triangle (D) Rectangle

(E) None of these

10. Find the smallest number from the following.

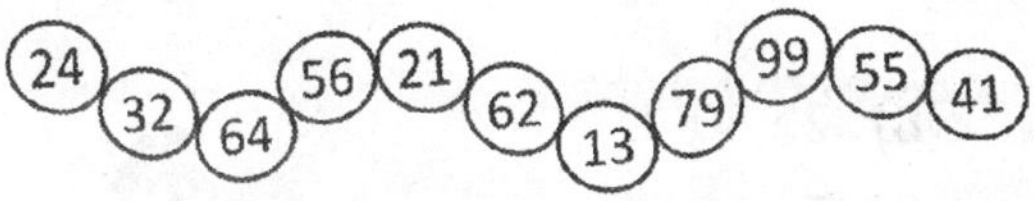

(A) 24 (B) 21

(C) 13 (D) 11

(E) None of these

11. Write the missing number.

15	18	21	24		30

(A) 28 (B) 29

(C) 26 (D) 27

(E) None of these

12. Choose the greatest number from the circle given below.

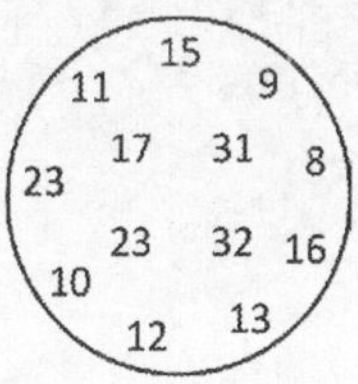

(A) 32 (B) 42
(C) 23 (D) 31
(E) None of these

13. Fill in the blank circle with the suitable number.

(5) (10) (15) (20) ( ) (30) (35)

(A) 22 (B) 25
(C) 23 (D) 24
(E) None of these

14. What is the time shown by the clock given below ?

(A) 3 : 30 (B) 2 : 30
(C) 4 : 30 (D) 5 : 30
(E) None of these

15. What is the length of the given figure?

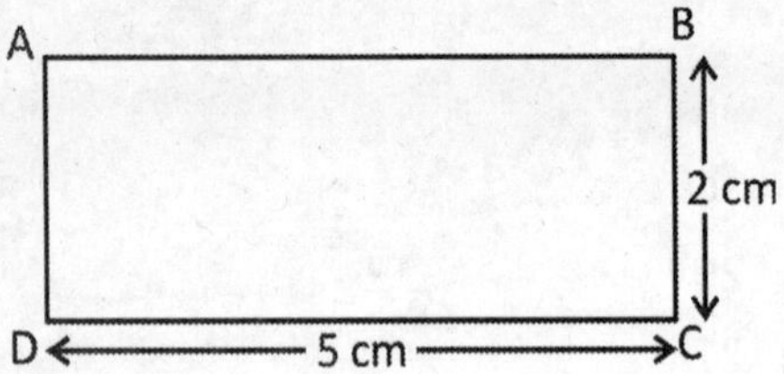

(A) 2 cm (B) 5 cm
(C) 4 cm (D) 3 cm
(E) None of these

Chapter 11

Mental Aptitude

Learning Objectives

- Introduction
- Concept of Patterns

Introduction

In mental aptitude, there are questions in which you have to think about the question in a logical way. The questions of mental aptitude may be based on numbering of alphabets, completing the patterns of drawings or shapes, finding the missing figures or finding the number patterns. There is a certain relationship between the things given in the patterns. You can easily answer such type of questions by observing that relationship given in the questions.

Concept of Patterns

In this chapter you will learn various patterns based on shape, size and number. Patterns are particular arrangements.

Ascending Order Pattern

It is the sequence of number from smaller to bigger. Let's see the following patterns of pencils shown below:

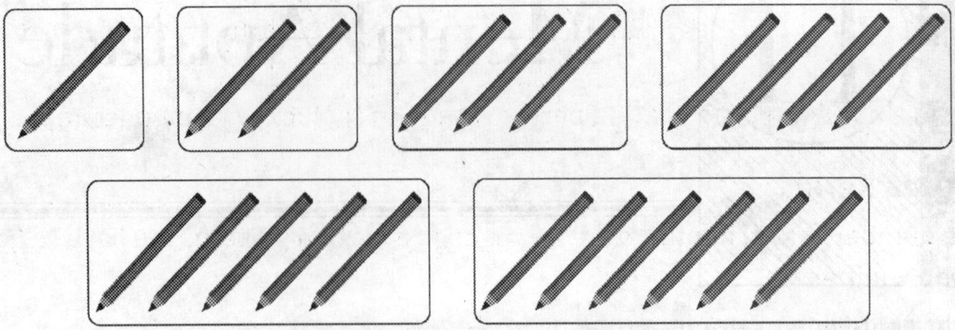

Here, number of pencils in each consecutive figures is increased by a gap of 1. It's a forth counting from 1 to 6.

Descending Order Pattern

It is the sequence of numbers from bigger to smaller. Let's see the following patterns of pencils shown below:

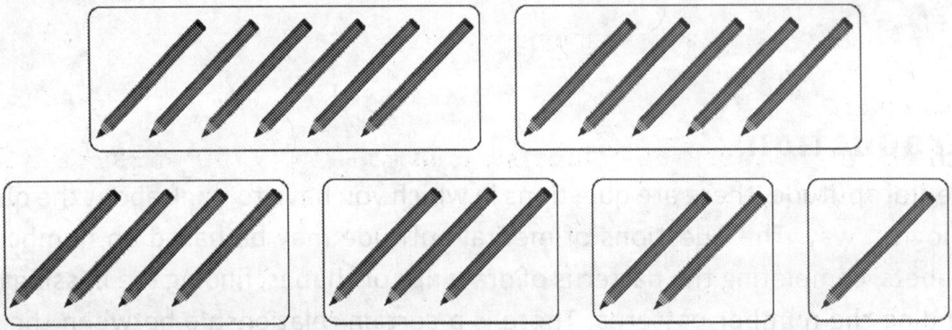

Here, number of pencils in each consecutive figures is decreased by a gap of 1. It's a back counting from 6 to 1.

Pattern Based on Rotation

Let us see another following patterns:

Here, each shape is rotated anti-clock wise direction in each next step. Or, we can say that each next figure is turned to its right.

Let's see another example:

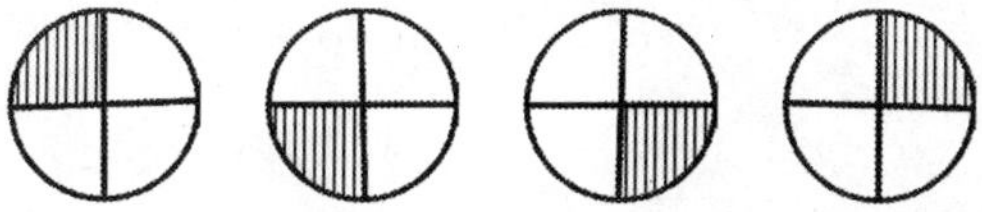

Here, in each figure, the shaded part is turned anti-clock wise by one step.

Number Series

In the number series, numbers are arranged in a certain pattern. You have to find the missing number.

See the following example:

Example: 1

Find the missing number.

[2], [4], [6], [8], [10] [?].

In the above given pattern, numbers are arranged in the gap of [2]. Counting from [2] you can find the missing number, that is [12]

Example: 2

Which one of the following numbers would you like to choose to complete the following number pattern?

[6] [12] [18] [24] [30] [?]

(A) 36 (B) 32 (C) 34 (D) 40

(E) None of these

Answer (A)

Explanation: In each next figure number increased by 6.

Example: 3

What will come in blank circle?

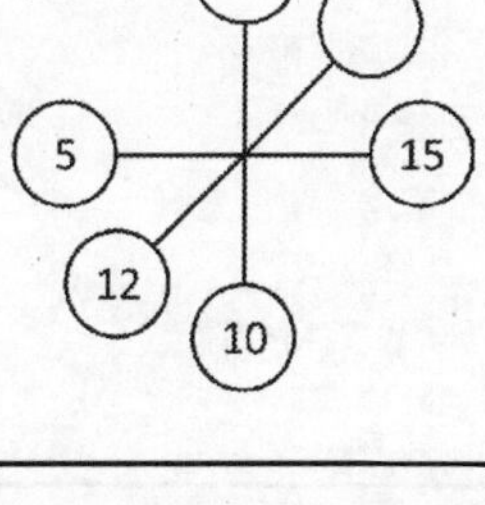

(A) 6 (B) 8

(C) 9 (D) 10

(E) None of these

Answer (B)

Explanation: Here, in each pair, the sum of the number is 20 as 5 + 15 = 20 and 10 + 10 = 20. So, 12 + 8 = 20

Summary

- ❖ Patterns are arrangements in particular style.
- ❖ Patterns can be made up of numbers, sizes, shapes ,etc.

Did You Know ?

- ❖ 1 googol is the number 1 followed by 100 zeroes. In fact Google's name came from misspelling of this word.
- ❖ On average you blink 25000 a day.
- ❖ Zero is the only number that can't be represented in Roman numerals.

Solved Problems

1. What may come next in the following pattern?

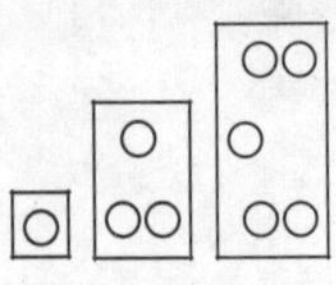

(A) 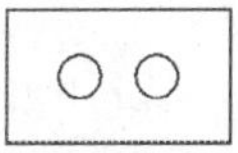

(B) 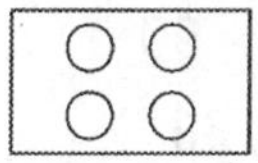

(C) 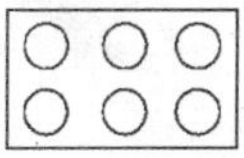

(D) 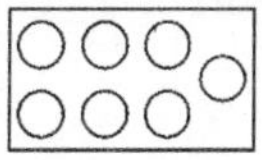

(E) None of these

Answer (D)

Explanation: Here, in each next figure number of circles increased by two.

2. What will come in place of question mark?

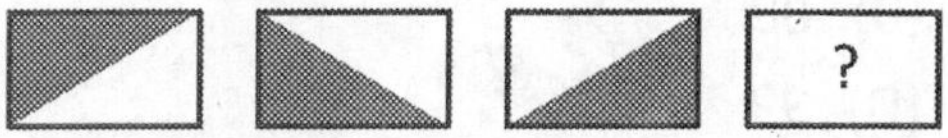

(A) 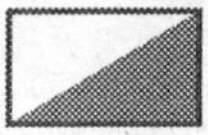

(B) 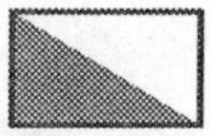

(C) 

(D) 

(E) None of these

Answer (C)

Explanation: In each next figure the shaded part rotates anticlockwise.

3. What will come in the place of question mark?

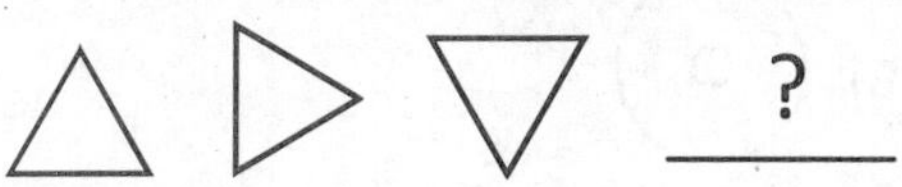

(A) 

(B) 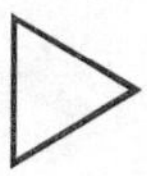

(C) 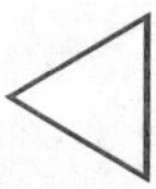

(D) All the above

(E) None of these

Answer (C)

Explanation: Here, in each next figure, the figure rotates clockwise.

4. Find the number series which is based on the gap of 5.

(A) 15, 20, 24, 27, 29, 30

(B) 5, 10, 14, 19, 23, 28

(C) 1, 5, 25, 50, 75, 85, 90

(D) 11, 16, 21, 26, 31, 36

(E) None of these

Answer (D)

Explanation: Clearly the series 11, 16, 21, 26, 31, 36 is based on the gap of 5.

5. Choose the correct number to fill in the blank.

11, 22, 44, ?

(A) 66 (B) 88

(C) 33 (D) 99

(E) None of these

Answer (B)

Explanation: Here the pattern is, 11 + 11 = 22, 22 + 22 = 44, 44 + 44 = 88.

6. Choose the correct option and complete the following series

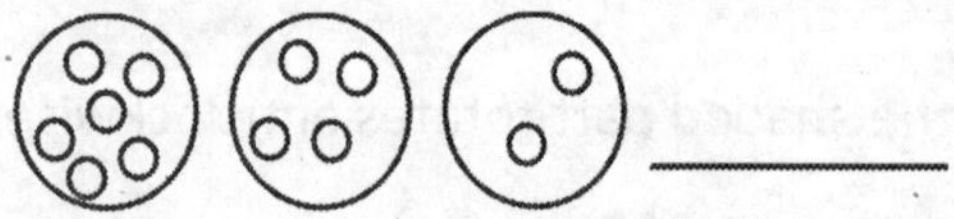

(A)  (B) 

(C) 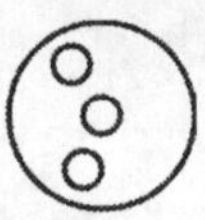 (D) All the above

(E) None of these

Answer (A)

Explanation: In each next figure, the number of smaller circles reduced by two.

7. Choose the correct option and complete the series

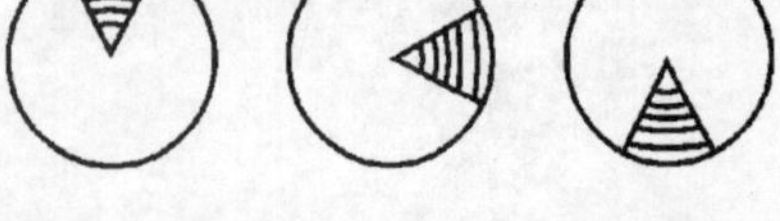

(A) 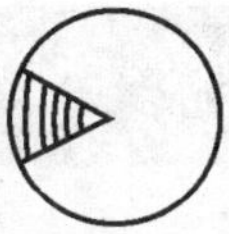

(B) 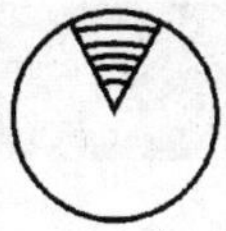

(C) 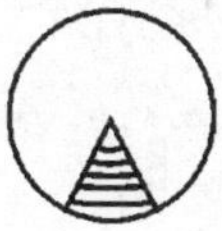

(D) All the above

(E) None of these

Answer (A)

Explanation: In each next figure, the circle rotates clockwise.

8. What will come in place of question mark?

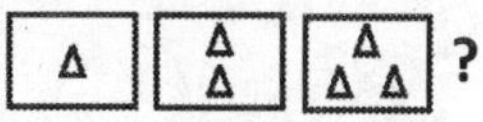

(A) 

(B) 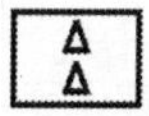

(C) 

(D) 

(E) None of these

Answer (C)

Explanation: In each next figure, number of triangles increased by one.

Practice Exercise 11

1. Choose the correct option and complete the following pattern.

11, 333, 5555, ______.

(A) 44444 (B) 66666

(C) 77777 (D) 99999

(E) None of these

2. Find the number series which is based on counting of 3.

(A) 3, 6, 9, 12, 15

(B) 3, 4, 5, 6, 7, 8

(C) 3, 9, 18, 97, 81

(D) All the above

(E) None of these

3. Fill in the blank: 1, 2, 4 , 8,______?

(A) 12 (B) 16

(C) 20 (D) 30

(E) None of these

4. Fill in the blank: 5, 12, 19, 26,________?

(A) 30 (B) 32

(C) 33 (D) 36

(E) None of these

5. Look at the following figure:

2	4	6
8	10	12
14	16	?

Which one of the following numbers will come in place of question mark?

(A) 18 (B) 3

(C) 5 (D) 8

(E) None of these

6. The table below shows the number of books read by Savita at the end of week.

Week	1st	2nd	3rd	4th	5th
No. of books read	3	6	9	12	?

If the pattern in the table continues, how many books she will read by 5th week?

(A) 9
(B) 12
(C) 15
(D) All the above
(E) None of these

Direction (7-9): In each of the following questions, find the figure, which comes next?

7.  ______.

(A) 
(B) 
(C) 
(D) 
(E) None of these

8.  ______.

(A) 
(B) 
(C) 
(D) 
(E) None of these

9. 10 20 40 80 ?

(A) 160
(B) 100
(C) 110
(D) All the above
(E) None of these

10.  ______ .

(A) 

(B) 

(C) 

(D) 

(E) None of these

11. Fill the blank in the series given below:

16, 18, 20, 22, 24, ______, 28, 30.

(A) 23

(B) 24

(C) 26

(D) 25

(E) None of these

12. Follow the pattern of figure -I to find the missing number in figure -2.

2 3 1

Figure I

8 9 ?

Figure 2

(A) 2

(B) 5

(C) 8

(D) 7

(E) 3

13. Study the first pattern to complete the second pattern:

9
12
3

Pattern- 1

9
14
?

Pattern- 2

(A) 0

(B) 2

(C) 5

(D) 3

(E) None of these

14. Complete the following pattern:

 ______ .

(A) 

(B) 

(C) 
(D) 

(E) None of these

15. Complete the following pattern 18, 15, 12, 9, 6, ______

(A) 2

(B) 3

(C) 5

(D) 4

(E) None of these

Model Test Paper-1

1. What does □ represent in the given question?

□ + □ = 16

(A) 8 (B) 4

(C) 12 (D) 16

(E) None of these

2. Jack has 10 toffees. He eats 6 toffees. How many toffees are left with him?

(A) 4 (B) 6

(C) 10 (D) 16

(E) None of these

3. Add 6 tens and 4 ones.

(A) 69 (B) 46

(C) 40 (D) 64

(E) None of these

4. Which one of the following options is correct to complete the numbers in the ladder?

50		48			45		43

(A) 49, 47, 46, 44 (B) 49, 56, 42, 36

(C) 50, 48, 45, 43 (D) 43, 45, 48, 50

(E) None of these

5. Counting by 2 which one of the following option is correct for missing number in the box?

13	15					25

(A) 17, 19, 21, 23 (B) 23, 19, 21, 17
(C) 13, 15, 25, 27 (D) 23, 16, 17, 11
(E) None of these

6. What is the time in the clock?

(A) 2 : 00 (B) 1 : 00
(C) 12 : 00 (D) 10 : 00
(E) None of these

7. Which day is the last day of the week?

(A) Sunday (B) Monday
(C) Saturday (D) Friday
(E) None of these

8. How many months in a year have 31 days ?

(A) 9 (B) 11
(C) 7 (D) 4
(E) None of these

9. The pictures of coins are shown in the given figure. Count the money and write in the box

1 Rupee 5 Rupee 1 Rupee = ₹ [ ]

(A) ₹1 (B) ₹6
(C) ₹7 (D) ₹8
(E) None of these

10. How many paise are there in 10 rupees note?

(A) 1000 paise (B) 100 paise
(C) 10 paise (D) 1 paisa
(E) None of these

11. Given below the picture of two huts. Which one of the following options is correct for huts?

(A)

(B)

(A) Hut A is bigger than hut B.
(B) Hut B is bigger than hut A.
(C) Both hut A and B are of same size.
(D) All the above
(E) None of these

12. Which one of the following number is equal to 9 more than 7?

(A) 14 (B) 15
(C) 16 (D) 17
(E) None of these

13. Which of the following has conical shape?

(A) Football and ball (B) Book and note book
(C) Pencil and eraser (D) Birthday cap and icecream cone
(E) None of these

14. How many corners are there in the given triangle?

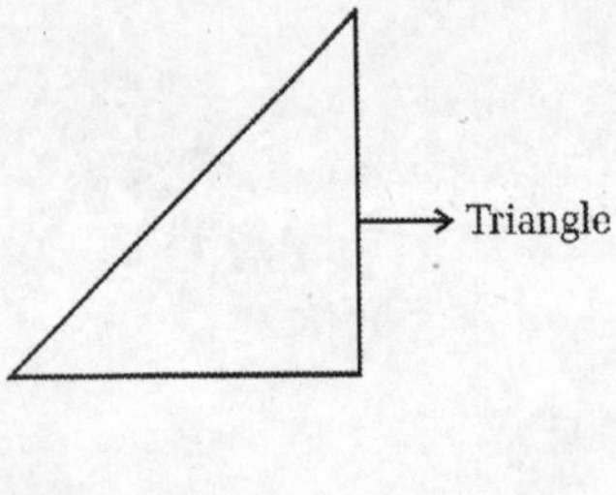

(A) 1 (B) 2
(C) 3 (D) 4
(E) None of these

15. A branch of tree has 4 mangoes. After some time 6 more mangoes grow up. Find the total number of mangoes in that branch.

(A) 10 (B) 6
(C) 4 (D) 14
(E) None of these

16. Smith has ₹18. He spends ₹6 to buy toffees. How much money is left with him now?

(A) ₹18 (B) ₹6
(C) ₹10 (D) ₹12
(E) None of these

17. How many ones make a ten?

(A) 1 (B) 10 (C) 100 (D) 0
(E) None of these

18. Counting by 1 complete the given series.

(A) 443, 445, 447, 448 (B) 449, 446, 442, 444
(C) 442, 443, 444, 445 (D) 100, 200, 300, 400
(E) None of these

19. Count by 5 and fill the boxes.

10 15 ☐ ☐ ☐ ☐

(A) 35, 15, 10, 5 (B) 15, 10, 5, 10
(C) 10, 15, 20, 25 (D) 20, 25, 30, 35
(E) None of these

20. When do you take your dinner?

(A) Morning (B) Evening

(C) Night (D) Afternoon

(E) None of these

21. The next day after Monday is _______.

Monday	→	

(A) Sunday (B) Tuesday

(C) Friday (D) Saturday

(E) None of these

22. Which one of the following months comes between April and June?

April	→		→	June

(A) April (B) June

(C) May (D) July

(E) None of these

23. How many 2 rupees coins are there in 20 rupees?

(A) 5 (B) 2

(C) 20 (D) 10

(E) None of these

24. Smith wants to buy an umbrella and the cost of umbrella is ₹100. How many 10 rupees note is required to buy this umbrella?

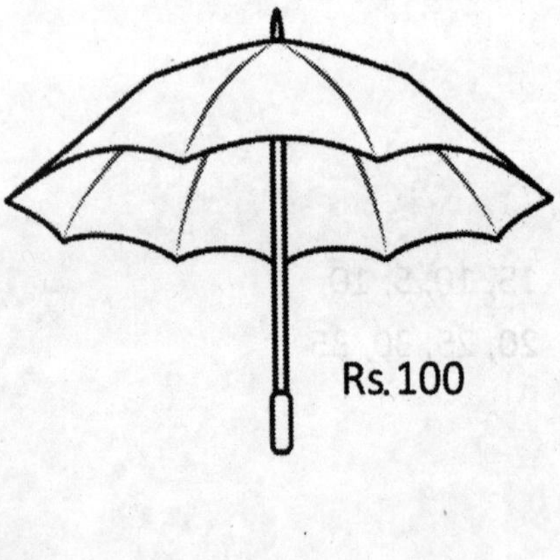

(A) 10 (B) 5

(C) 4 (D) 13

(E) None of these

25. Two stars are shown below. Which star is bigger?

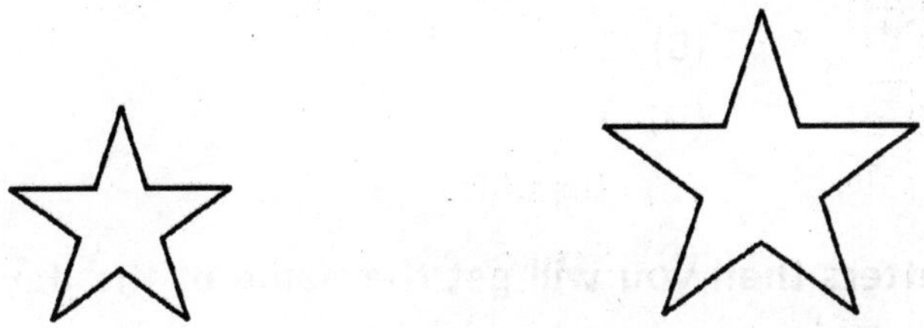

A B

(A) Star A is bigger

(B) Star B is bigger

(C) Both star A and B are of same size

(D) All the above

(E) None of these

26. How many types of geometrical shapes are there in the figure shown below?

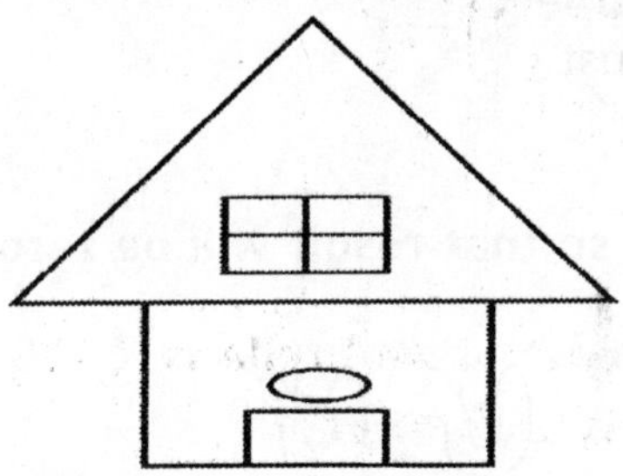

(A) 2 (B) 4

(C) 3 (D) 1

(E) None of these

27. Name the shape of the figure given below.

(A) Square (B) Rectangle

(C) Circle (D) Cone

(E) None of these

28. Add the following:

$$\begin{array}{r} 5 \\ +\ 2 \\ +\ 1 \\ \hline \square \end{array}$$

(A) 5 (B) 2
(C) 8 (D) 3
(E) None of these

29. If you fill the box with letters then you will get the name of the day of a week. Name that day.

W		D			S	D		Y

(A) Sunday (B) Wednesday
(C) Tuesday (D) Friday
(E) None of these

30. Name the month when republic day is celebrated.

(A) June (B) July
(C) January (D) August
(E) None of these

31. Which sign will come in the place of "And" so that result will be zero?

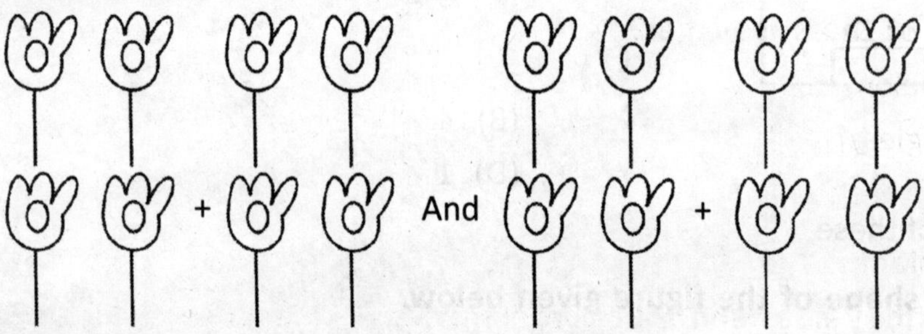

(A) + (B) –
(C) × (D) All the above
(E) None of these

32. Steve has 4 balls of cricket. Smith takes two from him. How many balls are left with him?

(A) 2 (B) 4
(C) 6 (D) 8
(E) None of these

33. 6 tens + 1 ones = 61, 6 tens + 2 ones = 62, 6 tens + ☐ ones = 60.

(A) 6 (B) 10 (C) 7 (D) 0
(E) None of these

34. A clock has two hands. The short hand is the hour and the long hand is the minute hand. The minute hand is at 12 and the hour hand is at 7. So the time in the clock is ☐

(A) 12 o'clock (B) 7 o'clock
(C) 12, 7 o'clock (D) 7,120 o'clock
(E) None of these

35. There are two fruits on the table. One is apple and another is watermelon. Which one of them is bigger?

(A) Watermelon (B) Apple
(C) Meaningless (D) All the above
(E) None of these

36. Fill in the blanks:

Square has four sides and four corners. Triangle has three sides and three corners. Circle has ____ sides and ____ corners.

(A) 2 (B) No
(C) 4 (D) 3
(E) None of these

37. 10 ones make a ten. How many tens is equal to 50 ones.

(A) 50 (B) 5

(C) 10 (D) 15

(E) None of these

38. A number is 7 more than 10. Find the number.

(A) 15 (B) 16

(C) 17 (D) 14

(E) None of these

39. Complete the series by replacing question mark.

2, 5, 8, 11, ?

(A) 12 (B) 13

(C) 14 (D) 15

(E) None of these

40. Take two numbers 10 and 5 and then subtract 6 from their sum. What is the resulting number?

(A) 5 (B) 7

(C) 9 (D) 6

(E) None of these

Model Test Paper-2

1. **Add the following and find the result.**

   9 + 1 = ☐

   (A) 10 (B) 9
   (C) 1 (D) 12
   (E) None of these

2. **A tree has 6 flower on a branch. 4 flowers fall down. How many flowers are left?**

   (A) 6 (B) 4
   (C) 2 (D) 1
   (E) None of these

3. **4 tens + 0 ones = ☐**

   (A) 26 (B) 14
   (C) 4 (D) 40
   (E) None of these

4. **Count by 1 and fill the missing numbers.**

28			31					36

   (A) 28, 29, 32, 34, 36, 37 (B) 36, 35, 34, 32, 33
   (C) 29, 30, 32, 33, 34, 35 (D) 35, 34, 33, 32, 30
   (E) None of these

5. **Count by 3 and fill the missing numbers in the box.**

22	25		31		37		43	

(A) 3, 5, 8, 11, 13
(B) 28, 34, 40, 46
(C) 43, 37, 31, 22
(D) 36, 46, 67, 72
(E) None of these

6. Write the time shown by the clock.

(A) 2 : 00
(B) 1 : 00
(C) 12 : 00
(D) 3 : 00
(E) None of these

7. Which one of the following days is the second day of a week?

(A) Tuesday
(B) Monday
(C) Wednesday
(D) Friday
(E) None of these

8. In which one of the following months 1 day is added in the leap year?

(A) April
(B) May
(C) February
(D) January
(E) None of these

9. Add the following money and fill in the box.

5 rupees

+

2 rupees

+

2 rupees

= ________.

(A) ₹ 10 (B) ₹ 9
(C) ₹ 12 (D) ₹ 4
(E) None of these

10. How many notes of Rs. 20 are there in Rs. 100?

(A) 1 (B) 4
(C) 5 (D) 6
(E) None of these

11. What is the shape of the ball A and ball B?

A

B

(A) Square (B) Round
(C) Flat (D) All the above
(E) None of these

12. How many circles are there in the figure?

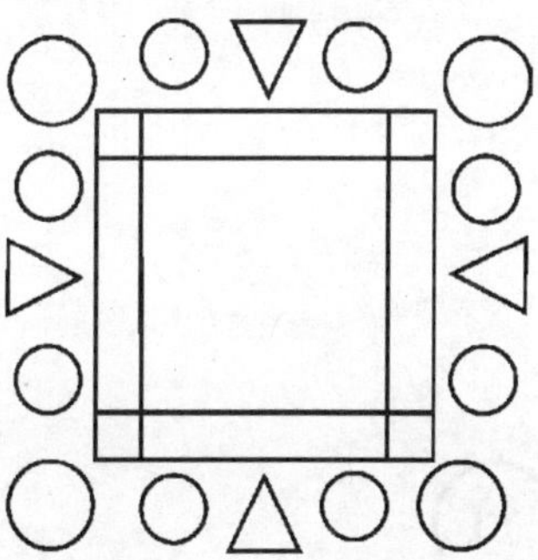

(A) 8 (B) 10
(C) 11 (D) 12
(E) None of these

13. Which one of the following numbers is 6 more than 7 + 3?

(A) 10 (B) 12

(C) 14 (D) 16

(E) None of these

14. Subtract 10 from the sum of 4 and 9.

(A) 1 (B) 5

(C) 2 (D) 3

(E) None of these

15. Find the sum of the following:

[6] + [2] + [2] = [ ]

(A) 4 (B) 6

(C) 8 (D) 10

(E) None of these

16. What does [ ] represent, if you subtract the following?

[7] – [4] = [ ]

(A) 7 (B) 4

(C) 3 (D) 10

(E) None of these

17. How many tens are there in 40 ones?

(A) 4 (B) 10

(C) 14 (D) 20

(E) None of these

18. Write the missing number.

(17) ( ) ( ) (14) ( ) ( ) (11)

(A) 17, 16, 15, 14 (B) 12, 13, 15, 16, 18

(C) 16, 15, 13, 12 (D) 14, 13, 12, 11

(E) None of these

19. Find the missing number counting by 2.

82		86		90		

(A) 82, 88, 89, 90
(B) 94, 90, 86, 82
(C) 84, 88, 92, 94
(D) 90, 46, 36, 42
(E) None of these

20. When do you take your breakfast?

(A) Night
(B) Morning
(C) Afternoon
(D) Evening
(E) None of these

21. Write the missing letters to get the name of a day. Name that day.

☐ AT ☐ R ☐ ☐ Y

(A) Monday
(B) Saturday
(C) Friday
(D) Thursday
(E) None of these

22. How Many months in a year have 30 days?

(A) 6
(B) 5
(C) 4
(D) 3
(E) None of these

23. How many 2 rupees coins are there in 10 rupees?

(A) 10
(B) 5
(C) 2
(D) 3
(E) None of these

24. Put the suitable sign in the box.

4 + 5 ☐ 3 +7

(A) >
(B) <
(C) =
(D) All the above
(E) None of these

25. The pictures of two plants are shown below. Which plant is bigger?

A  B 

(A) Plant A is bigger
(B) Plant B is bigger
(C) Both A and B are of same size
(D) None of these
(E) None of these

26. What is the shape of an egg?

(A) Circle
(B) Oval
(C) Triangle
(D) Square
(E) None of these

27. If circle = triangle and triangle = rectangle then rectangle is also equal to?

(A) Square
(B) Cone
(C) Circle
(D) All the above
(E) None of these

28. Jack's father gave 22 cookies to jack. Her mother also gave him 33 cookies. How many cookies Jack had now?

(A) 33
(B) 22
(C) 32
(D) 55
(E) None of these

29. Which one of the following is the last month of the year?

(A) May
(B) January
(C) November
(D) December
(E) None of these

30. Which day comes between Friday and Sunday?

Friday, ☐ ,Sunday

(A) Monday
(B) Friday
(C) Saturday
(D) Tuesday
(E) None of these

31. Which number will come in the blank box?

6	24	42
12	30	
18	36	54

(A) 60
(B) 47
(C) 49
(D) 48
(E) None of these

32. Which day comes next after Thursday?

(A) Friday
(B) Saturday
(C) Wednesday
(D) Sunday
(E) None of these

33. October is the tenth month of a year.
November is the ____ month of a year.

(A) Twelfth
(B) Eight
(C) Eleventh
(D) Ninth
(E) None of these

34. Lina has 20 toys, Smith has 40 toys, Zacob has 35 toys and Katherine has 10 toys.
Who has more toys?

(A) Lina
(B) Smith
(C) Zacob
(D) Katherine
(E) None of these

35. Complete the pattern:

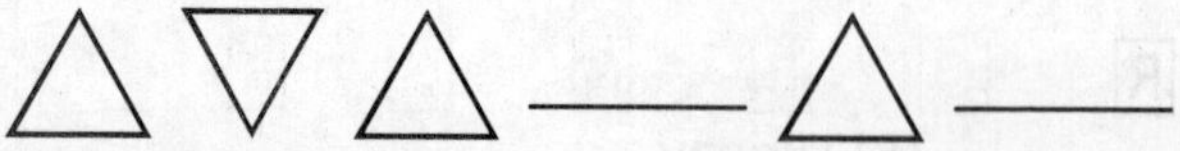

(A) 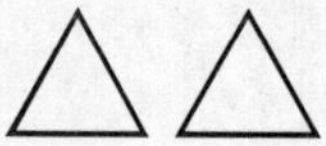

(B) 

(C) 

(D) 

(E) None of these

36. In Rectangle there are ____ corners and ____ sides.

(A) 4, 4
(B) 6, 4
(C) 3, 3
(D) no, no
(E) None of these

37. Which one of the following options is equal to the cost of the following figure?

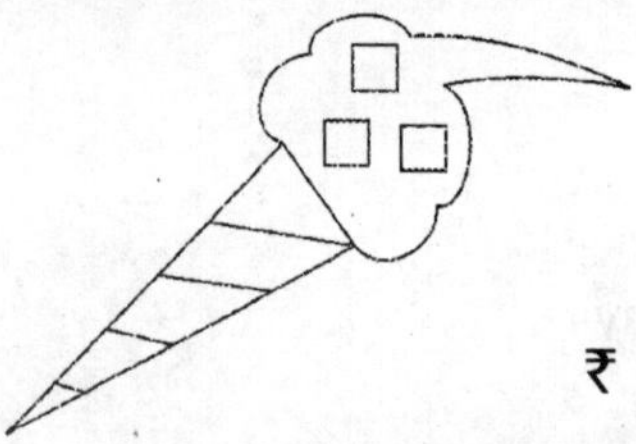

₹ 12/.

(A) ₹ 5 + ₹ 5 + ₹ 1
(B) 50 p + ₹ 10 + ₹ 1
(C) ₹ 5 + ₹ 5 + ₹ 2
(D) 25 p + 25 p + ₹ 10
(E) None of these

38. Which one of the following shapes has more sides?

(A) Trapezium 

(B) Triangle 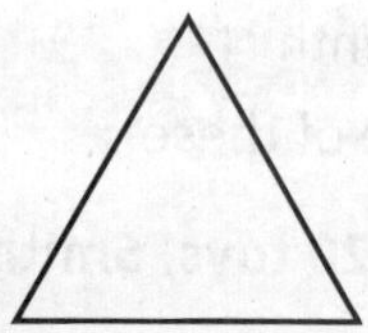

(C) Hexagon 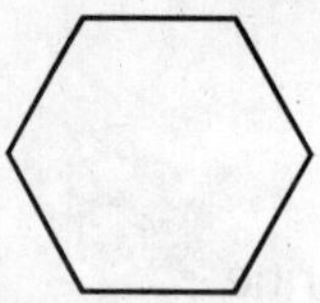

(D) Square 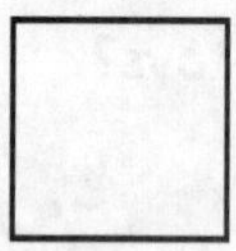

(E) None of these

39. In how many rectangles letter R is written?

G B R G R O B R G R

(A) 2 (B) 3

(C) 5 (D) 4

(E) None of these

40. If one triangle has 3 sides, then 4 triangles will have ____ sides.

(A) 6 sides (B) 9 sides

(C) 12 sides (D) 15 sides

(E) None of these

Model Test Paper-3

1. A number is 12 more than 12. Find the number.

(A) 22 (B) 26

(C) 24 (D) 36

(E) None of these

2. In which one of the following options result is 9?

(A) 6 – 3 (B) 8 – 3

(C) 7 – 3 (D) 12 – 3

(E) None of these

3. Fill in the blank:

___ tens + 7ones = 27

(A) 2 (B) 3

(C) 7 (D) 7

(E) None of these

4. In the following series which number will come at the place of question mark?

86, 87, 88, 89, ?

(A) 85 (B) 90

(C) 99 (D) 80

(E) None of these

5. Count by 7 and fill in the blanks.

7, 14, __, 28, 35

(A) 42 (B) 49

(C) 21 (D) 18

(E) None of these

6. Which one of the following clocks shows the time 4 : 00 i.e. 4 o' clock?

(A) 

(B) 

(C) 

(D) 

(E) None of these

7. Which day will come next in the given sequence of days?

Wednesday, Thursday, Friday, Saturday, Sunday, ________.

(A) Monday
(B) Thursday
(C) Tuesday
(D) Saturday
(E) None of these

8. Which one of the following is the correct spelling of second month of the year?

(A) Febury
(B) Febrauy
(C) February
(D) Febauary
(E) None of these

9. How many paisa are there in ₹8?

(A) 80 paisa
(B) 800 paisa
(C) 8000 paisa
(D) 18 paisa
(E) None of these

10. Which one of the following animals is biggest in size?

(A) Elephant (B) Lion

(C) Cat (D) Dog

(E) None of these

11. The circle on the trees shows fruits. Which one of the following trees has least number of fruits?

(A) 

(B) 

(C) 

(D) 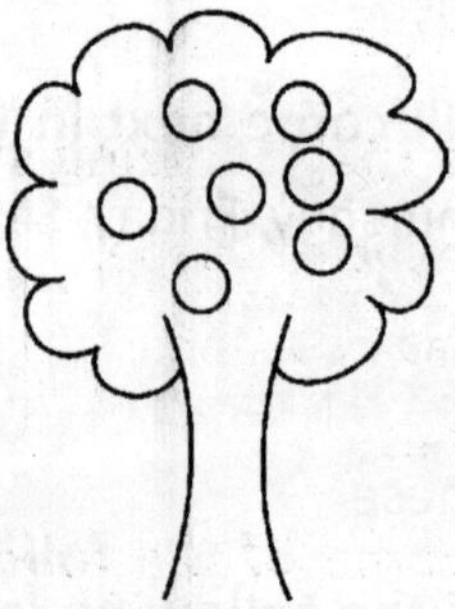

(E) None of these

12. How many triangles are there in the following figures?

(A) 8 (B) 7

(C) 9 (D) 14

(E) None of these

13. A square has 4 sides and 4 squares have 16 sides then 5 squares will have _____ sides

(A) 24 sides (B) 20 sides
(C) 28 sides (D) 30 sides
(E) None of these

14. How many sides are there in a given rectangle?

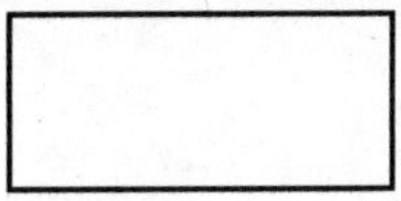

(A) 2 (B) 4
(C) 1 (D) 6
(E) None of these

15. Which one of the following statement is correct about circle?

(A) Circle is round in shape. (B) Circle is square in shape.
(C) Circle is flat in shape. (D) All the above
(E) None of these

16. What is the name of the following figure?

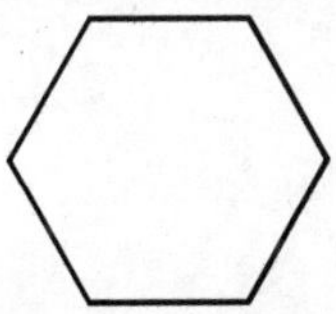

(A) Triangle (B) Octagon
(C) Square (D) Hexagon
(E) None of these

17. Find the sum of 6, 2, 3 and 4.

(A) 10 (B) 15
(C) 12 (D) 9
(E) None of these

18. 18 less than 25 is ________.

(A) 7 (B) 6
(C) 5 (D) 8
(E) None of these

19. Name the digit at one's place in the number 182.

(A) 1 (B) 2
(C) 8 (D) All the above
(E) None of these

20. How many pens are there in the given figure?

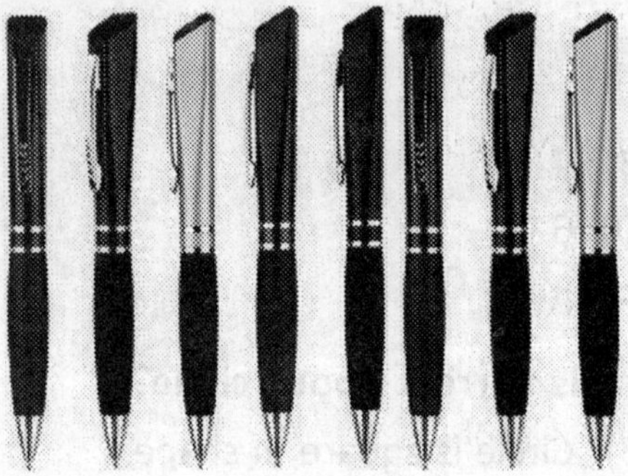

(A) 7 (B) 8
(C) 6 (D) 10
(E) None of these

21. Count by 4 and fill in the blank box.

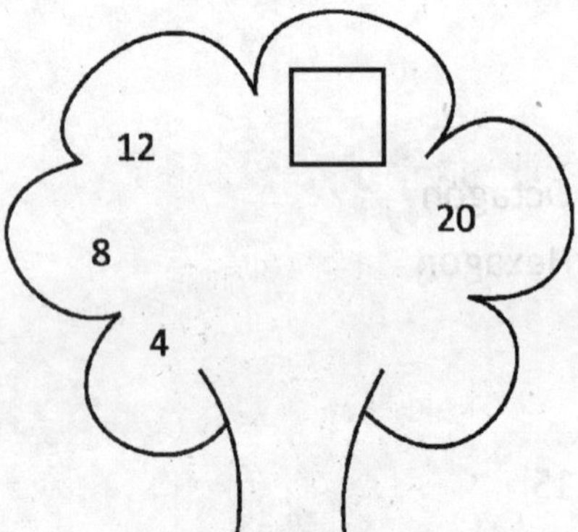

(A) 15 (B) 18
(C) 24 (D) 16
(E) None of these

22. What does the shortest hand of the clock show?

(A) Second
(B) Hour
(C) Minute
(D) All the above
(E) None of these

23. What comes after Saturday and before Monday?

(A) Sunday (B) Friday
(C) Thursday (D) Monday
(E) None of these

24. What comes after June and before August?

(A) September (B) June
(C) July (D) October
(E) None of these

25. What will be the total amount when you add ₹5 + 50 p + ₹10 + 25 p is______.

(A) ₹10.50 (B) ₹15.75
(C) ₹60.30 (D) ₹25.60
(E) None of these

26. Which one of the following is used to write?

(A) Pencil 

(B) Book 

(C) Eraser 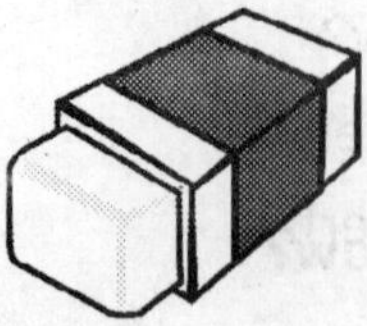

(D) Scale 

(E) None of these

27. Smith has 7 marbles, Steve has 5 marbles, Zacob has 14 marbles and Lina has 12 marbles. Who has the least number of marbles?

(A) Steve
(B) Smith
(C) Lina
(D) Zacob
(E) None of these

28. Which one of the following is the shape of a square?

(A) 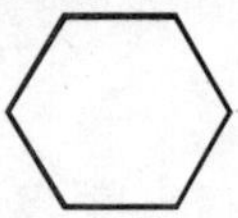

(B) 

(C) 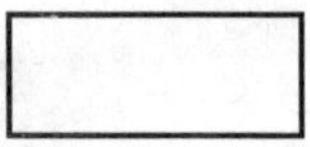

(D) 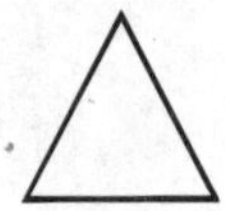

(E) None of these

29. How many triangle(s) are there in the following figures?

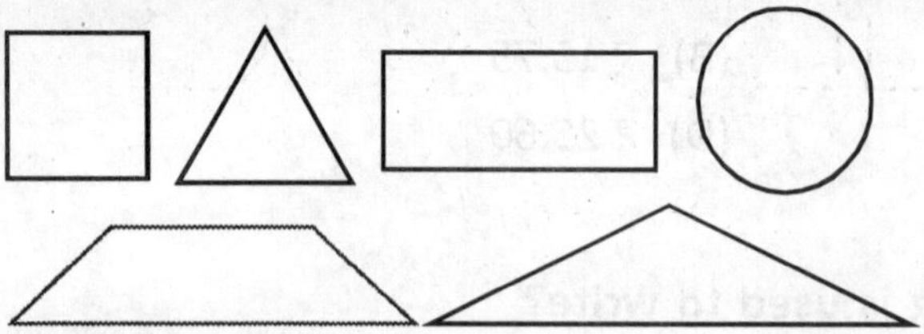

(A) 3
(B) 2
(C) 1
(D) 4
(E) None of these

30. If one D has 3 sides, Two D have 6 sides, Three D have 9 sides, Then four D have_______ sides

(A) 15
(B) 18
(C) 16
(D) 12
(E) None of these

31. There were 5 butterflies in a garden. 4 more butterflies joined them. How many butterflies are there in the garden now?

(A) 7 Butterflies
(B) 8 Butterflies
(C) 9 Butterflies
(D) 1 Butterfly
(E) None of these

32. In a class of 28 children, 16 are boys? How many girls are there in the class?

(A) 12 girls
(B) 44 girls
(C) 44 boys
(D) 12 boys
(E) None of these

33. Which one of the following options is equal to 75 paisa?

(A) 25 p + 50 p + 10 p
(B) 10 p + 20 p + 20 p + 20 p
(C) 10 p + 20 p + 25 p
(D) 15 p + 40 p + 20 p
(E) None of these

34. Which one of the following animals is the smallest?

(A) Cat
(B) Dog
(C) Cow
(D) Rat
(E) None of these

35. How many circles are there in the following figures?

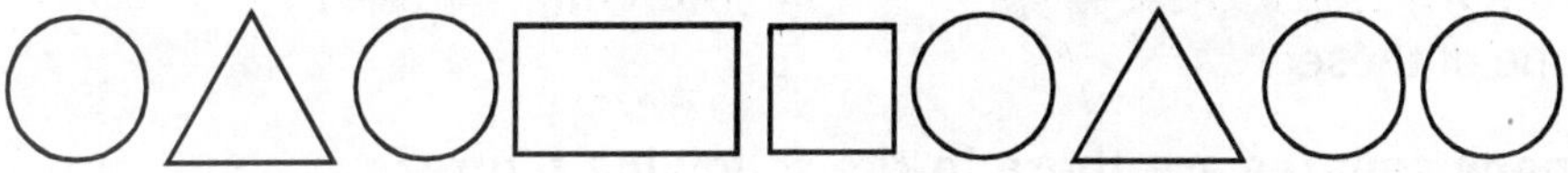

(A) 5 circles
(B) 2 circles
(C) 3 circles
(D) 6 circles
(E) None of these

36. Fill in the missing numbers.

10, 9, 8, 7, ____, ____, ____, 3, ____, ____

(A) 5, 4, 2, 1, 0
(B) 8, 9, 3, 4, 6
(C) 1, 2, 5, 4, 8
(D) 6, 5, 4, 2, 1
(E) None of these

37. What comes next after November?

(A) October
(B) December
(C) January
(D) September
(E) None of these

38. Which one of the following options shows the correct price of kite?

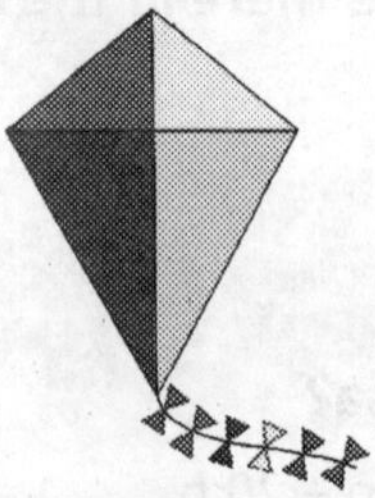

₹8

(A) ₹1 + ₹4 + ₹4
(B) ₹2 + ₹3 + ₹4
(C) ₹5 + ₹2
(D) ₹2 + ₹3 + ₹3
(E) None of these

39. Which one of the following has least money?

(A) James has ₹ 100
(B) Smith has ₹ 54
(C) Jack has ₹ 50
(D) Steve has ₹ 56
(E) None of these

40. How many squares are there in the following figure?

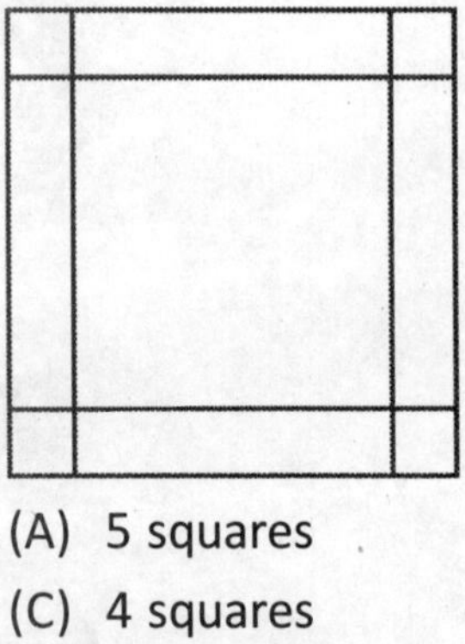

(A) 5 squares
(B) 6 squares
(C) 4 squares
(D) 7 squares
(E) None of these

Model Test Paper-4

1. **A number is 3 more than 12. Find the number.**

(A) 14 (B) 18
(C) 15 (D) 12
(E) None of these

2. **Find the remainder if we take away 4 from 12?**

(A) 6 (B) 8
(C) 4 (D) 9
(E) None of these

3. **Which one of the following options does the figure represent?**

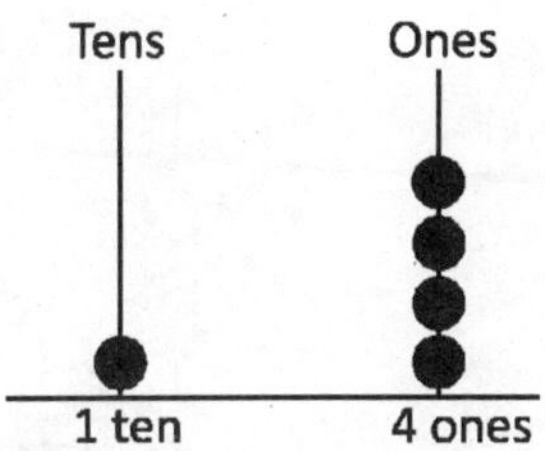

(A) 12 (B) 16
(C) 8 (D) 14
(E) None of these

4. **Fill the numbers and climb up ladder.**

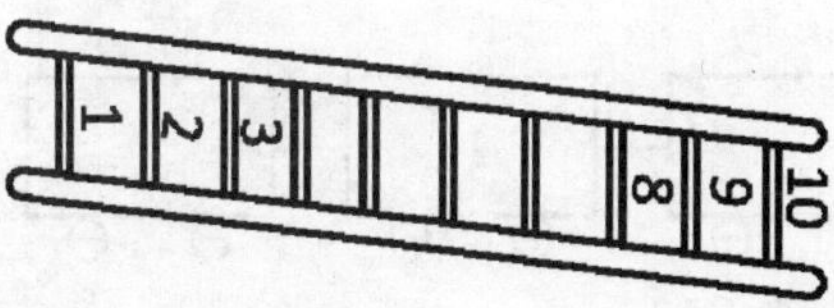

(A) 4, 5, 6, 7 (B) 7, 6, 5, 4
(C) 6, 7, 8, 9 (D) 1, 2, 3, 4
(E) None of these

5. Which one of the following is the largest and the smallest number?

116, 104, 100, 109, 136

(A) Largest 104, Smallest 100
(B) Largest 136, Smallest 116
(C) Largest 100, Smallest 109
(D) Largest 136, Smallest 100
(E) None of these

6. What is the sum of all the numbers given in the figure?

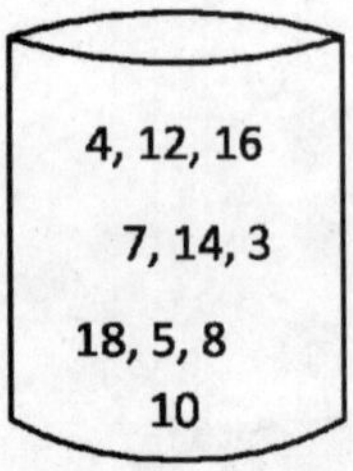

(A) 95
(B) 96
(C) 97
(D) 98
(E) None of these

7. How many circles are there in the given figure.

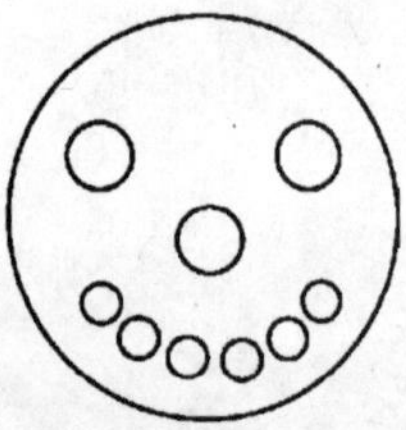

(A) 5
(B) 10
(C) 9
(D) 6
(E) None of these

8. Fill in the boxes by counting 2.

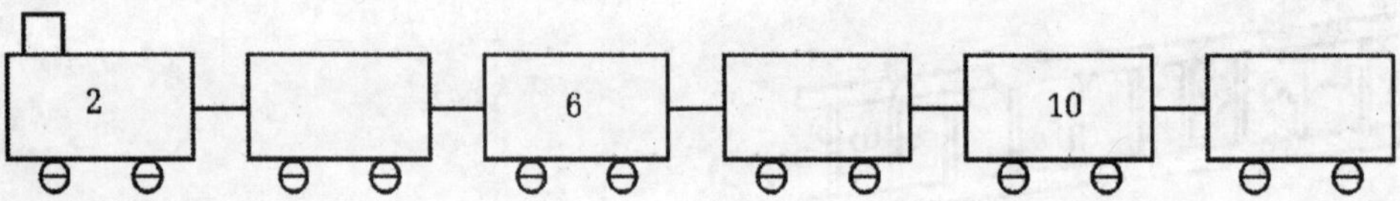

(A) 3, 7, 9
(B) 4, 8, 11
(C) 1, 5, 6
(D) 4, 8, 12
(E) None of these

9. Which month has least number of days?

(A) January
(B) November
(C) February
(D) August
(E) None of these

10. How many days does a leap year have?

(A) 346
(B) 366
(C) 336
(D) 356
(E) None of these

11. Which one of the following is the smallest number on the number line?

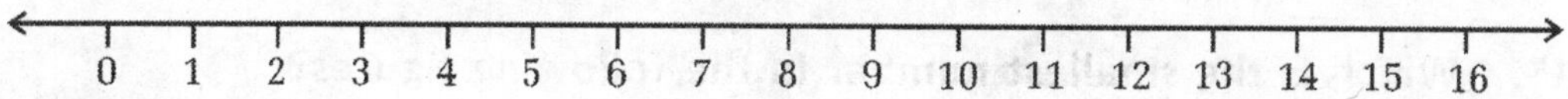

(A) 0
(B) 1
(C) 2
(D) 3
(E) None of these

12. There are eight cherries, Steve takes three cherries. How many cherries are left?

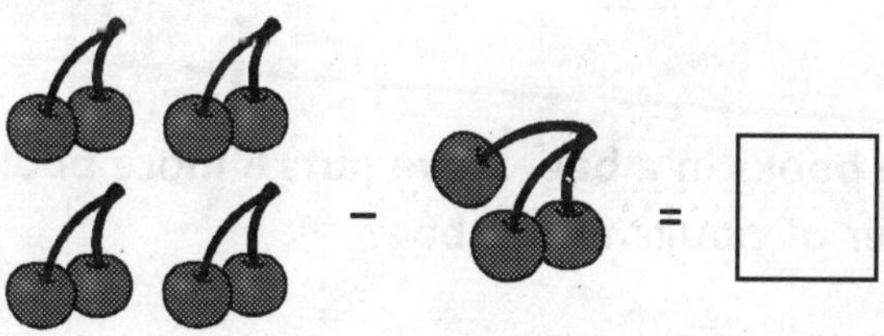

(A) 8
(B) 5
(C) 4
(D) 6
(E) None of these

13. Which one of the following numbers will come before the circled number?

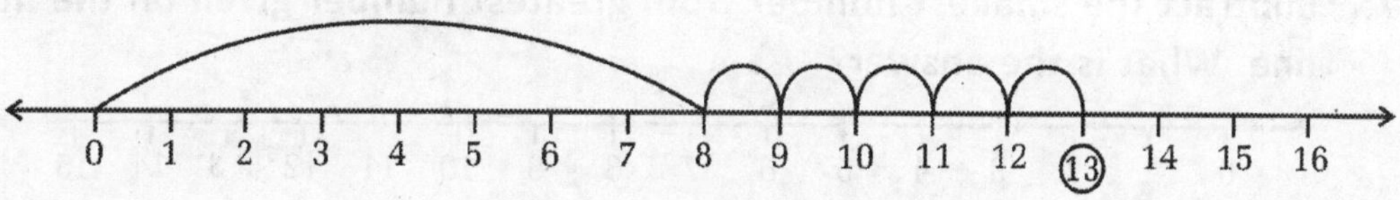

(A) 11
(B) 12
(C) 10
(D) 9
(E) None of these

14. In the following figure how many numbers are greater than 60?

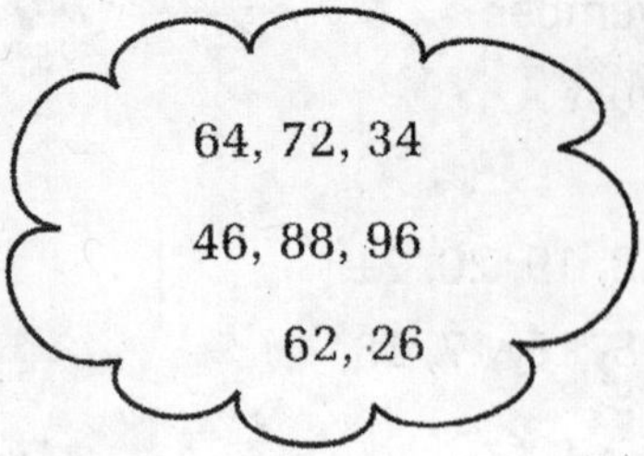

(A) 4 (B) 3
(C) 5 (D) 6
(E) None of these

15. Which is the smallest number in the following figures?

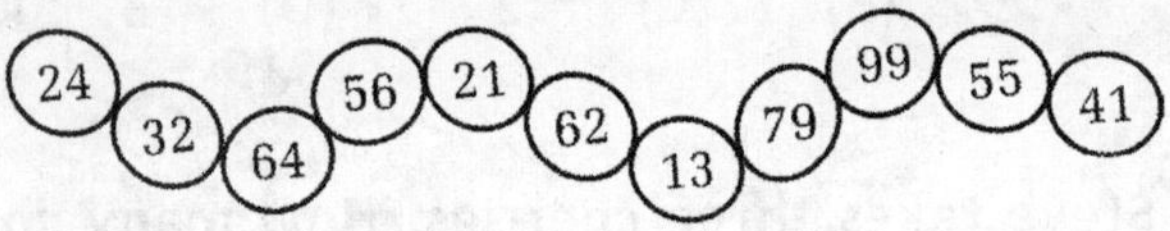

(A) 24 (B) 21
(C) 21 (D) 13
(E) None of these

16. There are 3 books and 2 note books in a bag. Steve puts 8 more books in it then what is the total number of books in the bag?

(A) 10
(B) 12
(C) 14
(D) 11
(E) None of these

17. Subtract the smallest number from greatest number given on the number line. What is the answer?

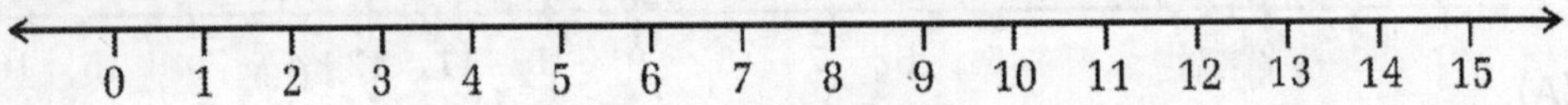

(A) 6 (B) 12
(C) 8 (D) 15
(E) None of these

18. Complete the following figure by counting 1.

(A) 12, 13, 15, 16, 19
(B) 17, 18, 19, 20, 21
(C) 11, 12, 13, 14, 15
(D) 14, 15, 16, 17, 18
(E) None of these

19. How many tens are there in the figure?

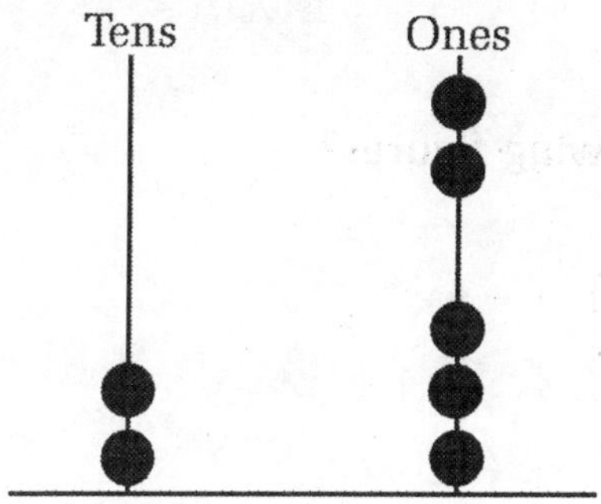

(A) 1
(B) 5
(C) 2
(D) 3
(E) None of these

20. Which is the largest numbers in given numbers?

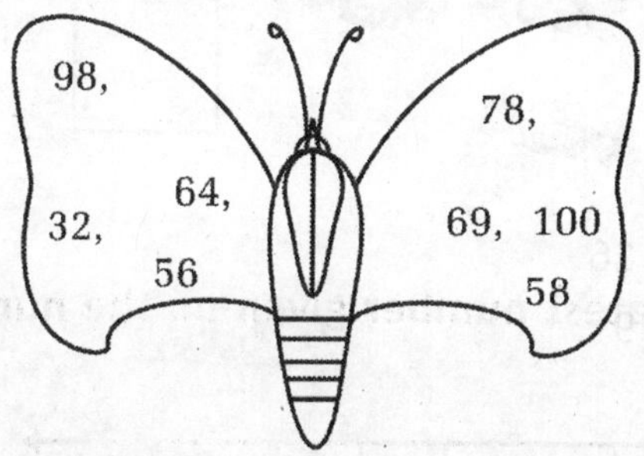

(A) 98
(B) 78
(C) 100
(D) 64
(E) None of these

21. Insert the correct symbol in the box.

5 + 9 ☐ 22-11

(A) <

(B) >

(C) =

(D) All the above

(E) None of these

22. What is the difference between the greatest and smallest number given in the figure?

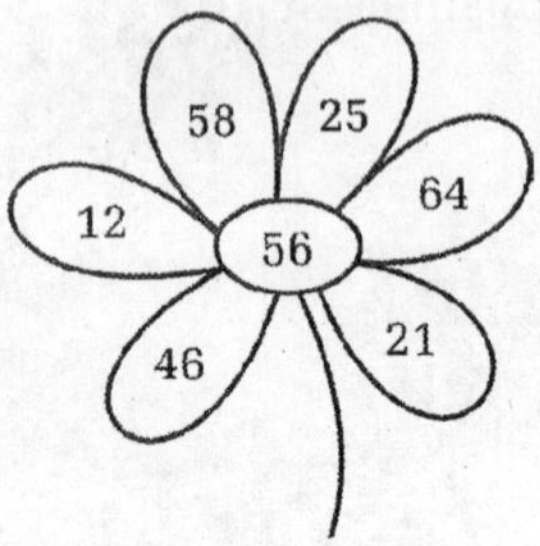

(A) 48

(B) 49

(C) 51

(D) 52

(E) None of these

23. James has five toffees, if Smith gives him four more toffees. How many toffees James have now?

(A) 6

(B) 16

(C) 18

(D) 9

(E) None of these

24. If 15 is taken away from 45, then what is the resulting number?

(A) 23

(B) 30

(C) 26

(D) 50

(E) None of these

25. How many ones and tens are there in the number 96 ?

(A) 9 ones 6 tens (B) 9 tens 6 ones

(C) 96 tens and 6 ones (D) None of these

(E) None of these

26. Few numbers are listed below:

99, 105, 140, 102, and 118.

Write the largest and the smallest number.

(A) Largest 118, smallest 140 (B) Largest 99, smallest 102

(C) Largest 140, smallest 99 (D) Largest 105, smallest 99

(E) None of these

27. Which of the following numbers are more than 15 but less than 20?

(A) 14, 15, 16, 17 (B) 16, 17, 18, 19

(C) 11, 12, 13, 14 (D) 15, 16, 17, 18

(E) None of these

28. Fill in the blanks by counting 3.

3 __ 9 __ 15 __

(A) 4, 5, 6 (B) 6, 12, 18

(C) 7, 8, 9 (D) 4, 8, 10

(E) None of these

29. By adding which two consecutive numbers on given number line gives you 19?

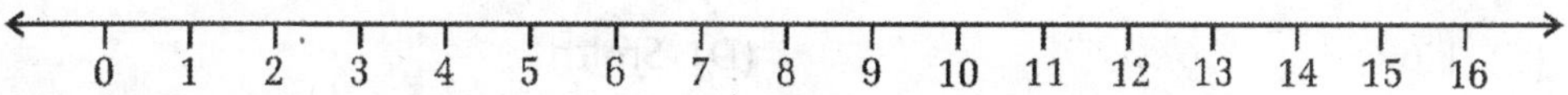

(A) 16 and 3 (B) 17 and 2

(C) 12 and 7 (D) 10 and 9

(E) None of these

30. There are ten birds on a tree, three birds fly away. How many birds are left on the tree?

(A) 8 (B) 6

(C) 7 (D) 3

(E) None of these

31. During Independence Day 56 balloons were left in the sky. 25 balloons were burst soon. How many balloons were left?

(A) 32 balloons
(B) 30 balloons
(C) 31 balloons
(D) 35 balloons
(E) None of these

32. Fill in the blank with missing numbers.

	26	27	28	29	31	31	32	33

(A) 23 (B) 34
(C) 24 (D) 25
(E) None of these

33. Fill in the blank by counting 3.

3, 6, 9,______, 15

(A) 18 (B) 12
(C) 21 (D) 24
(E) None of these

34. Juli has 20 balls, Robert has 12 balls, Lina has 25 balls and Smith has 23 balls. Who has the maximum number of balls?

(A) Juli (B) Robert
(C) Lina (D) Smith
(E) None of these

35. Which one of the following is a trapezium?

(A)  (B) 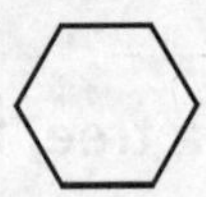

(C)  (D) 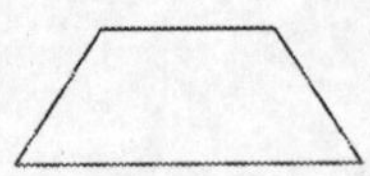

(E) None of these

36. If ABC = 123 then BCD = ?

(A) 1234
(B) 134
(C) 234
(D) All the above
(E) None of these

37. 12 tens + 10 ones = ________

(A) 120
(B) 140
(C) 130
(D) 150
(E) None of these

38. How many months are there in a year?

(A) 12 months
(B) 7 months
(C) 10 months
(D) 31 months
(E) None of these

39. Which one of the following options has least number of toffees?

(A) 

(B) 

(C) 

(D) 

(E) None of these

40. How many triangles are there in the given figure?

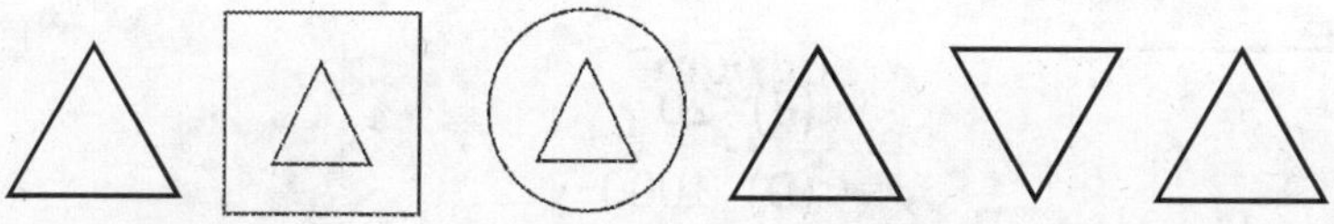

(A) 6 triangles
(B) 5 triangles
(C) 4 triangles
(D) 7 triangles
(E) None of these

Model Test Paper-5

1. Which is the biggest number in the circle?

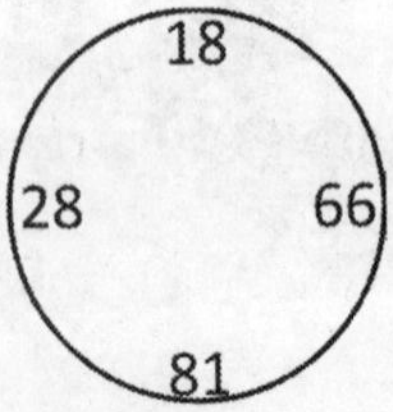

(A) 39 (B) 18
(C) 81 (D) 66
(E) None of these

2. Which one of the following is the smallest number?

64, 60, 63, 69, 65

(A) 64 (B) 69
(C) 63 (D) 60
(E) None of these

3. How many alphabets are there in the word MOTHER?

(A) 3 (B) 4
(C) 5 (D) 6
(E) None of these

4. 10 tens make __________.

(A) 100 (B) 20
(C) 30 (D) 1000
(E) None of these

5. Add the following:

$$\begin{array}{r} 73 \\ +\ 19 \\ \hline ? \\ \hline \end{array}$$

(A) 82 (B) 92
(C) 66 (D) 84
(E) None of these

6. On a tree 7 butterflies are sitting and 9 are flying around. How many butterflies are there in all?

(A) 14 (B) 15
(C) 16 (D) 17
(E) None of these

7. In an exam for 1 mark teacher gives 1 star. Smith has scored 10 marks. How many stars will he get?

(A) 5 (B) 10
(C) 15 (D) 20
(E) None of these

8. Subtract the following:

18 – 15 = ?

(A) 1 (B) 2 (C) 3 (D) 4
(E) None of these

9. Smith's grandfather is 58 years old. His grandmother is 5 years younger than his grandfather. What is her age?

(A) 64 (B) 42
(C) 52 (D) 53
(E) None of these

10. Which one of the following options is equal to 54?

(A) 68 – 45 (B) 41 + 13
(C) 68 – 25 (D) 32 + 42
(E) None of these

11. 12 months have ______ weeks and ______ day.

(A) 50 weeks 0 days (B) 52 weeks 1 days
(C) 51 week 2 days (D) 52 week 0 days
(E) None of these

12. If  **= 4 so find the sum of**

.

(A) 8 (B) 6 (C) 4 (D) 2

(E) None of these

13. What is the time in the watch shown below?

(A) 9 o'clock (B) 8 o'clock

(C) 10 o'clock (D) All the above

(E) None of these

14. When the long hand is at 12 and the short hand is at 1, it is ____ o'clock.

(A) 2 (B) 12

(C) 1 (D) 5

(E) None of these

15. Add the following:

2 + 3 + 4 + 5

(A) 11 (B) 12

(C) 13 (D) 14

(E) None of these

16. Complete the series by writing next number.

16, 21, 26, 31, ________

(A) 33 (B) 41

(C) 36 (D) 35

(E) None of these

17. Complete the series.

3, 13, 23, 33,________

(A) 43 (B) 63 (C) 53 (D) 23

(E) None of these

18. Which has a square face?

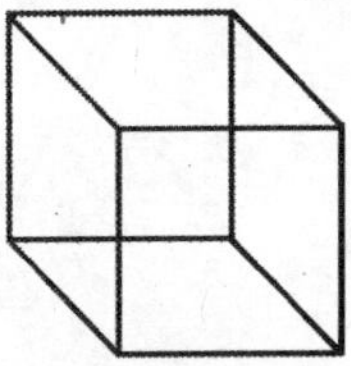

Box

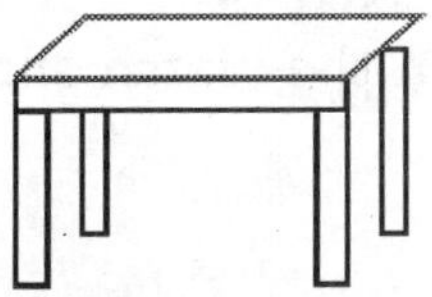

Table

Cylinder

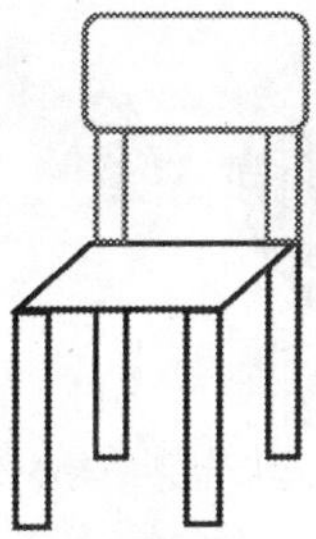

Chair

(A) Box (B) Table

(C) Scnergy (D) Chair

(E) None of these

19. How many different types of geometrical shapes are in the picture?

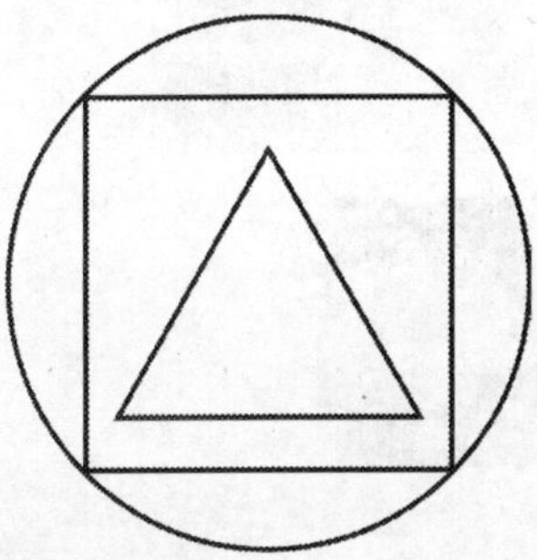

(A) 4 (B) 2 (C) 3 (D) 5

(E) None of these

20. Which one of the following coins has the highest value?

25 Paise 1 Rupee 2 Rupee 50 Paise

(A) 25 p. (B) ₹ 1

(C) ₹ 2 (D) 50 p.

(E) None of these

21. Find out total value of the coins.

25 Paise 25 Paise 50 Paise

(A) 1 Rupee (B) 90 paisa

(C) 75 paisa (D) 80 paisa

(E) None of these

22. Which one of the following notes has the least value?

(A) ₹ 1 (B) ₹ 5

(C) ₹ 500 (D) ₹ 20

(E) None of these

23. Which month comes after December and before February?

(A) September (B) December

(C) February (D) January

(E) None of these

24. Which one of the following is a month of summer season in India?

(A) August (B) July

(C) June (D) All the above

(E) None of these

25. If you add this vertically or horizontally the result is 18. Find the missing number.

4	9	5
7	6	5
7	?	8

(A) 5 (B) 6

(C) 3 (D) 4

(E) None of these

26. What comes just before Friday?

(A) Saturday (B) Thursday

(C) Monday (D) Sunday

(E) None of these

27. What is the time in the clock?

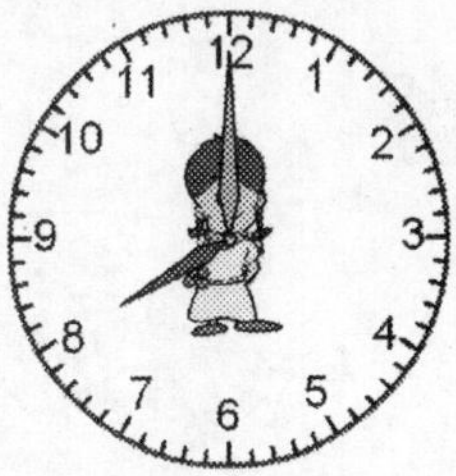

(A) 12 o'clock (B) 7 o'clock
(C) 12 : 35 (D) 8 o'clock
(E) None of these

28. 90 = □ + □

(A) 9 + 0 (B) 0 + 9
(C) 90 + 0 (D) 00 + 0
(E) None of these

29. Arrange in ascending order 39, 34, 38, 40

(A) 40, 38, 34, 39 (B) 39, 38, 34, 40
(C) 34, 38, 39, 40 (D) 40, 39, 38, 34
(E) None of these

30. Insert the correct symbol.

14 + 5 □ 18-2

(A) < (B) >
(C) = (D) All the above
(E) None of these

31. Which one of the following numbers is equal to 19 less than 27 more than 7?

(A) 11 (B) 10
(C) 15 (D) 12
(E) None of these

32. How many circles are there in the figure?

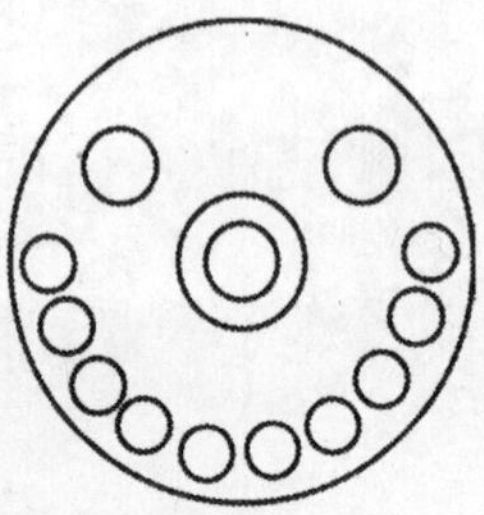

(A) 15 (B) 16
(C) 13 (D) 14
(E) None of these

33. 7 tens + 4 ones = ?

(A) 704
(B) 74
(C) 11
(D) 84
(E) None of these

34. Write in words.

17 < 52

(A) Seventeen is greater than fifty two
(B) Seventeen is equal to fifty two
(C) Seventeen is less than fifty two
(D) All the above
(E) None of these

35. Write '100' in words.

(A) Hundred
(B) Ninety
(C) Eighty
(D) All the above
(E) None of these

36. Study the pattern and choose the correct option?

50, 52, 54, 56.......

(A) Skip counting (2)
(B) Skip counting (5)
(C) Skip counting (3)
(D) Skip counting (1)
(E) None of these

37. Which one of the following day comes next after Sunday?

(A) Saturday
(B) Monday
(C) Tuesday
(D) All the above
(E) None of these

38. There are 3 books and 2 note books in a bag. Steve puts 8 more books in it then what is the total number of books in the bag?

(A) 10
(B) 13
(C) 14
(D) 11
(E) None of these

39. 5 tens and 9 ones – 2 tens and 6 ones = ?

(A) 3 tens 2 ones

(B) 3 tens 5 ones

(C) 3 tens 3 ones

(D) All the above

(E) None of these

40. Which one of the following options is equal to 75 paisa?

(A) 25 paisa + 50 paisa + 10 paisa

(B) 10 paisa + 20 paisa + 20 paisa + 50 paisa

(C) 10 paisa + 20 paisa + 25 paisa

(D) 15 paisa + 40 paisa + 20 paisa

(E) None of these

Sample Question Paper

Section-A (Mathematics)

1. Arrange the numbers in descending order.

11, 15, 7, 4

(A) 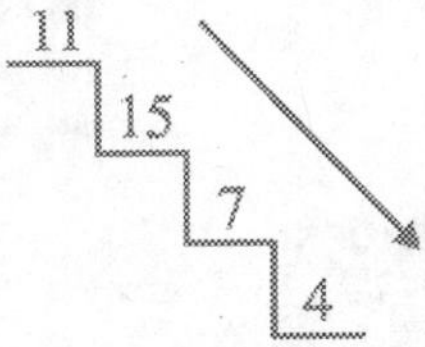

(B) 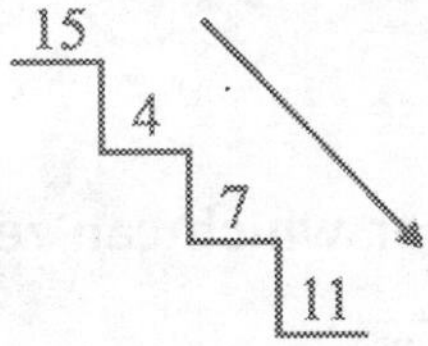

(C) 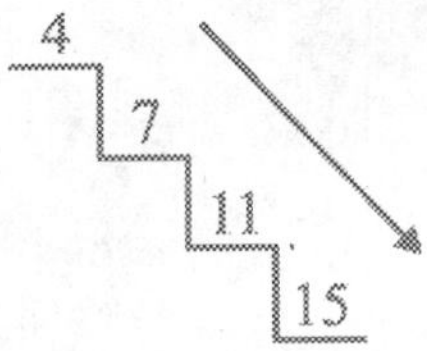

(D) 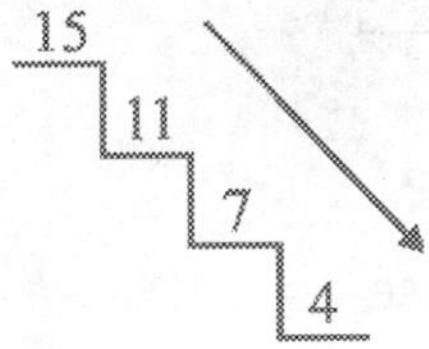

(E) None of these

2. Which one of the following statements is true?

(A) 7 is 1 less than 8

(B) 8 is 1 more than 7

(C) (8 + 7) is equal to (10 + 5)

(D) All of these

(E) None of these

3. The number shown on the abacus is ______.

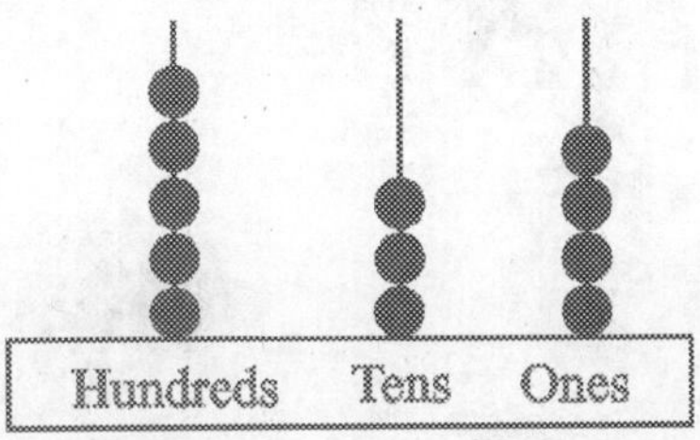

(A) 435

(B) 453

(C) 543

(D) 534

(E) None of these

4. Which one of the following two numbers when added gives 2 tens + 2 ones?

(A) 10 + 10 (B) 20 + 12

(C) 11 + 10 (D) 11 + 11

(E) None of these

5. Find the number which can replace the question mark.

6 + 7 + 4 = 7 + ?

(A) 6 (B) 4

(C) 10 (D) 17

(E) None of these

6. Which among the following is the heaviest ?

(A) 

(B) 

(C) 

(D) 

(E) None of these

7. In Gemini Circus, there are:

21 , 5  and 19 

How many animals are there in the circus?

(A) 54 (B) 45

(C) 35 (D) 53

(E) None of these

8. Find the correct way of counting by 7.

(A) 28, 42, 14, 21 (B) 42, 82, 21, 14

(C) 7, 14, 21, 28 (D) All of these

(E) None of these

9. Which of the following options is correct ?

(A) 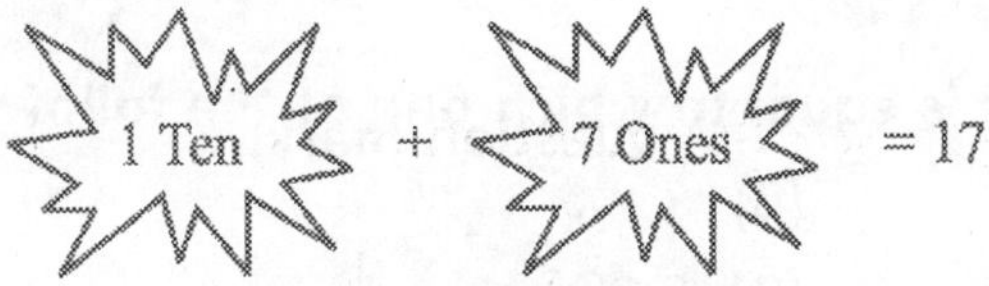

(B) 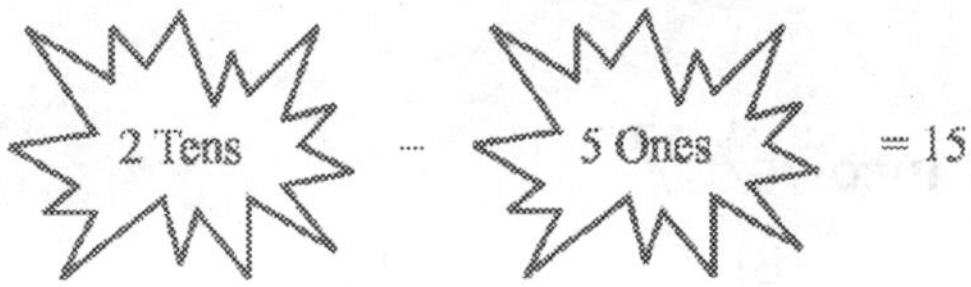

(C) 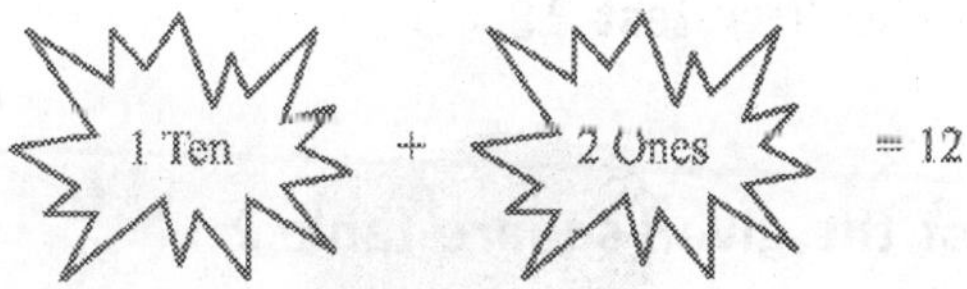

(D) All of these

(E) None of these

10. Which one of the following is equal to one and half minutes ?

(A) 30 seconds + 30 seconds (B) 60 seconds + 60 seconds

(C) 60 seconds + 30 seconds (D) All of these

(E) None of these

11. Which one of the following is correct?

(A) 1 + 1 = 11 (B) 1 × 1 = 11

(C) 1 × 0 = 10 (D) 1 × 1 = 1

(E) None of these

12. Which of the following arrangements is less than (7 + 5) but more than (7 + 3) ?

(A) 6 + 5 (B) 7 + 4
(C) 9 + 2 (D) All of these
(E) None of these

13. Which subtraction sentence gives same value as 11 – 7 ?

(A) 4 + 0 (B) 17 – 13
(C) 13 – 9 (D) All of these
(E) None of these

14. 3 tens 3 ones – 2 tens 5 ones is equal to which one of the following?

(A) 9 (B) 8
(C) 7 (D) 5
(E) None of these

15. Which one of the following is incorrect ?

(A) 111 – 11 = 100 (B) 91 – 11 = 80
(C) 111 + 11 = 122 (D) 12 + 18 = 32
(E) None of these

16. Which figure is in the centre of the given square table ?

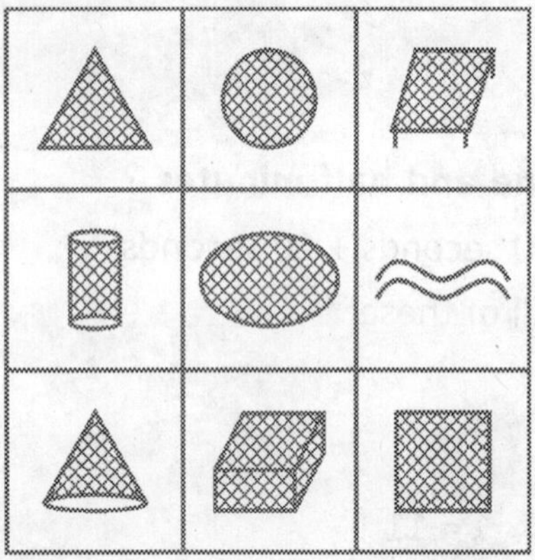

(A) Cylinder (B) Square
(C) Triangle (D) Oval
(E) None of these

17. Which abacus represents the number which is 21 more than 7 ?

(A) 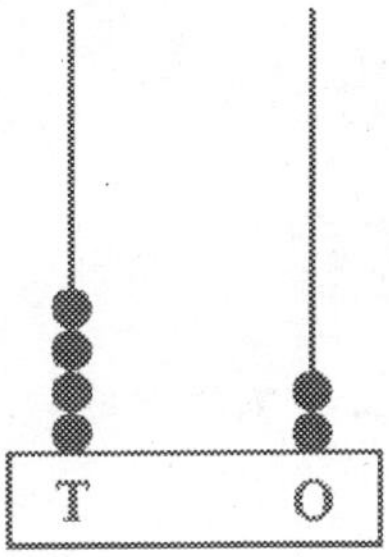

(B) 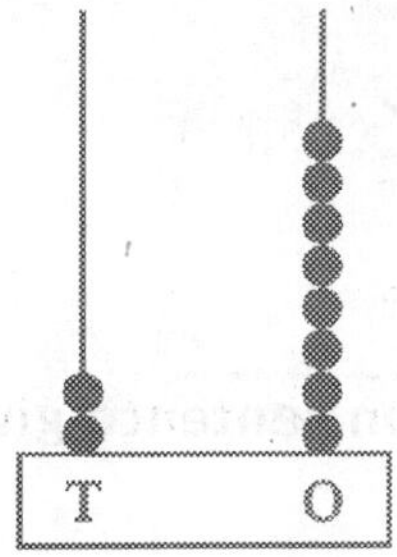

(C) 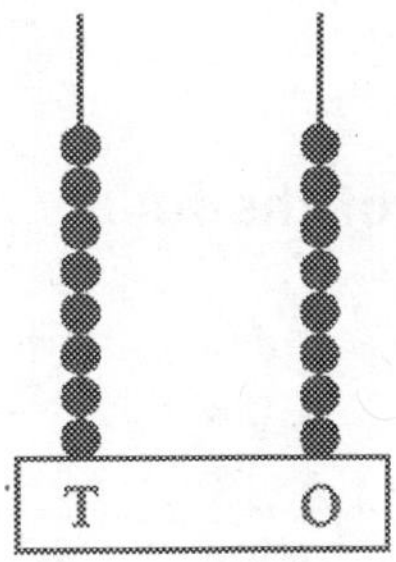

(D) 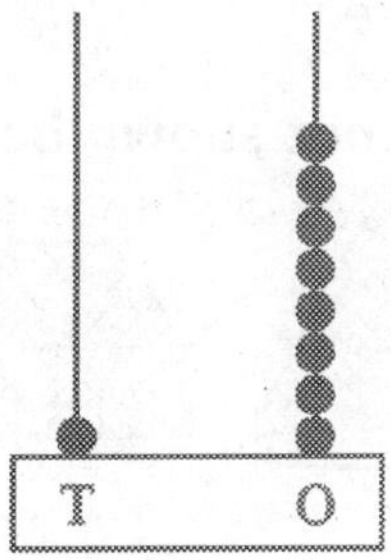

(E) None of these

18. If  **= 7 and**  **= 10, then which one of the following is correct ?**

(A) 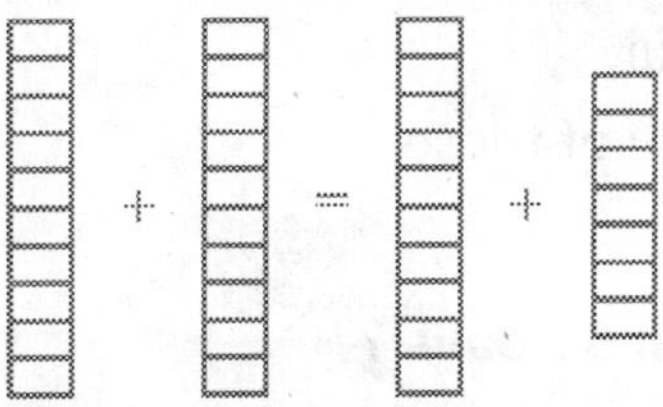

(B) 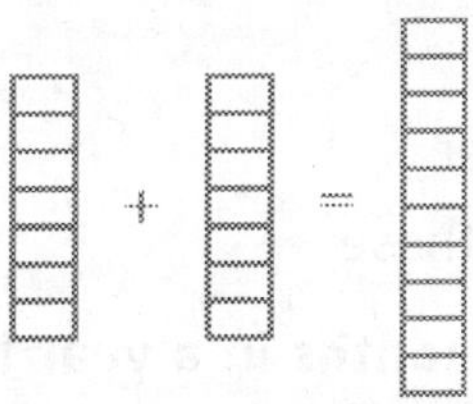

(C) 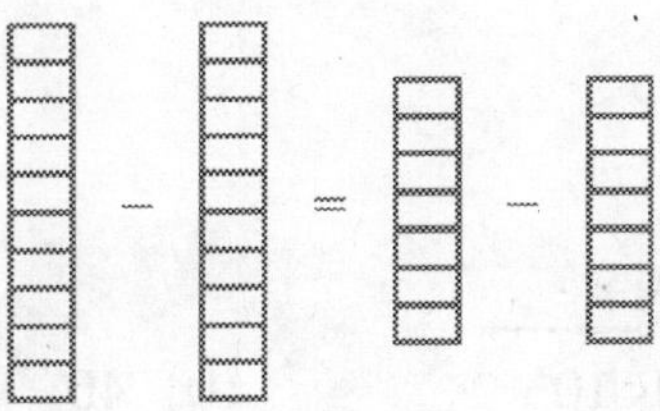

(D) All of these

(E) None of these

19. How many angles are there in the following figure ?

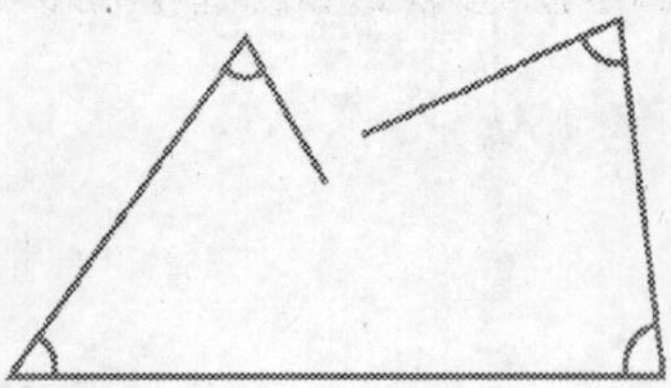

(A) 2 (B) 3
(C) 5 (D) 4
(E) None of these

20. Which figure is not shown below ?

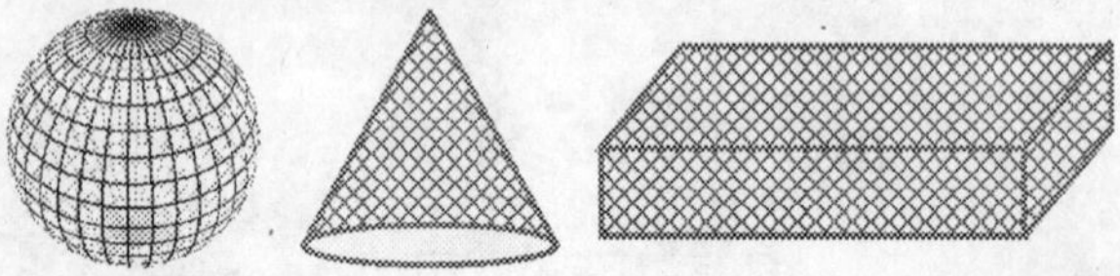

(A) sphere (B) cube
(C) cuboid (D) cone
(E) None of these

21. Find the correct way of counting by 9

(A) 9, 12, 18, 21 (B) 9, 18, 21, 24
(C) 9, 18, 27, 28 (D) 9, 18, 27, 36
(E) None of these

22. Which of the following months has 31 days ?

(A) May (B) July
(C) December (D) All of these
(E) None of these

23. How many months in a year has less than 31 days ?

(A) 7 (B) 4
(C) 5 (D) 12
(E) None of these

24. 10 + 10 + 10 gives the same value as 20 + _____

(A) 30 (B) 20 (C) 10 (D) 40
(E) None of these

Section-B (Mental Ability and Reasoning)

25. If ☆ + ☆ + ☆ = 9, then find the value of ☆.

(A) 2 (B) 3
(C) 5 (D) 7
(E) None of these

26. Complete the following pattern.

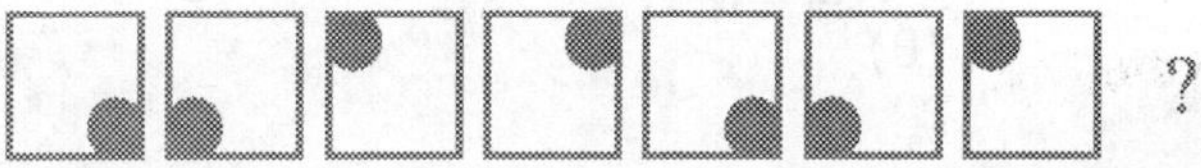

(A) 

(B) 

(C) 

(D) 

(E) None of these

27. How many squares are there in the following figure?

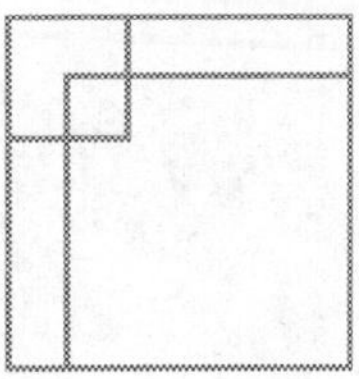

(A) 3 (B) 4
(C) 5 (D) 6
(E) None of these

28. What values for ● and ■ make both number sentences true ?

4 + ● = 9, ● + ■ = 11

(A) ● = 4 and ■ = 7 (B) ● = 5 and ■ = 6
(C) ● = 4 and ■ = 6 (D) ● = 3 and ■ = 5
(E) None of these

29. If ABC = 123 and BCD = 234, then find DEF.

(A) 654 (B) 564

(C) 456 (D) 567

(E) None of these

30. If 6 is related to 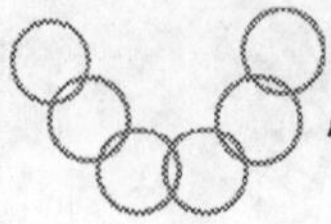 **, then 5 is related to ______**

(A) 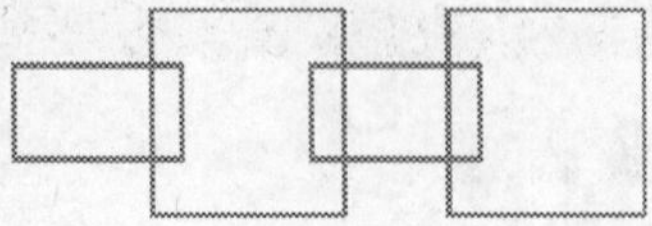

(B) 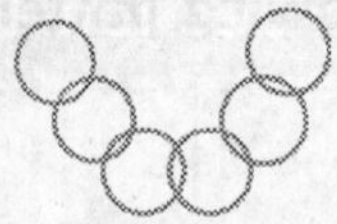

(C) 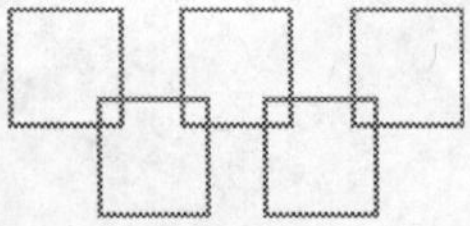

(D) 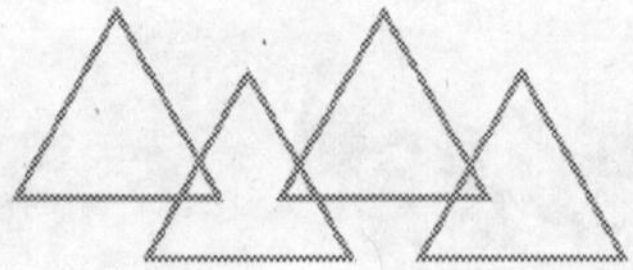

(E) 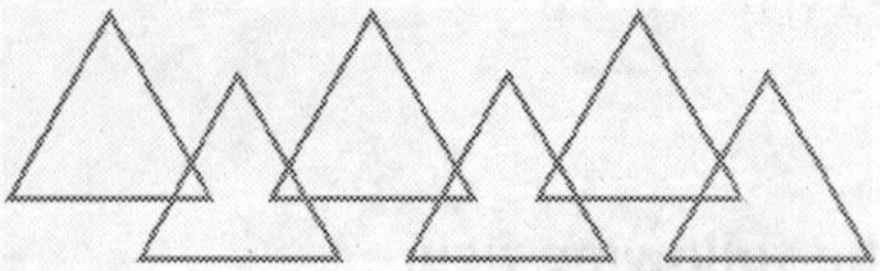

31. The puppy is ______ bricks heavier than the cat.

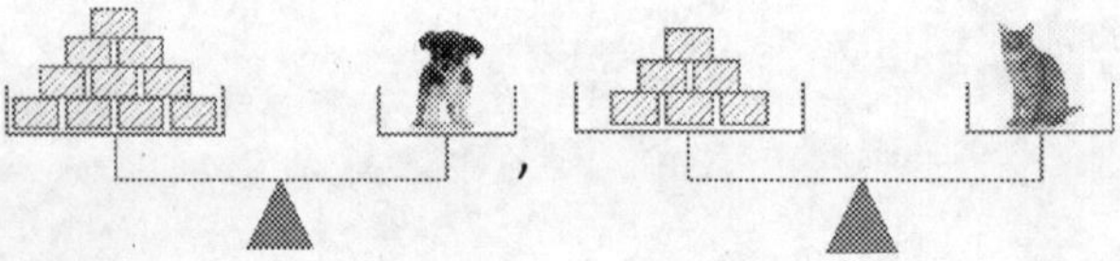

(A) 5 (B) 9

(C) 4 (D) 6

(E) None of these

32. Which of the following shapes has the least length and breadth?

(A) 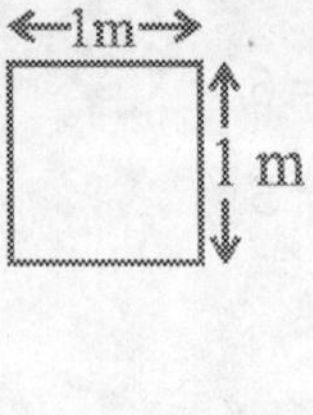

(B) 

(C) 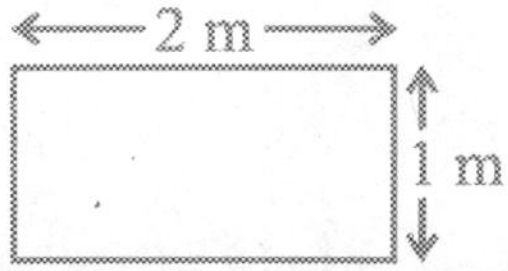

(D) 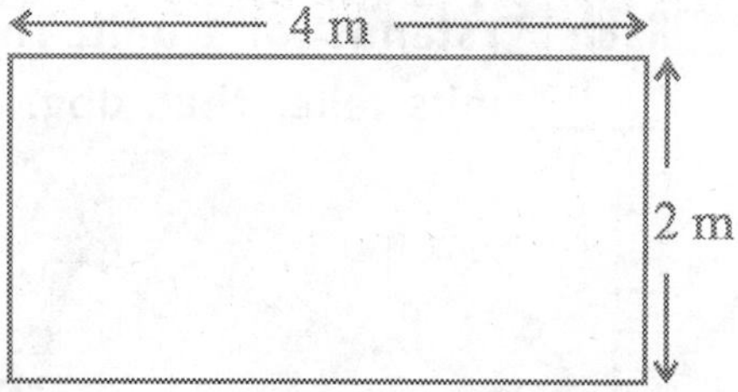

(E) None of these

Section-C (Scholar's Zone)

33. If  +  +  = 9 grams and

 +  +  +  = 12 grams,

then find the value of  + .

(A) 1 gram
(B) 4 grams
(C) 6 grams
(D) 12 grams
(E) None of these

34. Each group of balloons has:

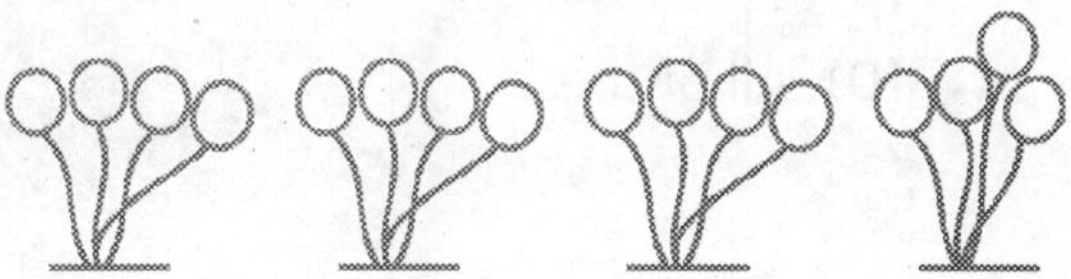

(A) 5 balloons
(B) 4 balloons
(C) 3 balloons
(D) 15 balloons
(E) None of these

35. Alex has 3 types of fruits. Number of apples he has is 5 more than that of bananas and number of oranges is 4 more than that of bananas. If he has total 4 bananas find the total number of fruits Alex has:

(A) 22
(B) 12
(C) 18
(D) 21
(E) None of these

36. **Each ☐ stands for 1 unit. The bull is _____ units shorter than giraffe and _____ units taller than dog.**

(A) 3 and 7
(B) 7 and 2
(C) 5 and 3
(D) 7 and 5
(E) None of these

37. **Which of the following is same as 138 ?**

(A) 338 – 200
(B) 238 – 100
(C) 388 – 250
(D) All of these
(E) None of these

38. **Fill in the blank with correct sign.**

17 ☐ 3 = 100 – 80

(A) +
(B) =
(C) ÷
(D) All of these
(E) None of these

39. **Which figure will complete the figure (x) ?**

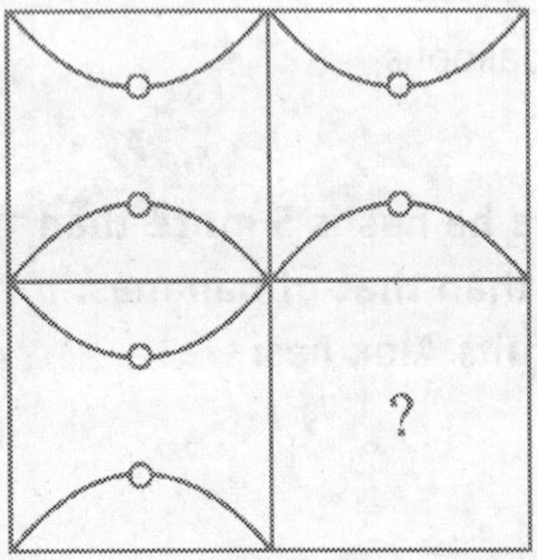

Figure (x)

(A) 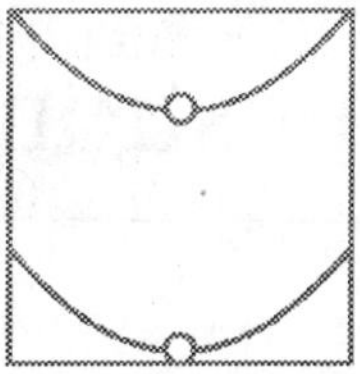

(B) 

(C) 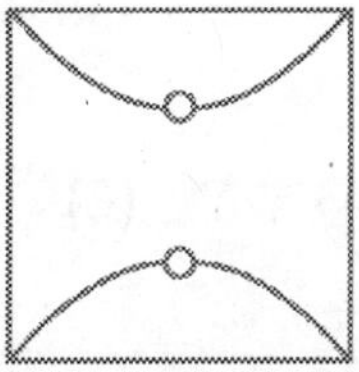

(D) 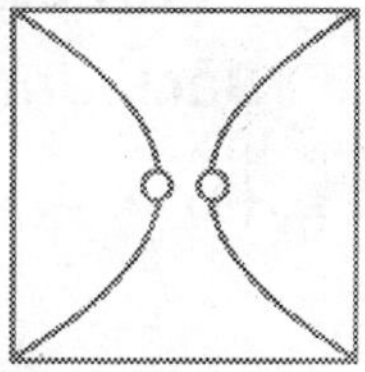

(E) None of these

40. If same rule is followed in A, B and C, then find the missing number.

1	2
4	3

A

8	12
20	16

B

3	6
?	9

C

(A) 21
(B) 14
(C) 5
(D) 12
(E) None of these

Practice Exercise Answers and Explanation for Selected Questions

Practice Exercise 1
Back and Forth Counting

1. (D) 2. (C) 3. (A) 4. (A) 5. (B) 6. (D) 7. (C) 8. (D) 9. (A) 10. (C)

Explanation for Selected Questions:

1. Option (D) is correct because forth counting from 5 to 10 goes as the following diagram:

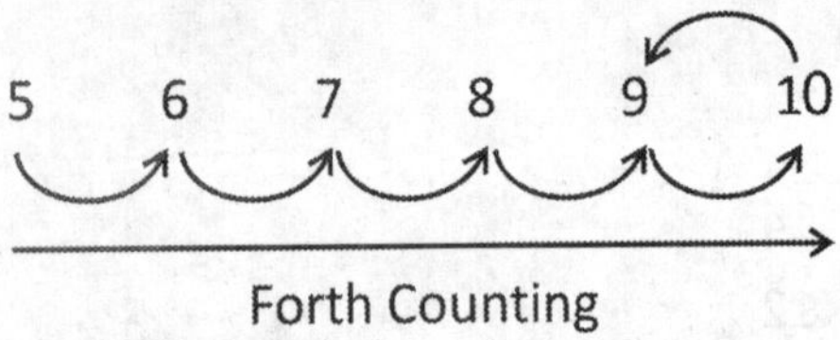

Option (A) is incorrect because 5 comes just before 6.

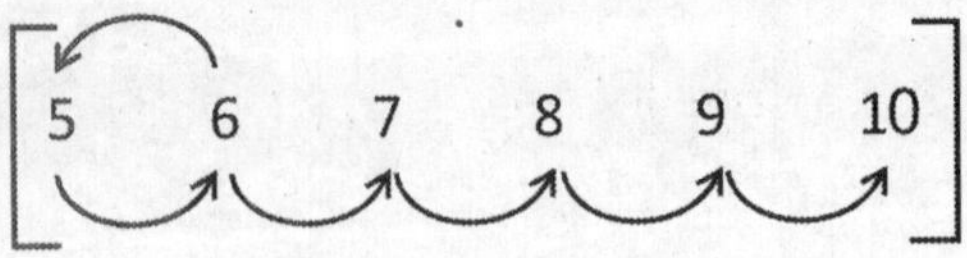

Option (B) is incorrect because 6 comes just before 7.

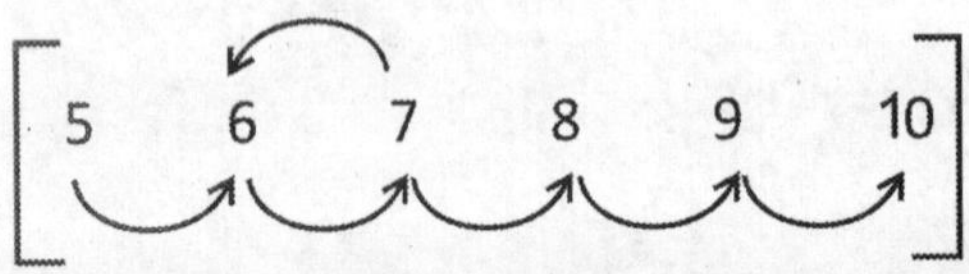

Option (C) is incorrect because 7 comes just before 8.

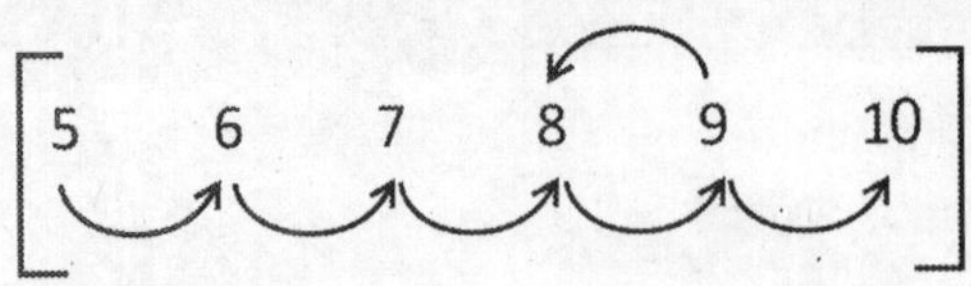

2. Option (C) is correct because it is clear from the following diagram :

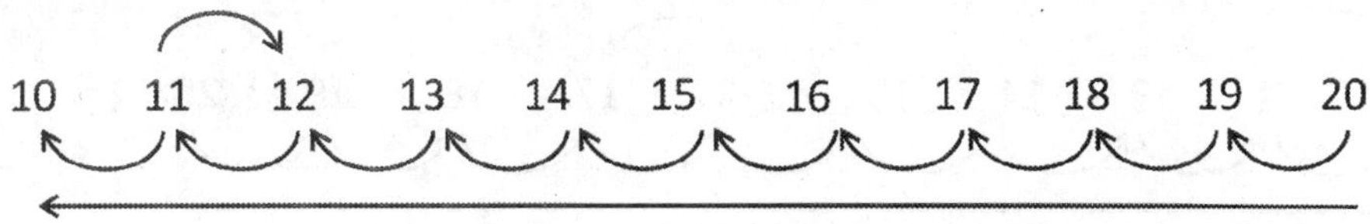

Back Counting

or

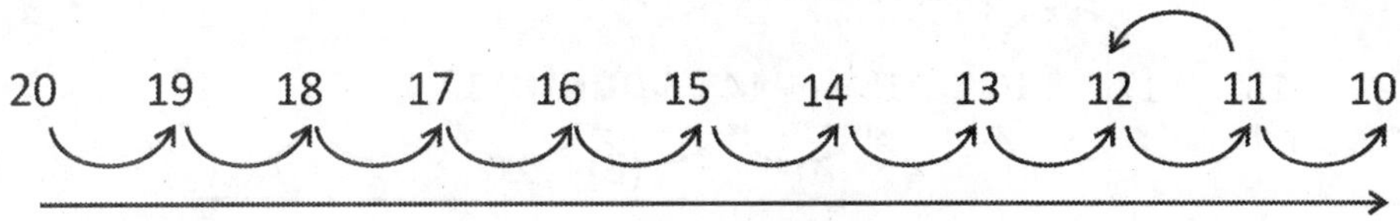

Back Counting

Option (A) is incorrect as it comes just before 12.

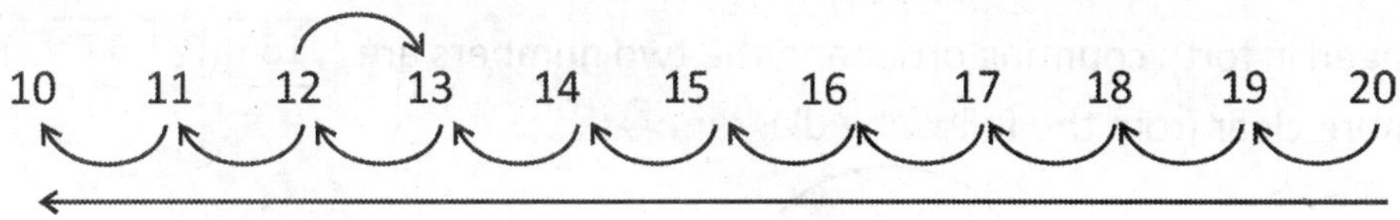

Back Counting

or

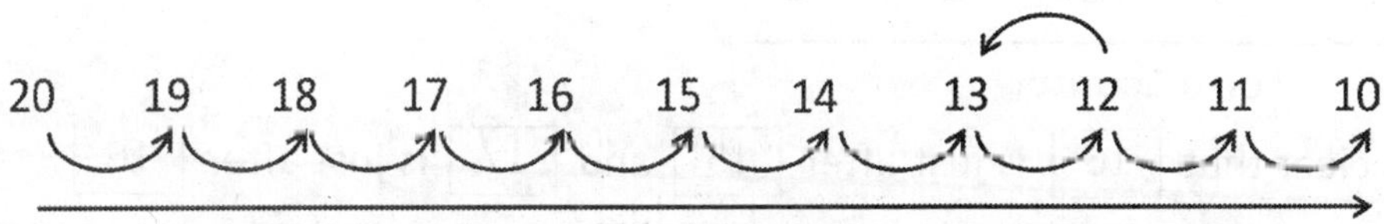

Back Counting

Option (B) is incorrect because it comes just before 17

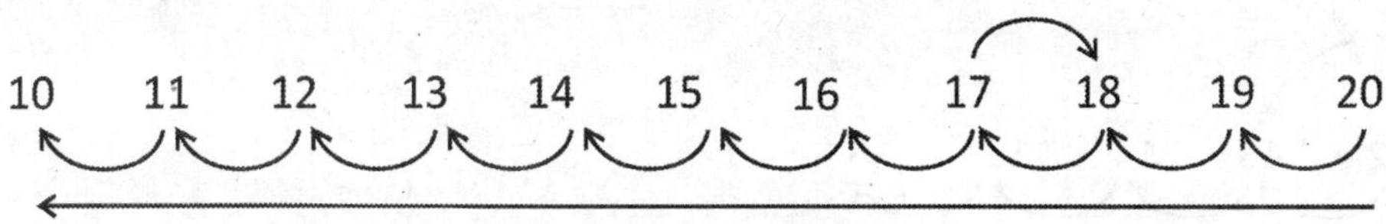

Back Counting

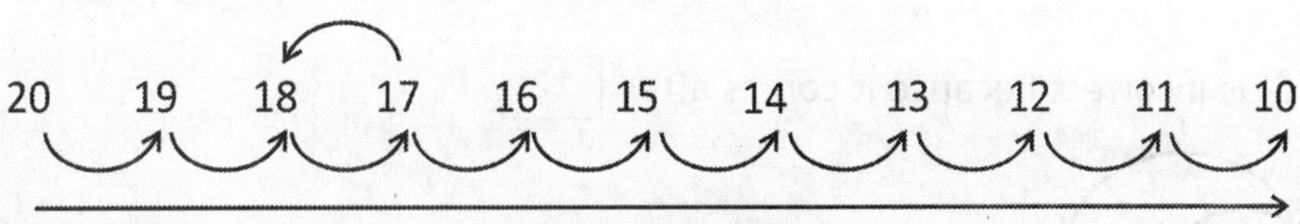

Back Counting

Option (D) is incorrect because it comes just before 16.

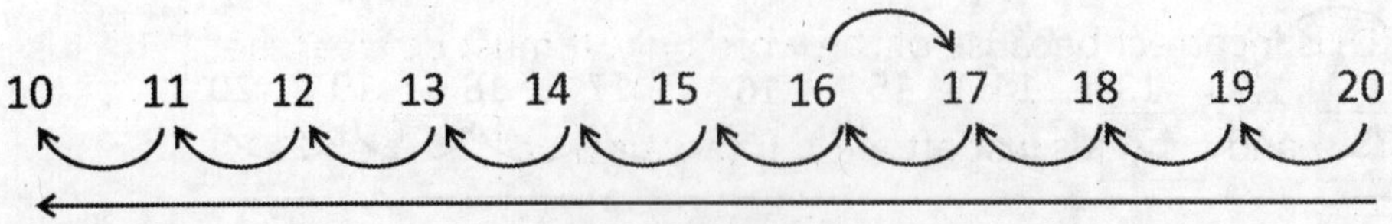

Back Counting

or

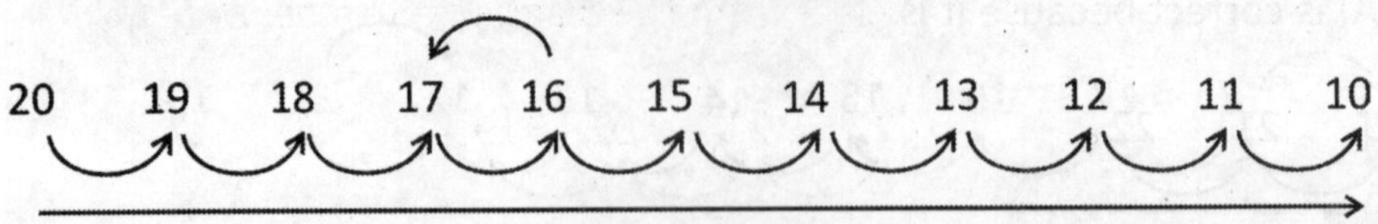

Back Counting

3. Option (A) is correct because there are two numbers after 15, when the numbers are arranged in forth counting order and the two numbers are 16 & 17. This will be more clear from the following diagram:

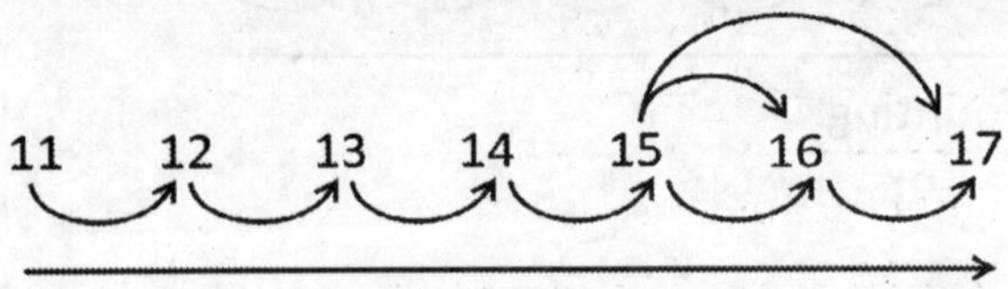

Forth Counting

Here, it is clear that 16 is just after 15 and 17 is just after 16.

Therefore, both the numbers 16 and 17 comes after 15.

Option (B) is incorrect because it comes after 11.

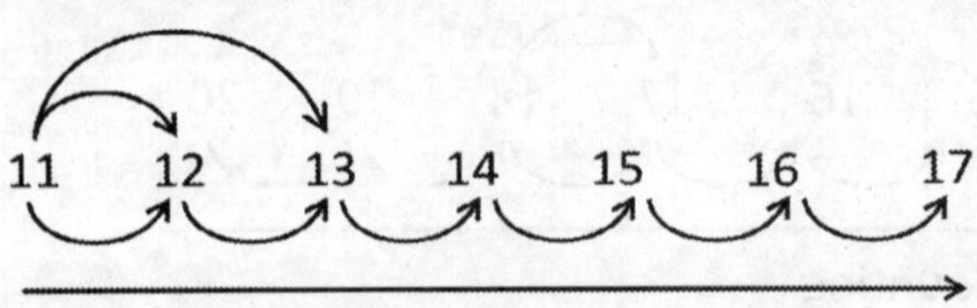

Forth Counting

Option (C) is incorrect because it comes after 12.

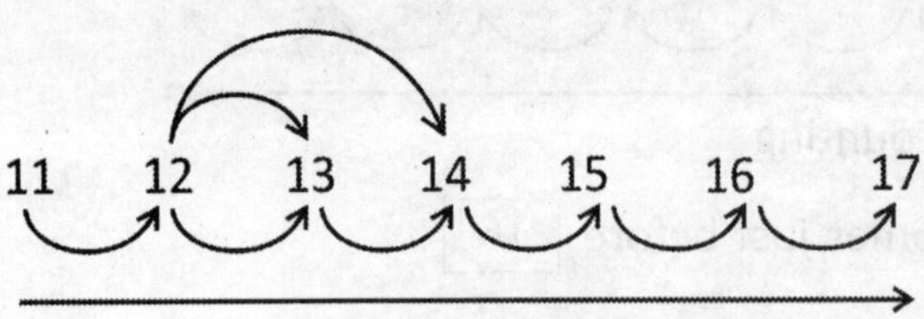

Forth Counting

Option (D) is incorrect because of the word only. It must be clear that 16 is just after 15 and 17 is just after 16. It means that 16 and 17 both come after 15.

4. Option (A) is correct because it is clear from the diagram given below:

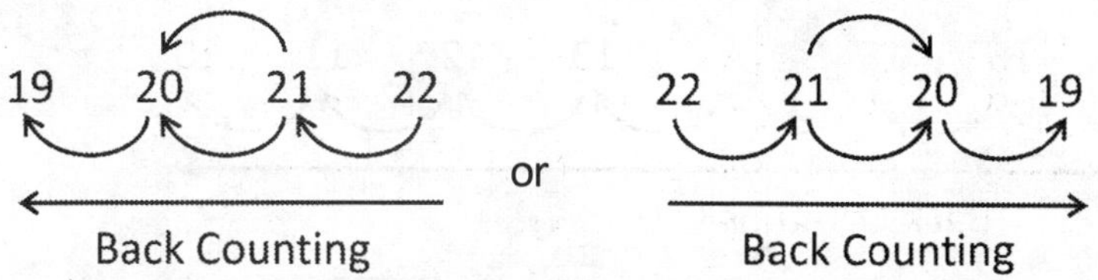

Option (B) is incorrect because it comes just after 20. The following diagram makes it more clear.

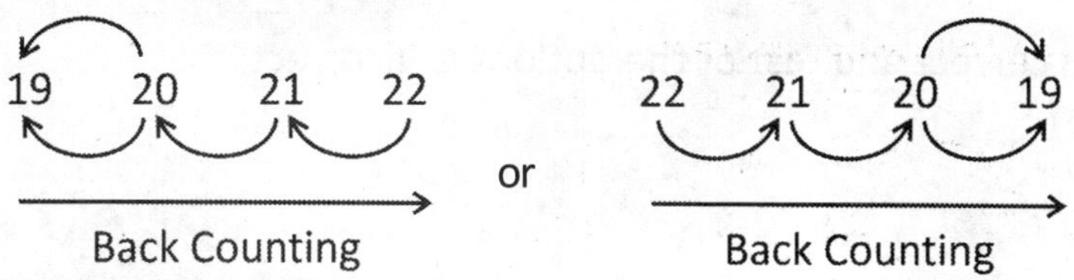

Option (C) is incorrect because the reverse or back counting starts with it.

Option (D) is incorrect because it comes just after 22. The following diagram makes it more clear.

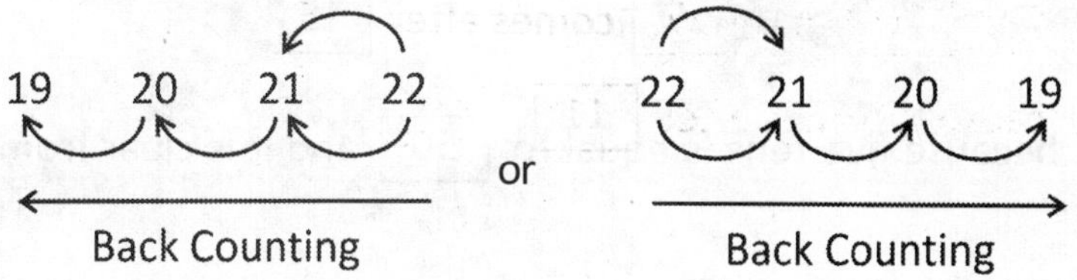

5. Option (B) is correct because it is clear from the following diagram:

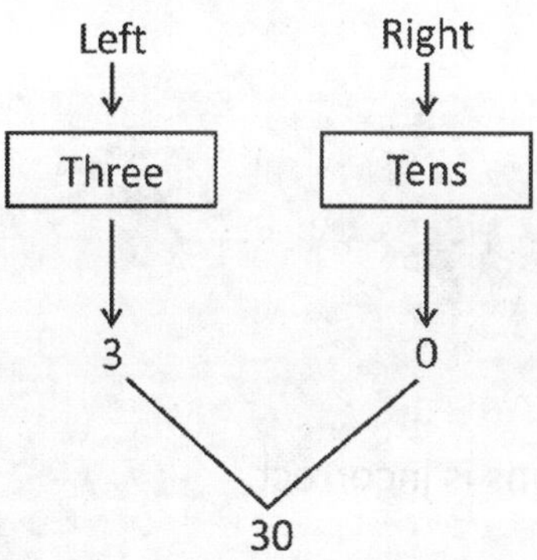

Option (A) is incorrect because one ten is equal to 10 and it is clear from the following diagram:

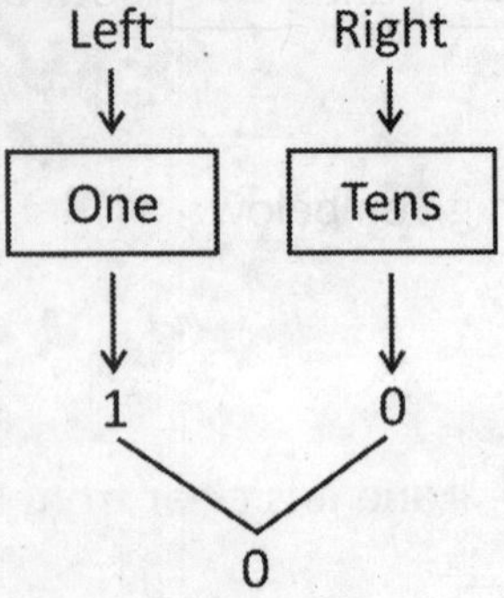

Option (C) is incorrect because two ten is equal to 20 and it is clear from the following diagram:

Therefore, option (C) is correct and rest of the options is incorrect.

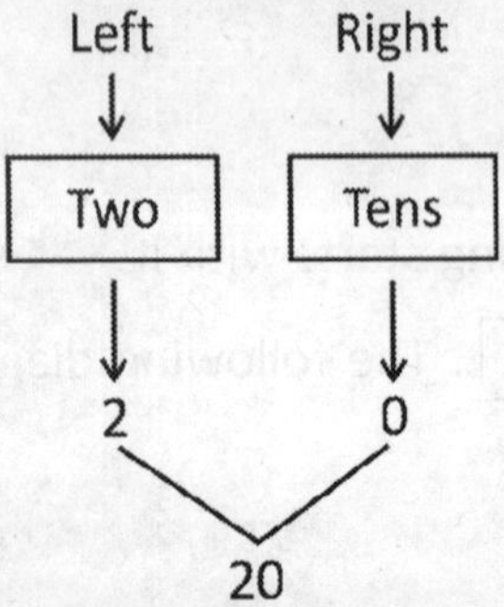

Option (D) is incorrect because five tens is equal to 50 and it is clear from the following diagram:

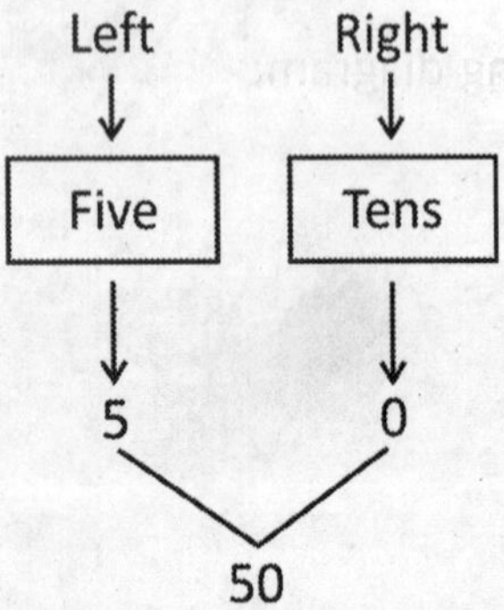

Therefore, option (A) is correct and rest of the options is incorrect.

6. Option (D) is correct. The following diagram makes it more clear:

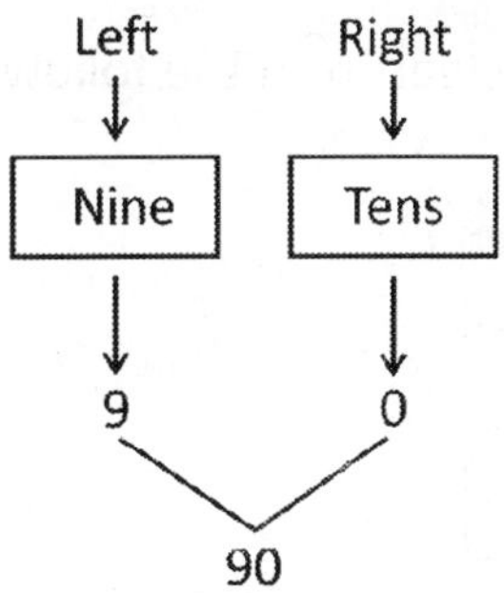

Option (A) is incorrect because ten tens is equal to 100 and it is clear from the following diagram:

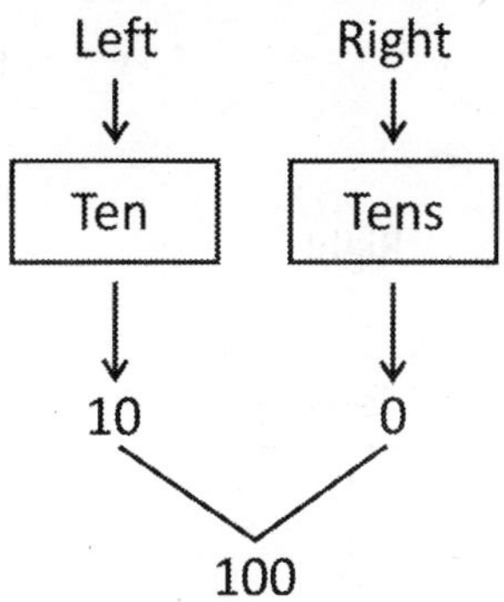

Option (B) is incorrect because seven tens is equal to 70 and it is clear from the following diagram :

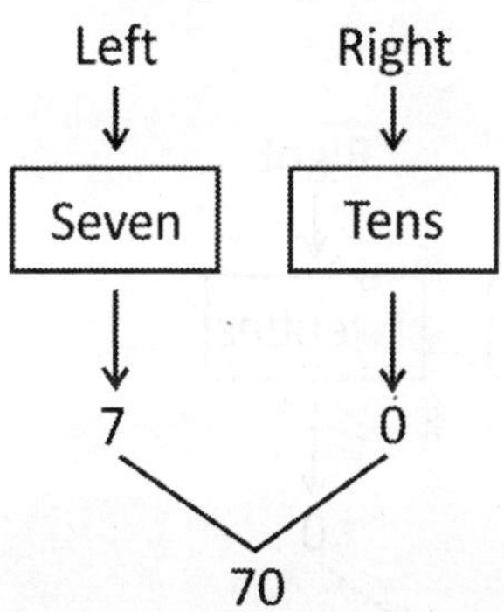

Option (C) is incorrect because seven tens is equal to 70 and it is clear from the explanation of option (B) that seven tens is equal to 70 .

8. Option (D) is correct because except this all are counted in twenties and tens both while option (D) or 30 is only counted in tens. It will be clear from the following diagrams for every options.

Diagram for option (A)

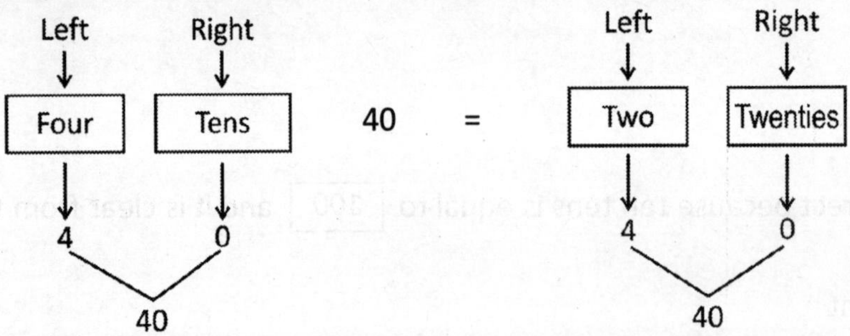

Diagram for option (B)

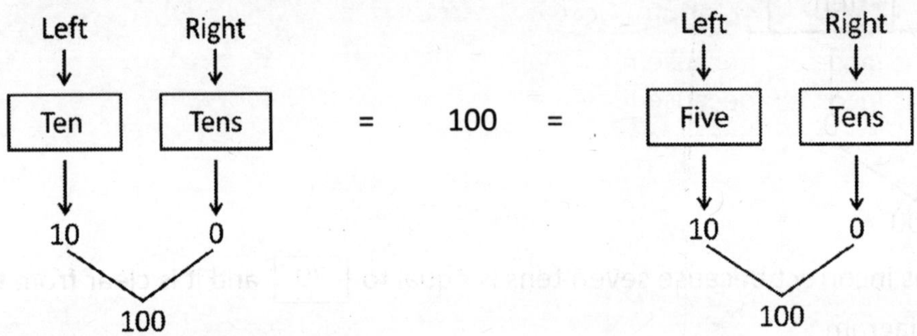

Diagram for option (C)

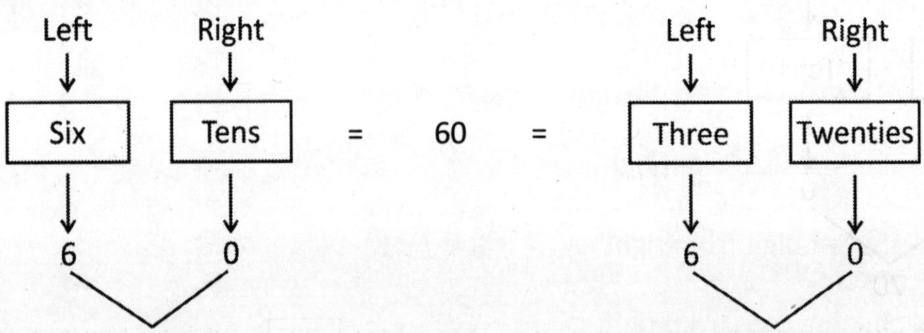

Diagram for option (D)

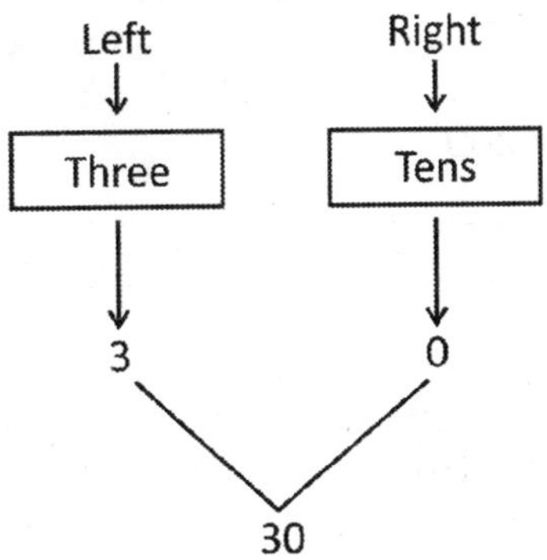

10. Option (C) is correct because the following diagram makes it clear.

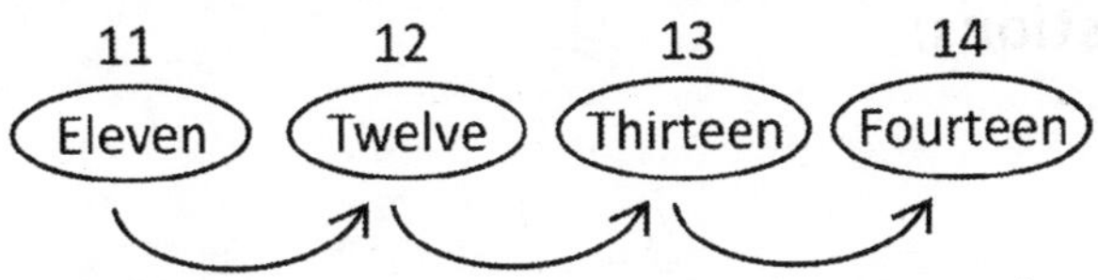

Option (A) is incorrect because it comes 4th
Option (B) is incorrect because it comes 1st
Option (D) is incorrect because it comes 2nd

Practice Exercise 2
Ones and Tens

1. (A) 2. (C) 3. (A) 4. (C) 5. (A) 6. (B) 7. (C) 8. (B)
9. (B) 10. (C)

Explanation for Selected Questions:

1. In 24 the first digit from right is 4 and hence, it is at ones place.

2. In 37 the 1st digit from right is 7 and hence, it is at ones place.

3. In 59 the 2nd digit from right is 5 and hence, it is at tens place.

4. In 12 and 17 the 2nd digit from right is 1 and hence, it is at tens place.

6. 2 tens + 6 ones = 26

7. 6 tens + 5 tens = 11 tens = 110 and 110 + 14 one = 124
8. 19 tens - 15 tens = 4 tens, 4 ones - 2 ones = 2 ones
10. 10 tens + 15 tens = 25 tens = 250
    5 ones + 5 ones = 10 ones = 1 ten = 10 $\Rightarrow$ 250 + 10 = 260

Practice Exercise 3
Addition

1. (A) 2. (D) 3. (A) 4. (B) 5. (A) 6. (A) 7. (B) 8. (C)
9. (D) 10. (C)

Explanation for Selected Questions:

1. 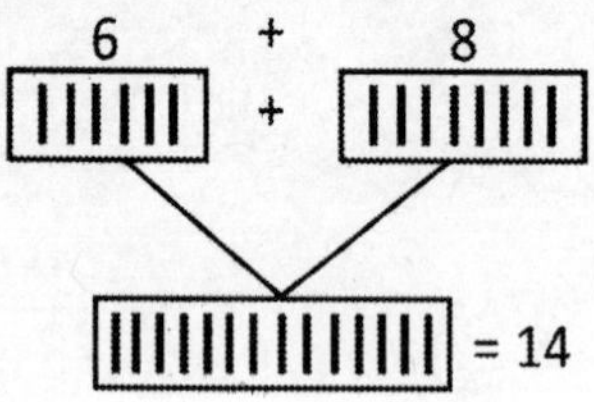

2. 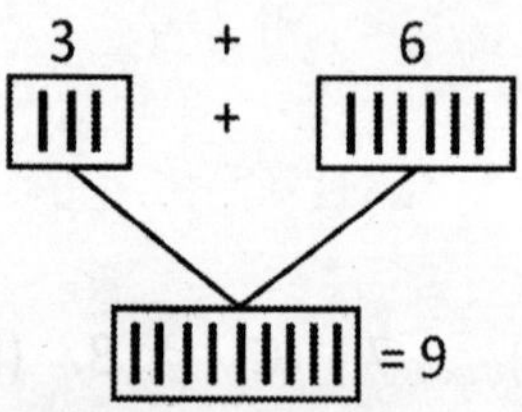

3. 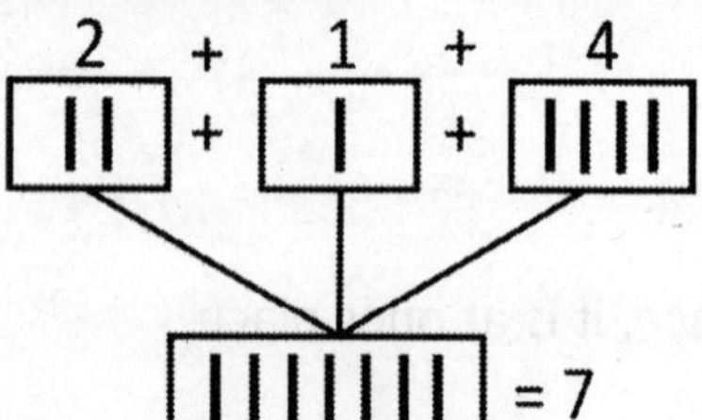

4. 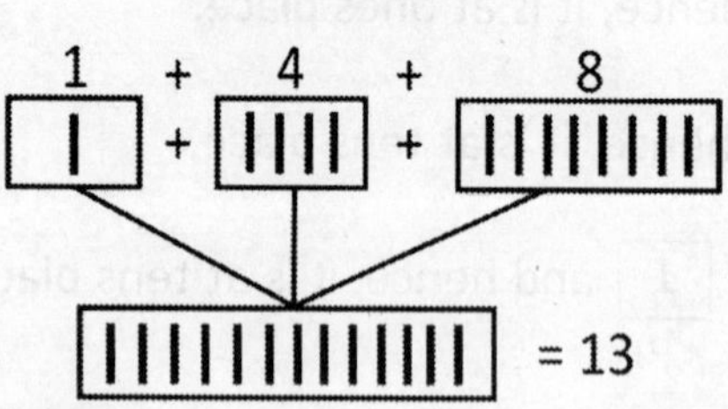

5. 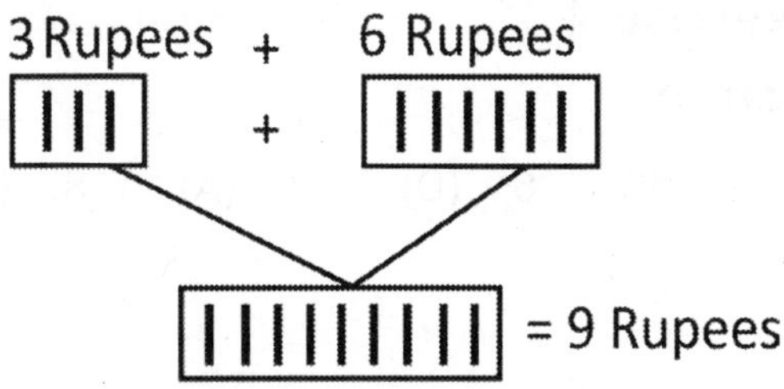

6. 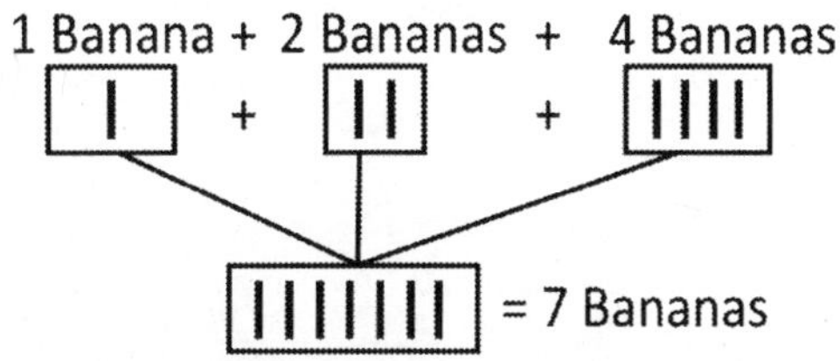

7. 

8. 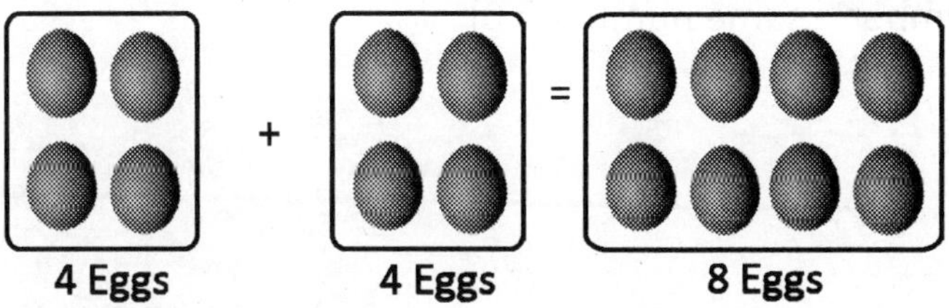

9. 1dozen = 12
   + 9
   2dozen=+24
   45 eggs

10. 17
   + 15
   + 18
   50

Practice Exercise 4
Subtraction

1. (B) 2. (B) 3. (D) 4. (C) 5. (B) 6. (D) 7. (A) 8. (B)
9. (A) 10. (C)

Explanation for Selected Questions:

1. 6 − 2

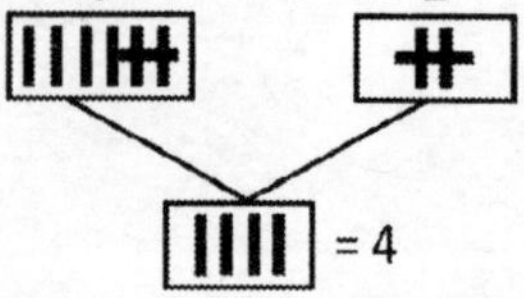

= 4

2. 8 + 1 − 9

(8 + 1) − 9

9 − 9 = 0 [same number − same number = 0]

3. Let's check (A)

4 − 3

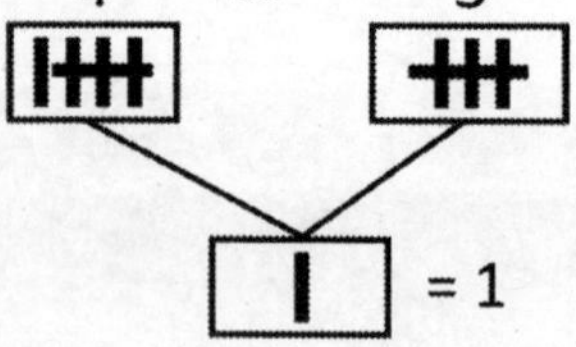

= 1

Let's check option (B)

4 − 4 = 0 because by the rule of subtraction

Same number − same number = 0

Let's check option (C)

7 − 5

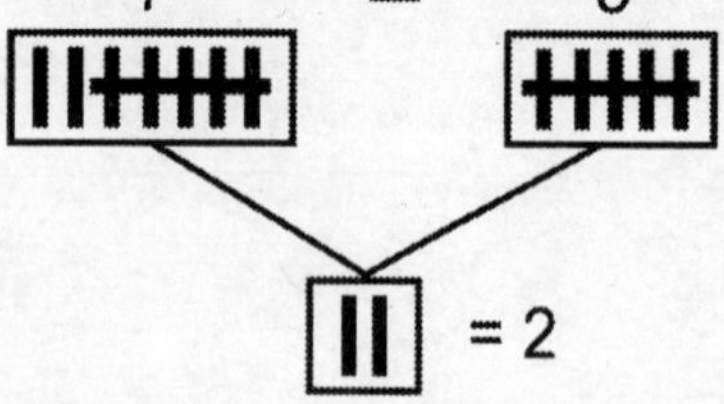

= 2

4. 15 – 8 – 6 = 15 – (8 + 6)

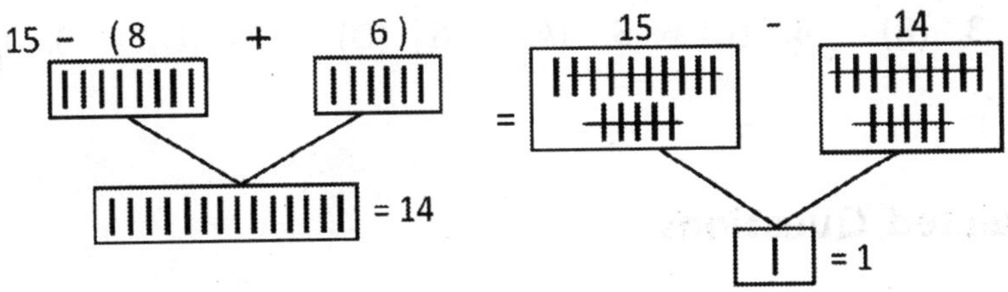

5.

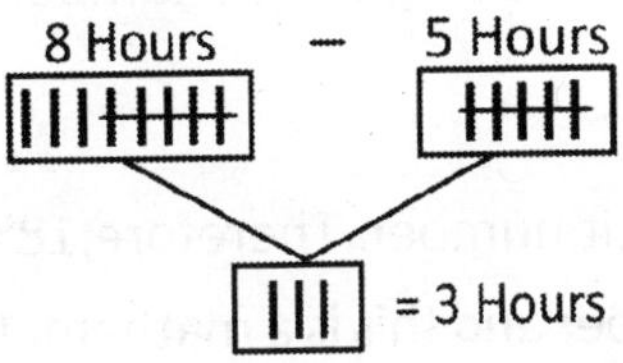

6.

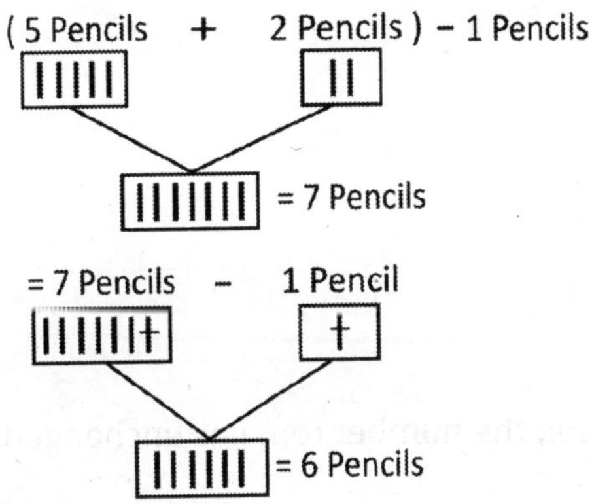

7.

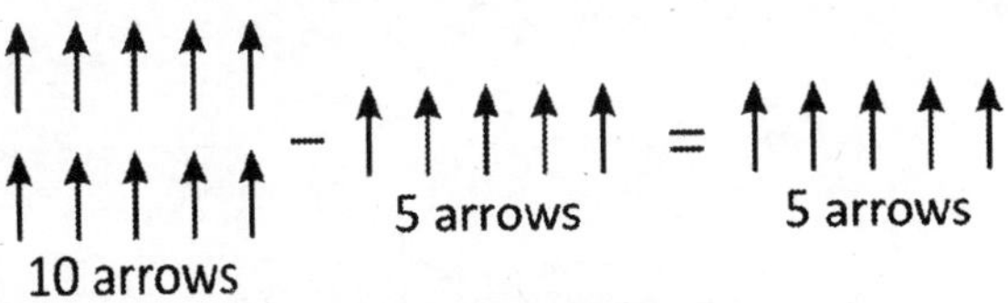

9. 48 + 10 – 7 = 58 – 7 = 51 birds.

10. 4 + 8 + 7 – 9 – 2 = 19 – 11 = 8

Practice Exercise 5
Comparison

1. (D) 2. (C) 3. (B) 4. (D) 5. (A) 6. (D) 7. (D) 8. (C)
9. (C) 10. (C)

Explanation for Selected Questions:

1. 17 is the two digit number which is always greater than a single digit number like 6. [Two digit number > single digit number].
2. Double digit number is always greater than a single digit number. Therefore,18> 7.
3. Out of the given options, option (B) is a double digit number and this is a mathematical fact that two digit number is always greater than a single digit number.
4. Option (D) is correct. Let's check it:

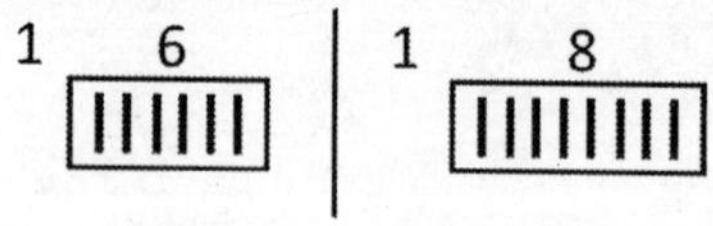

Clearly 6 < 8 or 8 > 6

Thus 16 < 18 or 18 > 16

5. If one or more zeroes is put before any number, the number remains unchanged.
6. Here zero (0) is after 8 and therefore, it is the number eighty which is very much bigger than 8.

7.

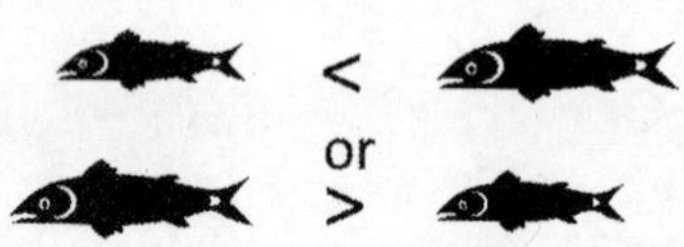

9.

$$\begin{array}{r} 27 \\ -\ 19 \\ \hline 08 \\ \hline \end{array}$$

Practice Exercise 6
Time and Calendar

1. (A) 2. (A) 3. (C) 4. (C) 5. (D) 6. (B) 7. (A) 8. (C)
9. (C) 10. (B)

Explanation for Selected Questions:

1. One day = 24 hours. Therefore,

   Three days = group of three 24 hours.

2. As 1 minute = 60 seconds

   Hence, 6 minutes = 6 times of 60 seconds

3. 1 hour = 60 minutes.

   Hence, 2 hours = 2 times of 60 minutes

4. After one hour the clock shows an increase of one hour. Therefore, after 5 O'clock one hour more is 6 O'clock.

5. When the clock gives time in complete round figure like, 1 O' clock, 2 O' clock, 3 O' clock, etc. then the minute hand is at 12.

6. Here the hour hand or shorter hand is between 2 and 3 while the minute or longer hand is at 6.

   It means that clock gives the time 2 : 30

7. 1 minute = 60 seconds

   5 minutes = 5 times of 60 seconds.

8. Hour hand of the clock is between 7 and 8.

9. 1 hour is equal to 60 minutes. Therefore, 4 hours is equal to group of 4 time 60 minutes.

10. [60] seconds [60] seconds [60] seconds

= [1] minute = [1] minute = [1] minute

Practice Exercise 7
Money

1. (A) 2. (D) 3. (B) 4. (A) 5. (D) 6. (C) 7. (A) 8. (D)
9. (A) 10. (B)

Explanation for Selected Questions:

1. [1] five rupees note = [5] rupees

   [2] five rupee note = [10] rupees

   [3] five rupee note = [15] rupees

2. One [10] rupees note = [10] rupees

   Two [10] rupees note = [20] rupees

   Three [10] rupees note = [30] rupees

   Four [10] rupees note = [40] rupees

3. One [10] paise = [10] paise

   Two [10] paise = [20] paise, Three [10] paise = [30] paise

4. One [20] paise = [20] paise

   Two [20] paise = [40] paise

   Three [20] paise = [60] paise

9. Option (A) is correct because cost of 3 oranges + cost of 2 apples
   = 5 rupees + 3 rupees = 8 rupees.

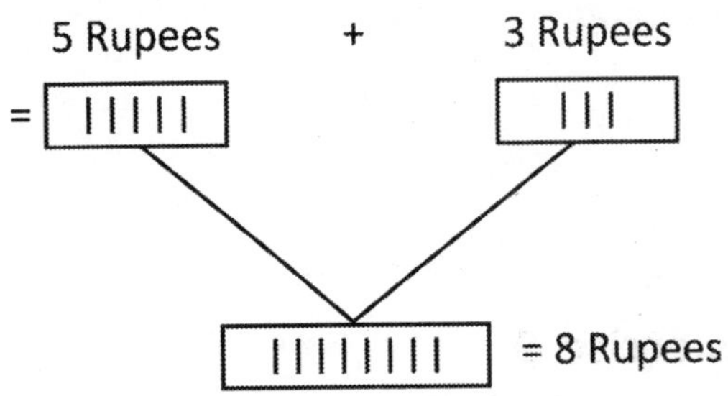

10. [7] rupees + [3] rupees = [10] rupees.

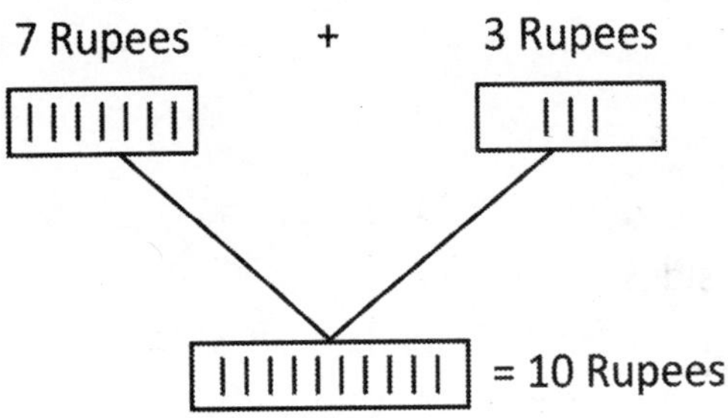

or,

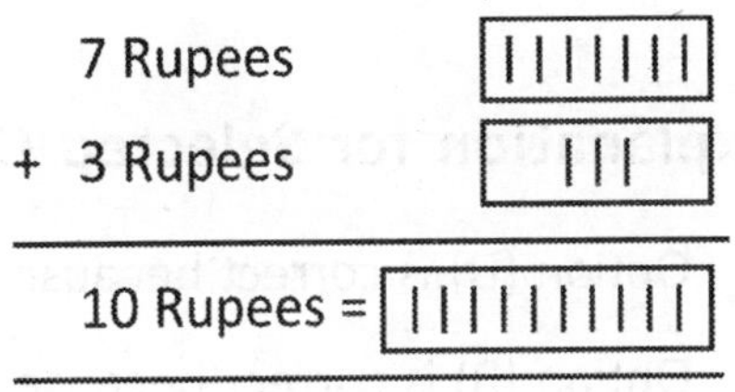

Practice Exercise 8
Measurement

1. (A) 2. (C) 3. (A) 4. (A) 5. (B) 6. (D) 7. (B) 8. (C)
9. (C) 10. (B)

Explanation for Selected Questions:

3. Breadth is the shorter dimension.
4. km > m > inches > cm.
5. [1] foot = one [12] inches.
8. [1] metre = one [100] centimetres.

   Therefore, [4] metres = [400] centimetres = [4] metres.
9. Breadth = 15 m

   Length = 7 m + 15 = 22 m

10. 4 m = 400 cm
+ 50 cm
450cm

Practice Exercise 9
Identification of Geometrical Figures

1. (A) 2. (A) 3. (B) 4. (D) 5. (D) 6. (B) 7. (A) 8. (D)
9. (B) 10. (B)

Explanation for Selected Questions:

5. Option (D) is correct because it has 4 sides.
6. Option (B) is correct because it is a triangle.
8. Option (D) is correct because this is a fact.
9. Rectangle has four sides.
10. Option (B) is a quadrilateral.

Practice Exercise 10
Applied Mathematics

1. (D) 2. (D) 3. (C) 4. (C) 5. (A) 6. (D) 7. (D) 8. (A)
9. (D) 10. (C) 11. (D) 12. (A) 13. (B) 14. (B) 15. (B)

Explanation for Selected Questions:

1. The greatest number in Box-1 and Box-2 both are 12.
   So, 12 + 12 = 24
3. Here, the pattern is 12 + 2 = 14, 14 + 2 = 16, 16 + 2 = 18
   18 + 2 = 20, 20 + 2 = 22, 22 + 2 = 24..
4. Here the result is 3 + 2 + 13 + 2 = 20.
6. Here, value of sum of the coins is
   5 + 1 + 5 + 2 + 2 + 5 = ₹ 20

7. Since, 8 + 8 = 16
   So, the value of ☐ is 8.

15. Here, the length is DC which is 5 cm.

Practice Exercise 11
Mental Aptitude

1. (C)	2. (A)	3. (B)	4. (C)	5. (A)	6. (C)	7. (C)	8. (A)
9. (A)	10. (A)	11. (C)	12. (D)	13. (C)	14. (D)	15. (B)	

Explanation for Selected Questions:

1. In each next number, number of digits is increased by 1 and the value of digit of the number increased by 2.
3. Here, the pattern is 1 + 1 = 2, 2 + 2 = 4, 4 + 4 = 8, 8 + 8 = 16.
5. Here, each next number in the row is increased by 2.
9. Here, the pattern is 10 + 10 = 20, 20 + 20 = 40, 40 + 40 = 80, 80 + 80 = 160.
12. Here, the pattern is,

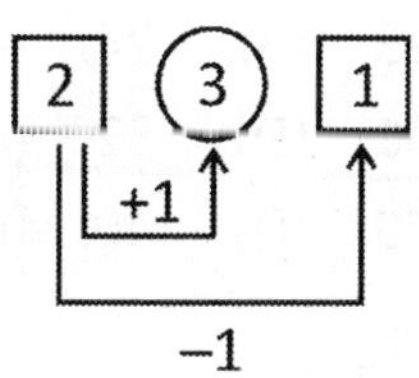

Similarly,

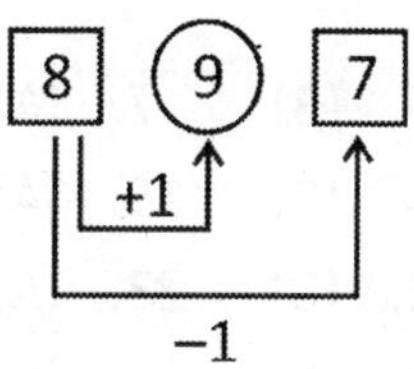

15. Here, the pattern is, 18 – 3 = 15, 15 – 3 = 12, 12 – 3 = 9, 9 – 3 = 6, 6 – 3 = 3

Model Test Paper Answer Keys

Model Test Paper – 1

1. (A)	2. (A)	3. (D)	4. (A)	5. (A)	6. (D)	7. (A)	8. (C)
9. (C)	10. (A)	11. (B)	12. (C)	13. (D)	14. (C)	15. (A)	16. (D)
17. (B)	18. (A)	19. (D)	20. (C)	21. (B)	22. (C)	23. (D)	24. (A)
25. (B)	26. (C)	27. (B)	28. (C)	29. (B)	30. (C)	31. (B)	32. (A)
33. (D)	34. (B)	35. (A)	36. (B)	37. (B)	38. (C)	39. (C)	40. (C)

Model Test Paper – 2

1. (A)	2. (C)	3. (D)	4. (C)	5. (B)	6. (C)	7. (A)	8. (C)
9. (B)	10. (C)	11. (B)	12. (D)	13. (D)	14. (D)	15. (D)	16. (C)
17. (A)	18. (C)	19. (C)	20. (B)	21. (B)	22. (C)	23. (B)	24. (B)
25. (B)	26. (B)	27. (C)	28. (D)	29. (D)	30. (C)	31. (D)	32. (A)
33. (C)	34. (B)	35. (C)	36. (A)	37. (C)	38. (C)	39. (D)	40. (C)

Model Test Paper – 3

1. (C)	2. (D)	3. (A)	4. (B)	5. (C)	6. (B)	7. (A)	8. (C)
9. (B)	10. (A)	11. (C)	12. (B)	13. (B)	14. (B)	15. (A)	16. (D)
17. (B)	18. (A)	19. (B)	20. (B)	21. (D)	22. (B)	23. (A)	24. (C)
25. (B)	26. (A)	27. (A)	28. (B)	29. (C)	30. (D)	31. (C)	32. (D)
33. (D)	34. (D)	35. (A)	36. (D)	37. (B)	38. (D)	39. (C)	40. (B)

Model Test Paper – 4

1. (C)	2. (B)	3. (D)	4. (A)	5. (D)	6. (C)	7. (B)	8. (D)
9. (C)	10. (B)	11. (A)	12. (B)	13. (B)	14. (C)	15. (D)	16. (D)
17. (D)	18. (A)	19. (C)	20. (C)	21. (B)	22. (D)	23. (D)	24. (B)
25. (B)	26. (C)	27. (B)	28. (B)	29. (D)	30. (C)	31. (C)	32. (D)
33. (B)	34. (C)	35. (D)	36. (C)	37. (C)	38. (A)	39. (C)	40. (A)

Model Test Paper – 5

1. (C)	2. (D)	3. (D)	4. (A)	5. (B)	6. (C)	7. (B)	8. (C)
9. (D)	10. (B)	11. (B)	12. (A)	13. (A)	14. (C)	15. (D)	16. (C)
17. (A)	18. (A)	19. (C)	20. (C)	21. (A)	22. (A)	23. (D)	24. (C)
25. (C)	26. (B)	27. (D)	28. (C)	29. (C)	30. (B)	31. (C)	32. (A)
33. (B)	34. (C)	35. (A)	36. (A)	37. (B)	38. (D)	39. (C)	40. (D)

Sample Question Paper

1. (D)	2. (D)	3. (D)	4. (D)	5. (C)	6. (A)	7. (B)	8. (C)
9. (D)	10. (C)	11. (D)	12. (D)	13. (D)	14. (B)	15. (D)	16. (D)
17. (B)	18. (C)	19. (D)	20. (B)	21. (D)	22. (D)	23. (C)	24. (C)
25. (B)	26. (B)	27. (B)	28. (B)	29. (C)	30. (C)	31. (C)	32. (A)
33. (C)	34. (B)	35. (D)	36. (C)	37. (D)	38. (A)	39. (C)	40. (D)

10001

SILVER ZONE FOUNDATION

OMR - ANSWER SHEET

PLEASE SEE INSTRUCTIONS OVERLEAF BEFORE FILLING THE ANSWER SHEET

PARTICIPANT'S NAME

FATHER'S NAME

SCHOOL NAME

PARTICIPANT'S ENROLLMENT NUMBER

PARTICIPANT'S CLASS

WRITE CLASS
Exp. 06 for class 6th

CLASS 01
CLASS 02
CLASS 03
CLASS 04
CLASS 05
CLASS 06
CLASS 07
CLASS 08
CLASS 09
CLASS 10
CLASS 11
CLASS 12

MOBILE NUMBER

TEST PAPER TYPE

Check 'Type' on Question Paper

A B C D

OLYMPIADS - SELECT YOUR SUBJECT

(I) Informatics Olympiad (iIO)
(M) Mathematics Olympiad (ISOM)
(S) Science Olympiad (IOS)
(E) English Language Olympiad (iOEL)
(G) GK Olympiad (SKGKO)
(F) French Language Olympiad (iFLO)
(T) Talent Hunt Olympiad (ITHO)
(H) Hindi Olympiad (ABHO)

STREAM FOR CLASS XI & XII OLYMPIAD - iIO ONLY

COMPUTER SCIENCE (C++) (S)
INFORMATICS PRACTICES (JAVA) (J)
COMPUTER SCIENCE (PYTHON) (P)
MULTIMEDIA & WEB TECHNOLOGY (M)

STREAM FOR CLASS XI & XII OLYMPIAD - iOS ONLY

PCB (B)
PCM (M)

MARK YOUR ANSWERS WITH HB PENCIL/BALL POINT PEN (BLUE/BLACK)

Q						Q						Q						Q					
1	A	B	C	D	E	11	A	B	C	D	E	21	A	B	C	D	E	31	A	B	C	D	E
2	A	B	C	D	E	12	A	B	C	D	E	22	A	B	C	D	E	32	A	B	C	D	E
3	A	B	C	D	E	13	A	B	C	D	E	23	A	B	C	D	E	33	A	B	C	D	E
4	A	B	C	D	E	14	A	B	C	D	E	24	A	B	C	D	E	34	A	B	C	D	E
5	A	B	C	D	E	15	A	B	C	D	E	25	A	B	C	D	E	35	A	B	C	D	E
6	A	B	C	D	E	16	A	B	C	D	E	26	A	B	C	D	E	36	A	B	C	D	E
7	A	B	C	D	E	17	A	B	C	D	E	27	A	B	C	D	E	37	A	B	C	D	E
8	A	B	C	D	E	18	A	B	C	D	E	28	A	B	C	D	E	38	A	B	C	D	E
9	A	B	C	D	E	19	A	B	C	D	E	29	A	B	C	D	E	39	A	B	C	D	E
10	A	B	C	D	E	20	A	B	C	D	E	30	A	B	C	D	E	40	A	B	C	D	E

SIGN. OF THE CANDIDATE & DATE OF EXAMINATION

SIGNATURE OF THE INVIGILATOR